HOW TO WRITE FUNNY

How to Write

FUNNY

EDITED BY JOHN B. KACHUBA

WRITER'S DIGEST BOOKS

CINCINNATI, OHIO

www.writersdigest.com

Visit our Web site at http://www.writersdigest.com for information on more resources for writers.

To receive a free weekly e-mail newsletter delivering tips and updates about writing and about *Writer's Digest* products, register directly at our Web site at http://newsletters.fwpublications.com.

05 04 03 02 01   5 4 3 2

Library of Congress Cataloging-in-Publication Data

How to write funny : add humor to every kind of writing / edited by John B. Kachuba.
  p.   cm.
  ISBN 1-58297-054-8 (pbk.: alk. paper)
  1. Wit and humor—Authorship. I. Kachuba, John B.
PN6149.A88 H69   2001
808'.7—dc21   2001026244
                                                                   CIP

Editor: Brad Crawford
Interior designer: Sandy Conopeotis Kent
Cover designer: Andrea Short
Cover illustration: © 2000 by Michael Witte
Production coordinator: Mark Griffin

ABOUT *the* EDITOR

John B. Kachuba is an editor, writer and journalist. He is the author of *Why Is This Job Killing Me?* His fiction has appeared in literary journals, and his nonfiction has appeared in *Poets & Writers*, *Civil War Journal* and other publications. He lives in Loveland, Ohio.

ACKNOWLEDGMENTS

Although it may seem like it at times, no writer works in a vacuum, and I need to recognize those folks who helped make this book happen. My thanks, first and always, to my wife, Mary, for her patient support and encouragement and for helping to transcribe some of the author interviews. Second, to my friend Jack Heffron at F&W Publications, who is doing his best to keep this writer out of the poorhouse. To Brad Crawford for producing such a great-looking book. To all the wonderful writers who so generously contributed their experiences to the book and finally, thanks to my writer pals at The Establishment for teaching me how to joke with the executioner . . . just a little off the top, please.

TABLE *of* CONTENTS

PART III: *The Interviews*

INTRODUCTION

When Jack Heffron at Writer's Digest Books asked me to edit *How to Write Funny*, I thought sure, why not? How hard could it be? I'm a funny guy, even when I'm sober.

I soon discovered that editing the book was a lot like herding cats. I found out that there were more ways to use humor in writing than I thought possible and that exactly how humor was written varied immensely from one writer to another. But my dilemma was a boon for you, because all these various ideas and thoughts, formerly running wild, have been corralled for you in this one book.

I also learned quickly just how subjective humor could be. Here's an example:

Two Uzbek shepherds meet in a bar. One says to the other, "Hey, great hat! Where'd you get it?"

"From the People's Collective," the other says. "Where did you get yours?"

His friend looks him squarely in the eye and says, "Kmart."

OK, me neither, but I'm told in Uzbekistan that this is a hoot.

All of the writers I interviewed for this book said their upbringing, their culture, their personal identities—all subjective aspects of their character—played some role in the formation of their sense of humor. Their life experiences not only helped them define what they thought was funny but, in many cases, provided them the vehicles to deliver their humor to a larger audience through their writing.

As an example, the storytelling tradition of his people influenced Native American writer Sherman Alexie, but so did reruns of *The Brady Bunch*.

Growing up in Hawaii, Japanese-American writer Lois-Ann Yamanaka heard her elders "talk story"; that pidgin patois carries much of the humor in her novels.

Romanian-born Andrei Codrescu's humorous writings on the absurdity of our society could not have been written without his personal experiences coming of age in a repressive country.

Roy Blount Jr.'s southern gentility is evident in his subtle and self-effacing humor, while Joe R. Lansdale's east Texas roots come to life in his roughneck, low-life—and humorous—characters.

The other writers I interviewed—Lee K. Abbott, Melissa Bank, Tom Bodett, Peg Bracken, Bill Bryson and John Dufresne—also acknowledged that they drew from the well of their personal experiences to form their senses of humor.

What all this means is that each of us has life experiences that make us unique as writers and informs our writing. There are positive and negative experiences, encouraging and demoralizing ones, uplifting and depressing. Together, they make up our writing psyche, that intangible something that compels us to put pen to paper, or fingers to keyboard, and write. Somewhere among all those disparate parts, the glue holding it all together, is humor.

In other words, there is humor in all of us. Some of us may have to dig deep to find it, but it's there.

How to Write Funny tells you how you can find the humorous side of yourself and how you can inject that humor into your writing. This book will not teach you to be a stand-up comic or a joke writer for Leno or Letterman; that's not its purpose. Its purpose is to show you how to add humor to whatever you write, fiction or nonfiction, to make your writing better.

Ah yes, I was afraid you would ask that. It's not easy to define *better*, but here are some ways in which the writers in this book have used humor to improve their writing:

Some use humor to allow them to discuss painful or depressing subjects without directly inflicting that pain or depression upon their readers. The chuckle in the middle of such serious material is the written equivalent of whistling in the graveyard.

Some use humor to poke fun at the human condition and to establish a common bond with their readers, while others inject a bit of levity into characters or situations that are too grim, that may emotionally overburden their readers.

Some writers use a wise-guy kind of humor as a veneer to protect their own or their characters' weaknesses and vulnerabilities, while other writers say being humorous is simply who they are; they know no other way of writing.

In addition to these brand-new interviews, *How to Write Funny* contains informative articles from writers working in an eclectic mix of genres—mainstream fiction, science fiction and fantasy, romance, children's, newspaper editing, and TV and radio scriptwriting. Together, they give you practical information, including handy tips and techniques, that will help you use humor more effectively in your writing. There are articles by David Bouchier, Patricia Case, Jennifer Crusie, David Evans, Esther M. Friesner, David A. Fryxell, Mel Helitzer, Robin Hemley, Dinty Moore, Josip Novakovich, Connie Willis and J. Kevin Wolfe. Plus, the workshop by Jennifer Crusie is a great hands-on exercise that will hone your humor-writing skills and maybe give you a few laughs as well.

So, enough chatter. If you want to learn how to punch up your writing with humor, read this book. If you think you've already mastered how to write funny, read this book anyway—I could use the money.

And don't forget, next time you're in Uzbekistan, the punch line is "Kmart."

—John B. Kachuba

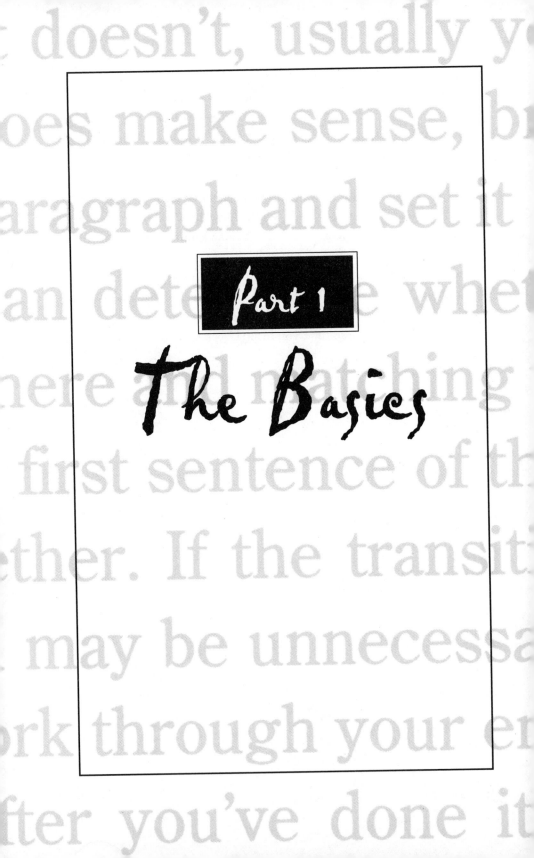

Part 1

The Basics

CHAPTER I

Relaxing the Rules of Reason

BY ROBIN HEMLEY

Unlike tragedy, a sense of humor is determined by myriad factors: our age, our socioeconomic backgrounds, our culture. What most of us consider tragic is fairly static, though something tragic can be *made* funny by comic techniques such as repetition. In Nathanael West's *A Cool Million*, the hero keeps losing limbs and other parts of himself as he makes his way in the world until there's very little that's left of him. You lose one limb or all your limbs at once, that's tragic. But if you lose them little by little, as well as an eye, your teeth, your hair, you start defying logic, and once you've transcended logic, most people will laugh in spite of themselves, even if they find something a little horrifying at the same time.

Simply put, tragedy has serious and logical consequences. Cause and effect. Comedy usually doesn't. You throw a person off a tall building in a comedy, he bounces. You throw someone off a building in a tragedy, don't wait for the bounce. Aristotle understood this in his "Poetics" when he wrote, "The causes of laughter are errors or deformities that do not pain or injure us; the comic mask, for instance, is deformed and distorted but not painfully so."

Comic Principles

People have been thinking about the comic for as long as there's been laughter, and the principles of comedy have been well defined. Of course, knowing and doing are two different things, but it's useful to have some understanding of what human beings see as funny, if not why. Henri Bergson defined some of the basic forms of comedy in his famous essay "Laughter," published in 1900. Chief among these forms are the Snowball, Repetition, Inversion, the always-popular "Reciprocal Interference of Series" and Transposition. Ironically, Bergson—genius though he may be—is no laugh riot. Still, for some of the theory behind laughter, his essay is an important resource for the fledgling humorist.

Form vs. Content

My six-year-old daughter, Isabel, has been telling "knock knock" jokes for more than two years now and still doesn't quite have the hang of it.

"Knock knock," she'll say from the back seat as we're driving somewhere.

"Who is it?" I say, honoring the ritual of it.

"Tree."

"Tree who?"

"Tree, don't you know you're going the wrong way, buddy!" She laughs hysterically at this even though it makes absolutely no sense. The funny thing is, I laugh, too. I don't know why, though I think we're laughing for different reasons. I'm not quite sure why *she's* laughing. I'm laughing because she understands the form of the knock knock joke, but not the content, and what results is something sublimely ridiculous—most of the time.

I admit there are times when Isabel's sense of humor gets a little irritating, after she's told seven of these non sequitur knock knocks in a row and the freshness has worn off. Apparently, I'm not the only one who grows tired of her jokes sometimes. Recently, she reported that a boy at her bus stop runs when he sees her "because he says he hates my jokes, Daddy." She says this proudly, not with any hint of insecurity. Personally, I love the fact that my daughter has discovered bad jokes as a source of personal empowerment. Maybe someday she'll run seminars on the subject.

Isabel, in her absurd knock knock jokes, is following Bergson's idea that "a comic meaning is invariably obtained when an absurd idea is fitted into a well-established phrase form."

Of course, Izzy loves to discuss Bergson every chance she gets.

"Tell me about Reciprocal Interference of Series again, Daddy," she often begs me before bedtime.

"No more Bergson," I say. "We did Bergson last night. Don't you ever get tired of Reciprocal Interference of Series? Hey, I've got an idea! Let's talk about humor as a defense mechanism, a way of turning . . ."

She rolls her eyes. "Freud," she says.

"OK, Bergson. *A situation is invariably comic when it belongs simultaneously to two altogether independent series of events and is capable of being interpreted in two entirely different meanings at the same time.*"

"Thank you, Daddy," she says. "Now I can get to sleep."

Funny Is Where You Find It

Writing funny is a matter of perspective. How you see the world. It's not simply a matter of knowing the right formulas—it's hardly that at all. We laugh at what we find strange, unusual, illogical. When I write something funny, I generally don't set out to do so. I write, and because I see the world a little bizarrely, I suppose, it comes out funny.

What's remarkable is that in spite of the fact that humor depends on so many variables (age, era, culture), many humorous works *do* survive the ages. We still read the works of the ancient Greek playwright Aristophanes, and of course, Shakespeare's romantic comedies are produced quite often, as are works such as French playwright Molière's *The Imaginary Invalid.* And of course, our most revered author in America was essentially a humorist, Mark Twain. Humor survives the ages for many of the same reasons that great tragedies survive. The great humorists have an understanding of our common human foibles and frailties. If you want to write funny, you have to have some understanding of your own foibles first.

Start with an idea or concept or even a journal observation that you think is funny. A friend of mine once told me about a guy who murdered his first wife and put her in a freezer. He had her in a storage locker and his second wife stopped paying the bill for it, so the contents were auctioned off, and one lucky buyer purchased a freezer with a dead woman inside.

Gruesome certainly, but I could easily imagine a darkly comic story about such a situation.

What one person finds funny another person finds deranged.

I just found that idea as I was flipping through my journals. It was something that I thought was bizarre enough to take note of, regardless of whether it would ever show up in a story of mine. If you want to write, funny or otherwise, keeping a journal is a good idea. Things that are funny happen around us all the time, just about every day. The trick is being receptive to the world around you. There are some things you hear that you'll never forget and other things that are lost unless you write them down. Take, for example, the following dialogue I recorded in my journal on October 25, 1997:

I saw two women with five children ranging in age from seven to two running between, around and ahead of their mothers on a narrow walk through the grounds of a hotel where I was staying.

One woman said, "I've known parents with kids who've lost their front teeth playing a sport and then they have to go their whole lives with fake teeth."

"Oh, I know!" said the second woman.

"And isn't that just the worst look when someone's missing a front tooth and they don't replace it?"

"Oh, I know!"

I'm not sure why this amused me—it's not fall-down funny, but it's funny enough that I thought it worthy of being placed in my journal (a dubious honor, I realize). Part of what I think I find funny here is the repetition of the second woman's "I know's." There's also a kind of potential pattern here, something I'm sure I recognized more or less intuitively at the time—this kind of "dissing" is one of our more laughable and common traits as humans. One can imagine this conversation building, snowballing out of proportion. People like to have others agree with them, and that's what the second woman was doing with the first. Thus encouraged, I can imagine the first woman continuing on with "looks" that she finds awful. "And what about those children who never wipe their noses. I mean, they're just like faucets. You'd think their parents would teach them a thing or two about hygiene."

"Oh, I know!"

"That is *the* worst look, bar none."

"Oh, I know!"

"And some parents will let their kids eat anything—I mean anything, like Little Debbie donuts by the forklift, until they . . ."

Here, I could imagine an unfinished sentence, maybe a pause on the pathway as the first mother realizes too late that she's said something that might offend her friend. She *was* going to criticize parents who "allow" their children to grow chubby, but maybe one of the five children running around them is a little overweight, and now, instead of just saying "I know!" after each nasty observation, the second mother grows silent, maybe defensive. Perhaps, if the story went on from here, the situation might deteriorate into a shouting match, with each mother insulting the appearance of the other's children, down to the way they dress. Who knows? But the point is that this situation was presented to me unexpectedly as I was innocently walking from my hotel room to the hotel lobby.

Funny Situations

Sometimes, too, you find yourself in a situation that starts off serious but becomes absurd. When this happens, take it as a gift and write it down.

Once, I was called to serve on a jury when I lived in North Carolina. At 8:30 A.M., I found the jury lounge in the courthouse, which, according to my journal, contained about seventy-five to one hundred seats. I sat down along with about fifty other potential jurors, and I filled out the appropriate forms. The jury clerk explained the jury procedures to us at a podium with a microphone. Beside her was a Hitachi TV set on which you could see her replicated. This was my first clue that the day was going to be a bizarre one. I wondered why one would need *both* a live person explaining the proceedings *and* a TV image of them at the same time. This was not the kind of wide-screen TV that one sees at outdoor rock concerts or when the Pope comes to town so that the millionth person in the farthest corner of the venue has a chance of seeing what they came to see. This was a small TV in a small room beside a woman who could be seen and heard perfectly well without her image being projected onto the screen beside her. I decided the image must be for potential jurors who were reality-impaired.

After she was done explaining what we had already filled out, she stepped aside and a video came on the TV, a video on jury duty, of course. The video started out with a song titled "I Call North Carolina Home." I loved the lyrics, which went:

> I call North Carolina home.
> Lord, it's just like livin' in a poem.
> I like calling North Carolina home.

When the video was over, the TV switched to Regis and Kathy Lee. Then the clerk swore us in and told us to turn in our Bibles. Apparently, past jurors had taken home Bibles as souvenirs.

And on it went. The day grew increasingly bizarre, hitting its odd crescendo perhaps when I sat in the courtroom during jury selection and watched the potential juror beside me cock her thumb and index finger into a make-believe gun and blow away the defendant about whom she was supposed to feel impartial. Thankfully, she was excluded. But I wasn't, and I eventually wrote an article about my experiences for a local paper.

Anecdotes

A story I wrote that won *Story* magazine's Humor Award began as an anecdote a friend told me once. My friend Max Childers told me that he had once had a story accepted by a magazine in Atlanta, and he waited for over a year for the magazine to publish it. This in itself isn't unusual or funny, but then he received a letter from the editor saying that the magazine was folding and that the story would appear in its last issue. Another year passed. Then the editor wrote again and he said that a terrible thing had happened—the last issue of the magazine was at press when a deranged printer, in love with a woman who was a horrendously bad poet, took out all of the real contents of the magazine and substituted his girlfriend's awful poetry. Outraged, the editor showed up on the printer's lawn, called him outside and punched him in the nose. Now he was facing assault charges.

This, I thought, was gold—one of the funniest situations I had ever heard. I asked, maybe begged Max for permission to use his anecdote, and then I wrote the story from the printer's point of view. The reason I chose the printer was because he was the one in love, driven by passion. He was the one in whom the irony of the situation resided. In other words, he didn't really think what he was doing was wrong. Or, he thought his deep love for his girlfriend excused his behavior. And furthermore, he thought his girlfriend's poetry was great.

I changed a few of the details. I made the magazine a much larger one than in the real story, a magazine like *The New Yorker*, with a formidable reputation. This situation could be believable because there are plenty of magazines that are printed hundreds of miles from their editorial offices— the printers often mail the magazines directly to subscribers and distribution centers from their printing plants. And so it wasn't beyond the realm of possibility that something like this could happen. I chose to exaggerate the situation in this way because it made the stakes higher, the consequences of the lovelorn printer's actions all the funnier.

I started the story after the damage was done, with the editor on the printer's lawn.

> A man on my lawn in a white suit and a Panama hat is calling me down. He's a little chicken-headed fellow with a bow tie. He's holding a hip flask in one hand and a rolled-up copy of a magazine in another. He's one of the scrawniest fellows I've ever seen and his gray hair hangs to his shoulders.

The most pleasurable part of writing this story was the invention of the poems by the printer's girlfriend. It's a lot more difficult than one might imagine to write bad poetry, at least a poem that's earnestly bad. In other words, to be *really* funny I knew I needed to write a poem in character, a poem that I could imagine someone writing and thinking was completely profound and meaningful. After many tries, I came up with the following:

Mother Nature's Abortion

Wood nymphs and sprites are dying of pollution
So are unicorns and fairies
Oh, what is the solution?

Smokestacks belch their foul fumes
While Puck and Bacchus gag
The leprechauns and elves are doomed!

Once-mighty Zeus drinks acid rain
Hobbits hobble around on crutches
Even happy Buddha cannot hide his pain

Mother nature has had an abortion
No one even tried to stop
This ecological disaster of immense proportions.

In the course of one's life as a writer, one sees many bad examples of writing, and I have seen my share of puerile writing even worse than this. Frankly, I wrote a few such earnestly bad poems in high school. My goal wasn't to make fun of bad poets per se—too easy a target and rather mean on my part. The bad poems in my story (there's one more, titled "The Plight of the One-Legged Pony") served a larger purpose in my mind. I didn't want to make fun of anyone really. It was the main character's misguided but true love that I found so funny, and which, in a strange way, I wanted to celebrate. If I was making fun of anyone, it was the pompous editor of the magazine who showed up on the lawn of the lovelorn printer.

Relaxing the Rules of Reason: Daydreams, Dreams and Fantasies

I've always had a bit of an attention-span problem. If I find something boring, I turn away or retreat inside myself and invent something funny. As a kid, I daydreamed all the time, and while this habit had some unfunny consequences when I was a child, the daydreaming habit has served me well as a writer.

Once I dreamed that the Queen of England had a secret love-child, a Jamaican man who was a couple of years older than Charles. Who knows where this stuff comes from? I thought the dream was bizarre, even slightly embarrassing that I would dream something so ridiculous, but there's hardly anything too ridiculous to be written down and considered for a story. Don't be afraid of your ideas. If you have a strange dream or wild thought, write it down, pursue it, see where it goes.

How you pursue it, as we've seen, determines how funny the piece is. Exaggeration. Repetition. Snowballing. These are three of the comic writer's invaluable tools. But you must also allow yourself to be illogical, to make something impossible possible, if only for the time it takes to read your story. Bergson said we laugh when there is a relaxation in the rules of reason. Comic absurdity is dreamlike in this way, and it gives us the impression of playing with ideas, perhaps of relaxing the rules and conventions of society as well. That's why, in all those wonderful old Marx brothers movies, there's always a society matron or a judge or someone else who represents Reason and Order being lampooned. Comedy of this kind, the farce, is anarchic and subversive. The comedian who fools with our expectations of order, decency and logical reasoning is the well-meaning enemy of propriety. How does one "relax the rules of reason"? One might as well ask, How does one dream? In your dreams, all of your usual self-consciousness and self-censors have been turned off. In the same way, you need to relax these censors and your own fear of being a fool in order to relax rules of reason. Take a situation you know well, maybe your work situation, and turn it on its head. What if your boss issued a memo one day ordering everyone to do something ridiculous? In the film *Bananas*, Woody Allen's crazy dictator issues a directive to the people of the nation that from now on, underwear must be worn on the outside of people's clothes. And I was once told of the chair of an English department, who on having a nervous breakdown, started issuing bizarre orders to his staff such as, "Make a list!" No mention of what was supposed to be on the list. Simply, "Make a list!"

Don't be afraid to write something stupid. Undoubtedly, someone will think what you're writing is stupid. Someone else will think it's a riot.

Follow through. The bigger the limb you walk out on the better. In other words, don't be afraid to write something illogical. And if you write something illogical, don't be halfhearted about it. Push the situation for all it's worth. The dream about Queen Elizabeth's love child was one I turned into a bizarre little short story. And in another instance, I had a student at the time, blonde haired and blue eyed, who claimed to be descended from some Germanic tribe, though I can't remember which one. I thought it was somewhat amusing that this privileged kid was trying, in my opinion, to cash in a bit on identity politics. So I started daydreaming about the situation. What if some long-forgotten tribe came forward now, appearing out of the woodwork, and reclaimed its heritage? What would be the most unusual tribe, a tribe that one might not normally think of? I started with all the European and Asian tribes that I had learned of in history class—the Goths, the Visigoths—no, not so funny. The Tartars, the Vikings, the Mongols. Not funny. Then I remembered the Vandals. The Vandals. Funny. Really funny, I thought, because the Vandals had not only disappeared, they also had to be the most maligned tribe in history. They had sacked Rome, and their name was now synonymous with senseless damage to other people's property. It didn't make sense that anyone would be proud of being a Vandal, but that's exactly what made it funny. It didn't make sense.

So I wrote a story, which was eventually anthologized and read on National Public Radio, about a college student who appears in the office of a professor of classical history. The story is told from the point of view of the professor who is confronted by his Vandal student for spreading vicious lies about her people. I decided to write the story from his point of view so we wouldn't be sure whether she was really a Vandal or just a clever student doing a snow job on her meek professor in order to get an extension on a paper and a better grade. I also decided that I would wait until about halfway through the story before I divulged what her claim was.

> "I'm here to better my people," she said, looking around the office as though her people had gathered around her.
>
> "Your people? Are you a Mormon?"
>
> "No."
>
> "You're not . . . I mean, you don't look. . . ."
>
> "I'm a Vandal, Dr. Radlisch."
>
> I put my chin in my hand. "A vandal," was all I could manage to say.
>
> "Part Vandal," she said. "Over half."
>
> "You deface property?" I said.
>
> "Another lie," she said. "Another stinking Roman lie." She spat on my carpet.
>
> "You spat on my carpet," I told her, and pointed to it.
>
> "I'm a Vandal, Dr. Radlisch," she said. "If you only knew the truth about us."
>
> "Amy," I said calmly. "I'm not doubting you, of course. But what you're telling me is that you're a Vandal. V-A-N-D-A-L. Vandal. Like the tribe? The one that disappeared from history in the sixth century when Belisarius defeated them and sold them into slavery?"

"Pig," she said. "Dog. Roman dung. Belisarius." And she spat again.

"Please stop spitting on my carpet," I asked her.

She nodded and folded her arms primly in her lap.

Surprising Yourself

When I was pondering writing this piece, I lay in bed one morning thinking of principles of comedy that I thought were important for other writers to know. What came to my mind, first and foremost, was *cream cheese.* There it was, floating around in my head, *Philadelphia Brand Cream Cheese.* Lying in bed, I started to formulate the *Philadelphia Brand Cream Cheese Method of Comic Writing.* It seemed plausible at the time. Maybe I could even structure an infomercial around the concept. It had something to do with the idea that cream cheese eaten in large quantities makes people hilarious. Some enzyme in the cheese. A chemical interaction with that portion of your brain that controls your ability to write comically, a portion of the brain that has been isolated in laboratory animals. And most importantly, Philadelphia Brand Cream Cheese. Maybe it had to do with W.C. Fields's famous epitaph, "I'd rather be in Philadelphia." I don't know. It was funny at the time and I went with it, mulling over the possibilities as I lay in bed in that state between waking and dreaming. To me, that's at the heart of writing funny, being open to and exploring the possibilities of an idea, no matter how odd and absurd, seeing where it takes you.

Unpredictability. We laugh at what surprises us. The humorist takes the world as it is and shows it to us upside-down. Yet, even tipped upside-down the world is somehow recognizable, and from this perspective we're often shown truths about the human condition that we're blind to when we see the world right side up (i.e., Philadelphia Brand Cream Cheese, one of the four elements that make up the world, according to the ancient Chinese: Fire, Water, Air, Philadelphia Brand Cream Cheese). Whatever the humorist's tool: exaggeration, repetition, snowballing, a comic reversal, the result is still the same—we laugh because we have been shaken out of our normal perceptions. It's as though the humorist is shaking up sleepwalkers, shouting in our ears, "Hey, wake up, don't you see this is funny?" As a writer of humor, this is what your attitude must be, but you must surprise yourself first. You must be open to seeing the world upside-down, be a bit of an anarchist, someone who doesn't mind shouting a bit, or telling anti-knock knock jokes.

Robin Hemley is the author of several books of fiction and nonfiction, including the book on writing form, *Turning Life Into Fiction*. His work has won a number of awards, including the *Chicago Tribune*'s Nelson Algren Award for Fiction and two Pushcart Prizes. His work has also been heard on National Public Radio.

CHAPTER 2

The Comic Point of View:
Putting Humor in Your Fiction

BY DAVID BOUCHIER

I wasted the second-best years of my life trying to be a serious writer. How else could I communicate my deep insight into the meaning of things, the sadness of the human condition, the fragility of love and the pain of a sensitive soul doomed to live in a crass materialistic world? Thousands of tedious pages later, it dawned on me that these great truths were already old news in William Shakespeare's time, that I had nothing to add and that it was time to lighten up.

Shakespeare understood that life is funny at least as often as it is tragic. After every sad scene, he brings in the clowns. Contemporary writers too often forget to bring in the clowns, and one sure way to make your fiction more appealing is to add a carefully calculated dose of humor.

"Carefully calculated" is important. Humor does sell fiction, but only when it is used sparingly. "Funny books" without cartoons are not a big market. So this essay suggests how to add the comic point of view to your fiction without changing its essential themes or qualities.

The Nature of Humor

Humor is like sex: Everybody knows exactly what it is, but no two people ever agree. College professors have written dozens of books offering philosophical, psychological, sociological, historic, poststructuralist and even biological theories of humor. They all come to the same conclusion: We don't quite understand humor yet, and we require generous funding for further research.

Therefore, I will ignore the profound intellectual question of what humor is and go straight for the trivial but practical question, How does humor work?

It certainly doesn't work on everybody. "Everyone has a sense of humor" is one of those daft cliches, like "Every cloud has a silver lining" and "Every child has a special gift," that vanishes in a puff of smoke the moment we think about it. My father-in-law doesn't have a sense of humor. There are whole nations and whole professions without a sense of humor—think of Serbs, IRS inspectors and proctologists, for example.

A sense of humor is a special gift. It gives you, as a writer, the magical power to make people laugh, whether they like it or not. Anyone with a sense of humor can write humor, although history shows that it helps to be a depressive, an alcoholic or a drug addict, and preferably all three (think of the roll call of great humorists, and you'll see what I mean). It also helps to forget about your self-esteem, if you are lucky enough to have any. And don't expect it to be easy. Sitting down at a keyboard to be funny in cold blood, as it were, takes some practice. There are no guarantees for the humorous writer. Some readers will find your most brilliant strokes of wit as entertaining as the Baltimore telephone directory. The same readers may gag with laughter over your most tragic passages.

The comic point of view is essentially that of the stranger or alien. It captures the amazement and curiosity we all feel when, for example, we travel in strange countries where everything seems odd, and even perverse. It's what social scientists call anthropological distance. All tribes have strange customs, and the writer's job is to become an anthropologist to his or her own tribe. The comic point of view is always the outsider point of view—the innocent, the unbeliever, the depressive, the misanthrope, the anarchist or the Antichrist who sees things as nobody else sees them.

Some writers think this way like breathing. Others have to make a conscious effort to get out of their conventional skin. But the basic operating principles of humor are the same for everyone.

Incongruity

Wit is the unexpected copulation of ideas. Humor can be as complicated as a play by Aristophanes or Tom Stoppard. It can be as simple as a pratfall or a pie in the face. The only quality all humor shares is the unexpected— it surprises us by subverting the commonplace. Oscar Wilde was a master of this technique: "If one tells the truth, one is certain sooner or later to be found out" or "The good end happily and the bad unhappily. That is what fiction means."

Incongruity is the basic, and in some sense the only, technique of the humorist. The reader must be surprised by an unexpected event, an unlikely connection, an inappropriate role performance or a bizarre viewpoint.

There are dozens of ways to do this in storytelling, and it may be useful to distinguish the most common humor devices. In reality, of course, these devices can be mixed and matched in any way the writer chooses.

Irony

Fiction without irony is like painting without perspective. Irony exposes the incongruities of everyday life—the half-truths, deceptions and self-deceptions that help us all get through the day. Things are never what they seem, and the essence of ironic humor is the lack of fit between life as it is and life as we imagine it should be. We think the world should make sense: It doesn't. We think life should be dignified: It never is. We think life should have a serious purpose, like football or lawn care: But of course the purpose always turns out to be very silly in the end. Irony is the writer's richest and most inexhaustible humor resource.

The genre of the campus novel, from Kingsley Amis to Richard Russo, is a perfect example. Higher education is meant to be a serious business; universities are meant to be serious places. So it's funny when, in Russo's *Straight Man,* the chair of the English department hides in the ceiling space over the faculty offices to eavesdrop on a meeting between his colleagues.

> It has to be ninety degrees up here among the rafters. I'm sweating profusely, and when I lean forward, a drop of perspiration from the tip of my nose finds the crevice I'm peering down through and lands with an almost audible plink in the center of the long conference table.

Another reason why irony is such a powerful source of humor is that, as Voltaire observed long ago, life is absurd, but we try to make sense of it. This doomed effort creates some of the best comedy. One of the funniest books in this century (in my opinion) is Douglas Adams's *The Hitchhiker's*

Guide to the Galaxy, which is entirely based on the quest for "the meaning of life, the universe and everything" and comes up with the rather disappointing answer: "forty-two."

John Gay, the author of *The Beggar's Opera*, wrote, "Life is a jest and all things show it; I thought so once and now I know it." This is what the humorist focuses on: that everyday life is a precarious stage show with flimsy scenery and a badly edited script. The show is so fragile that it can always be subverted by the writer who pulls back the curtain and reveals the masquerade.

Word Games and Dialogue

We normally assume that one word means one thing or, in those cases where words have double and triple meanings, that the context will make it clear.

> When my love swears that she is made of truth
> I do believe her, though I know she lies

Thus begins Shakespeare's 138th sonnet, leading into a hall of mirrors and verbal paradoxes that play with the double meaning of "lie" in Elizabethan English. We laugh, perhaps a little uneasily, when the meanings become unsteady. Millions of ancient jokes rely on this technique.

A duck walks into a store and says, "Gimme some Chap Stick, and put it on my bill."

Word games are funny, up to a point. But, unless you are the next James Joyce, an extended piece of fiction cannot rest entirely on the dazzling elaboration of language. From the reader's point of view, it becomes tiresome and too much like hard work to figure out a deluge of puns, double entendres, oxymorons, palindromes and so on. Smart-talking characters, very facile with language, are a good way of bringing wordplay into your fiction. Consider this exchange between a mother and her four-year-old daughter, from Mark Leyner's story "Tinker, Tailor, Toddler, Spy."

> "One song and you go to sleep. One. That's it."
> "But Daddy sings me lots of songs."

"Your father's weak; he's easily manipulated."

"I know that, Mommy."

"It's wrong to take advantage."

"I know; he's so . . . so . . ."

"Acquiescent? Pliable? Docile? Spineless?"

"He's such a . . . such a . . ."

"Doormat? Patsy? Sucker?"

"Yeah. Sucker."

The precocious child, the superior mother and the idiot father are ancient comedy stereotypes. But we get a wry smile from this exchange, just because the words flow so well.

The Simple Truth Is Funny

"If I want to tell a joke, I tell the truth: There's nothing funnier," said Bernard Shaw. And it is possible to get a comic effect simply by writing the plain truth—saying things that everyone has been dying to say but didn't because they might be accused of political incorrectness or bad taste. We have so many sacred cows that if you start shooting you can hardly miss. The language is packed with wimpish euphemisms like "rest room," "correctional facility," "senior citizens" and "downsizing." Because euphemisms are both transparent and dishonest, they have great humor potential. Try losing the euphemisms and allowing one or more of your characters to talk in plain words.

Unfortunately, truth hurts, and it's all too easy for the humorist to be blamed for condoning racism, ageism, sexism, weightism and everything not nice. People write to me every week and say, "How dare you make fun of foreign taxi drivers" (or antique collectors, or gardeners, or old people, or joggers or whatever). I always reply courteously that I wasn't making fun but simply pointing out some unwelcome facts. There are so many groups just waiting to be offended by the most trivial slight that I despair of finishing the list in my lifetime. Ask yourself, What is usually not said? and you probably have an opening for humor.

Satire as a Lethal Weapon

Satire is the opposite of truth telling. Satire is a big lie mobilized to get a comic effect. Sometimes the lie is mere exaggeration, sometimes it is a complete invention. Either way, satire is an attack weapon. It inflates the faults and foibles of powerful people or conventional ideas, with the intention of making them look ridiculous. "Humor belongs to the losers," said Garrison Keillor, and that's what satire is about. It's a kind of revenge, often very sweet and always tinged with anger.

Jonathan Swift was the father of modern satire. In scathing books like *A Tale of a Tub*, *The Battle of the Books* and *Gulliver's Travels*, Swift mocked the pretensions and prejudices of his own time. His technique was quite simple and works as well today as it did in the 1700s. He picked his target, imagined a fantastic metaphor and exaggerated everything. For example, in *Gulliver*, he created a deadly satire on prejudice with the story of the "Big Endians" and the "Little Endians," two groups locked in eternal battle over which end to open a boiled egg.

Kurt Vonnegut and Joseph Heller crafted marvelous satires on the Second World War, using Swift's tools of exaggeration, fantasy and aggressive ridicule. But contemporary satire is harder. Politics and popular culture have moved almost beyond the reach of ridicule. It's difficult to come up with something so bizarre that it won't actually happen before your piece appears in print or even before you find a stamp and mail it. So satire can be risky for a fiction writer, who always risks being upstaged by reality.

Don't Forget the Visuals

Writing humor for readers is profoundly different from writing for a stage or TV performance. There's nothing to help your words along: no visuals, no funny acting, no sound effects or voice tricks, no reliable audience response. Cartoonist Gary Larson could surprise us into laughter with a simple sketch of cows drinking martinis in a field. Jerry Seinfeld or Jay Leno can reinforce their jokes with facial expressions and body language. But a writer has only words on paper and has to work twice as hard to get the same effect.

This is the classic case where you must show rather than tell. How do your characters look, how do they move, how do they sound, what damage are they doing to their immediate environment? Here's a scene from Michael Bond's mystery novel *Monsieur Pamplemousse on the Spot*. The setting is a very exclusive French restaurant, and Pommes Frites is a bloodhound.

> . . . a large, wet, freshly Vaselined nose reappeared on the other side of the window, and pressed itself firmly against a fresh area of glass. Monsieur Pamplemousse gave a sigh. Pommes Frites was being more than a little difficult that evening. He shuddered to think what the outside of the window would be like when it caught the rays of the morning sun.

Hold the Jokes

The joke is the primordial form of humor. When we want to be funny in company, we tell jokes, because jokes are economical, easy to remember and easy to understand. If you like telling jokes, keep them for the next party. They don't work well in fiction. Jokes are a performance art, and joke-telling characters are always a bore. Instead, create funny characters, who will naturally say funny things.

A Funny Character Is a Caricature

Funny characters are unusual, strange, odd, perhaps obnoxious and always extreme. Your friends and family are not funny characters, not even your eccentric Aunt Edna. A truly comic character is a caricature, a creature of the author's imagination. Consider how Charles Dickens introduces the character of Scrooge in *A Christmas Carol*.

> Oh! But he was a tight-fisted hand at the grindstone, Scrooge!
> A squeezing, wrenching, grasping, scraping, clutching, covetous old sinner. Hard and sharp as flint, from which no steel had ever struck out generous fire, secret and self-contained, and solitary as an oyster.

No modern author has the luxury of so many adjectives, and this description goes on in the same vein for another three hundred words! But the point is made. Scrooge is extreme in his prejudices and behavior, bizarre in his appearance and daily habits, and has a horrible effect on other people. Once you have met him, you can never forget him. That's the essence of a good caricature.

It helps if your character has a funny name, like Scrooge. The enchanted weaver in Shakespeare's *A Midsummer Night's Dream* is called Bottom. The two leading characters in Bond's successful series of French gastronomic mysteries, quoted previously, are Monsieur Pamplemousse (grapefruit) and his talented dog, Pommes Frites (french fries). It's hard to raise a smile with a character called Jones.

Funny characters are often divided or conflicted. They act one way and think another, play a role badly or try unsuccessfully to bring two aspects of their personalities together. A character who wants to be chaste but can't quite manage it, or who tries and fails to be promiscuous, is always good for a laugh. A funny character is eternally on the edge of the precipice, like James Thurber's everyman, with a precarious grip on reality. The character's struggle to cope with life is funny, because it is doomed to failure.

Cruel as it sounds, humor does come from tormenting your characters with psychological, sexual, social and financial conflicts. They have to suffer—to be humiliated, confused, worried. Noble and good characters are an unfunny bore. Miguel de Cervantes and Voltaire perfected the type of the naive character who understands nothing that is going on in the world (or pretends not to). James Thurber perfected the character who can never win.

Strange Settings and Awkward Situations

Although humor can be set anywhere, it can be helped into orbit by dropping your characters into a setting that's funny in itself. Look for the off-key, weird and inappropriate setting, a place where your characters don't quite belong, a setting rife with opportunities for tension, incongruity, disaster and embarrassment. Dump your characters in places where they don't understand the language or don't know how to behave. In his novel *East Is East*, T. Coraghessan Boyle has his protagonist, a young monoglot Japanese seaman, washed ashore on the coast of Georgia, in an artists'

How to Write Funny

colony surrounded on all sides by rednecks. In Samuel Beckett's *Molloy*, first love happens in a garbage dump.

Even a slight shift in perspective can bring out the humor in a familiar genre. The popular crime stories of Lindsey Davis are set in ancient Rome. Her wisecracking Roman detective, Marcus Didius Falco, knows how to set the scene. Here's the irresistible opening of *A Dying Light in Corduba*.

> Nobody was poisoned at the dinner of the Society of Olive Oil Producers of Baetica—though in retrospect, that was quite a surprise. Had I realized that Anacrites the Chief Spy would be present, I would myself have taken a small vial of toad's blood concealed in my napkin and ready for use. . . . Me first if possible. Rome owed me that.

Comical Plots and Unlikely Connections

Extreme characters in strange situations tend to create funny plots all by themselves. A perfectly straightforward genre plot—romance or mystery—can be full of humor created by character, situation and dialogue. Jane Austen and Charles Dickens wrote wonderfully funny fictions without ever resorting to crazy plot devices.

But if you can make the plot itself funny, so much the better. Simple twists and reversals on standard plotlines can be enough to bring out their comic possibilities (the hero is the villain, the corpse is not dead, the femme fatale is a transvestite). *The Hitchhiker's Guide to the Galaxy*, mentioned earlier, has an insanely complicated plot that begins with the destruction of the Earth and proceeds to trash and satirize every science fiction device ever invented.

Most fiction plots aren't like that. They have serious and funny passages, and the transition between the two can be a challenge. In a play, the scene can change. In a novel, the author can start a new chapter to smooth the bump between funny and serious. The short story writer has a problem that can best be solved by using bathos, the sudden, jolting drop from serious to funny. The reverse transition is almost impossible to manage gracefully in a short piece.

The Humor Writer's Tool Kit

The sources of humor are infinite. Make your own list of the devices that work best for you. But here's a starter tool kit: Reach into it whenever you are stuck for a humor idea. First, the two big ones.

EXAGGERATION

This is one of the oldest and most reliable humor devices. Take a look at the unlikely memoirs of Baron von Munchausen as told by Rudolph Erich Raspe, or any of Mark Twain's tall tales. Only a very little exaggeration is necessary. Consider this description of a New York cab ride by Dave Barry.

> . . . the taxi has some kind of problem with the steering, probably dead pedestrians lodged in the mechanism, the result being that there is a delay of eight to ten seconds between the time the driver turns the wheel and the time the taxi actually changes direction, a handicap that the driver is compensating for by going 175 miles an hour, at which velocity we are able to remain airborne almost to the far rim of some of the smaller potholes.

UNDERSTATEMENT

" 'Tis but a scratch," says the Black Knight, in *Monty Python and the Holy Grail,* when both his arms have been cut off. The imperturbable valet Jeeves in the stories of P.G. Wodehouse is never ruffled by any disaster. A narrator or character with the habit of relentless understatement is one of the oldest and most reliable comic devices.

But there are dozens of reliable humor techniques. Here are a few, and your imagination will suggest how to build the list.

Intrusion of the unexpected word, phrase, person or event.

Reversal or substitution of words, identities, conventional wisdoms or behaviors.

Anachronism: that particular form of incongruity where time is dislocated.

Failure and humiliation, incompetence and embarrassment.

Miscommunication and misunderstanding.

Absurdity and fantasy: Nothing is too wild to try!

Bathos: Pride comes before a fall.

Insane logical progressions, the most famous being Joseph Heller's manic explanation of "the catch" in *Catch-22*.

Parody: a tricky technique, because readers must know the original to understand the parody, but worth a try with mainstream culture themes.

Humor Writing Is Good Writing

Great humor writers were and are good writers first and foremost. Slow and difficult humor is a contradiction in terms. Humor must be easy to read and transparent. It should announce itself in the first line and move relentlessly forward with something funny in every paragraph.

George Orwell's famous advice in his essay "Politics and the English Language" is doubly true for humor: Use short, simple words, short sentences, the active voice, no cliches, and if you can cut, then cut. Shakespeare said it even more pithily: "Brevity is the soul of wit."

David Bouchier is the award-winning weekly essayist for National Public Radio stations WSHU, WSUF and WMMM and writes a weekly humor column called "Out of Order" for the regional editions of the Sunday *New York Times*. He teaches at the State University of New York at Stony Brook and the New School in New York and has led humor-writing workshops at the Iowa Summer Writing Festival, the Cape Cod Writers' Conference, the Chautauqua Writers' Conference and many others. His essays and short stories have appeared in many newspapers and magazines in Britain and the United States.

CHAPTER 3

Giving the Joke:

A Roundtable Discussion With Mark Leyner, Maggie Estep, James Finn Garner and P.J. O'Rourke

BY FRANK SENNETT

At the book fair panel sponsored by *New City*, the alternative weekly newspaper I work for, something funny is about to go on. At least I hope so. Humor is notorious for losing its humor when it's discussed, dissected, and advice about how to write it dispensed.

But the writers assembled for the panel discussion might just be the group able to put that notion to rest. We've got Mark Leyner, former *Esquire* columnist. His riotously absurd sense of humor is reflected in the titles of his five books: *I Smell Esther Williams, and Other Stories*; *Et Tu, Babe*; *My Cousin, My Gastroenterologist*; *Tooth Imprints on a Corn Dog*; and, most recently, *The Tetherballs of Bougainville: A Novel.*

And we have Maggie Estep, who used to perform her rawly personal humor at events such as the Lilith Fair tour of women rockers. Estep is the author of *Soft Maniacs: Stories* and *Diary of an Emotional Idiot: A Novel.*

The third writer who will tackle the unenviable task of talking funny about writing funny is James Finn Garner, who has followed up his bestselling comic-fable franchise *Politically Correct Bedtime Stories, Once Upon a More Enlightened Time: More Politically Correct Bedtime Stories* and *Politically Correct Holiday Stories*—with *Apocalypse Wow!: A Memoir for the End of Time.*

Rounding out the panel is perhaps the best-known writer of the bunch, humorist and malcontent P.J. O'Rourke, decidedly a writer of nonfiction (*Holidays in Hell, Parliament of Whores, Eat the Rich*). A founder of *National Lampoon*, O'Rourke doesn't write fiction, but he still makes use of its techniques to deliver his biting wit. Plus, he's just too damn funny to leave out.

As the audience settled into their seats, I began to ask the questions—then got out of the way as fast as I could.

Is there a feeling with humor writing that if it makes readers laugh, it can't be considered the stuff of literature?

MARK LEYNER: I have wondered the same thing. Books that are at minimum generous in their attempts to make people laugh are treated entirely differently than more serious works. I have no idea why. It certainly has an impact on my own status as a writer. I think humor is ghettoized like never before critically, not just where you look for it in the bookstore.

P.J. O'ROURKE: There's a lot of cat books in bookstore humor sections. Really funny. Lovely gifts.

JAMES FINN GARNER: I think people who have senses of humor take it for granted, especially putting it down on paper. Norman Mailer is never going to be very funny. He can work on a book for years and years, and he'll never be very funny. Anybody up here might write a serious book—and won't be taken seriously of course, because of what we've done before—but humor comes more naturally to us, so possibly we take it more lightly and don't stand up for it. But why should we?

O'ROURKE: I think it's ego. Part of the whole business of literature—a large part of it—is feeling important. "This is an important book that I'm reading, so I must be an important person reading this book." The whole business about giving out awards: "Here's someone who wrote this important book and that's important. And I read it and that makes me important. And now my important friends and I are going to give this important award." And you just can't do that with *101 Uses for a Dead Cat.* The likelihood of my ever getting a literary award of any kind is slim to none. But I do have a prepared acceptance speech, which is: "My life is over. This book has offended so few people that I wound up getting an award."

Humor's just one of many tools for a writer, and it happens to be the only tool I know how to use—for me it's sort of the Popeil Pocket Fisherman—so I just don't think that you can worry about this. Yeah, you're never going to make people feel important reading your book, but you'll actually sell some books. And people will enjoy them and people will read them instead of just saying they read them. I'd rather write something that was funny and people enjoyed and I had a good time writing, rather than something like *A Brief History of Time*, which just sits on people's coffee tables forever. I just don't think you should worry about that. I mean, obviously God had a sense of humor. Look at the Shroud of Turin. He so loved the world that he gave us his only begotten son—and a fitted top sheet.

MAGGIE ESTEP: I always think my writing is really tragic, mysterious and sad. And then people think it's funny—so they're laughing at my pain. But when something's funny, it doesn't seem like you've suffered enough. Like we're having too good a time out there.

The best humor you can write, if you're going inside yourself to find it, is brutally honest. Do you take a piece of yourself doing that?

O'ROURKE: I love doing that. That's the whole reason I do it. It's necessary, and that's what I think makes it universal, when you go to that primal thing.

James Finn Garner was obviously trying to deflate the balloon of political correctness with Politically Correct Bedtime Stories, *and P. J. O'Rourke has deflated a few balloons in his time. But are you usually just out to write something fun, or do you set out to do biting social commentary?*

GARNER: It depends on whether it's satire or not. Somebody asked me if comedy needs an object, and I answered no, but satire always does. But I was mad that not enough people got offended by the *Bedtime Stories*.

O'ROURKE: Somewhere in a vegetarian commune in California right now, they're seriously reading them.

GARNER: If you say you've got a higher goal, like puncturing a balloon, fine. But if it pisses people off, that's fun, too.

Humor is mainly channeled aggression. It's also a way of dealing with transgression, with breaking taboos. When you break a taboo in writing, you either have to get real funny or real serious. If it falls in the middle, you're just going to make people angry and uncomfortable. You have to either crank it up in the modern, "Mom was a drag queen and abused me and my sister and ate my little brother" school of memoir. . . ."

LEYNER: Then you get in the literary section.

How to Write Funny

GARNER: One of the ideas that I was going to talk about here is the short shelf life of humor. People read Twain and people might read Dorothy Parker, but nobody reads Robert Benchley or H.L. Mencken anymore. It seems to me that humor is often a very contemporary thing because it doesn't last a long time. And to be literary, you've got to last a long time. You've got to be dead.

ESTEP: But what about *Portnoy's Complaint*, where he's having sex with the liver? That's sort of timeless, isn't it?

GARNER: Sure, you've got Philip Roth, Terry Southern, Hunter Thompson. But anything written prior to 1960 meant to be humorous, no one reads anymore. Or am I wrong?

One of the distinctions Maggie makes with Portnoy's Complaint *is that humor about being human, living life, relationships, stands a better chance of being timeless than social commentary that's very particular to its time.*

O'ROURKE: Humor tends to be topical, because the effect you're striving for is a fast, involuntary thing. Humor has to work immediately; it has to hit little trip wires. And those trip wires tend to be things that are right on the front of people's minds; they tend to be highly topical things. The big element of a joke is surprise. And so the idea of an enduring joke is like the idea of an enduring surprise. That would be a pretty horrible thing, wouldn't it? It would be sort of like being in *Groundhog Day.* So it's no surprise that humor doesn't have the staying power tragedy does. It does, but only when it's about fundamental human concerns. Byron, for instance—the only part of Byron that's worth reading anymore is the funny stuff. When he's funny, he's very funny indeed. But in that case, the serious stuff is what's topical.

How tough is it to write humor when the headlines out of Washington, for instance, are so bizarre?

O'ROURKE: You can't keep ahead of it. You can't keep ahead of this bunch in Washington. Just when you think you've got a really good Clinton joke, he actually does it.

GARNER: When it was leaked that some tobacco company was going to market a root beer-flavored cigarette to entice teenagers, I wrote an essay quitting the business. Because this guy was a savant, obviously. He just popped up in a meeting and said, "Let's make a root beer-flavored cigarette!" That's perfect, that's what they're going to walk away with. I can't elaborate on that—except with maybe a vanilla cigarette to make a nice root beer float for the kids.

O'ROURKE: You need really strong issues to do satire. Satire is by definition humor with a moral point of view. I've never done any because I just don't have any morals. But when you have fuzzy issues and gray areas and everybody being sort of wrong about things . . . there won't be a whole bunch of good affirmative action jokes. The arguments are just too complex. Something like Vietnam or Nixon, and Watergate or even Monica—these things make pretty good jokes. But a complex issue like tax reform does not make a good joke.

Why, invariably, is the funniest, best piece in a magazine at the back?

LEYNER: I was on the back at *Esquire*, but then I lost it for a while to the editor's wife, who wanted it. Then I got it back for a while. Why? Look, most of the magazines we write for suck. And if someone can go right to the back page and read your piece without having to brave the rest of the magazine. . . . I think it's a coveted place, actually. I've never thought of it as being marginalized.

O'ROURKE: I used to be a magazine editor, and that last page is absolutely crucial. It is probably the first thing people see when they open the magazine besides the cover. And the cover, of course, doesn't have any actual content, so it is often the first thing people read. And it's very important in magazine economics because advertisers traditionally want the front of the book—they want the inside of the cover. But by putting something strong on the last page of a magazine, which is the idea of putting humor back there, you can sell the inside of the back cover for as much as you sell the inside of the front cover.

LEYNER: I even recommended that the *New England Journal of Medicine* have a funny back page.

Is there any fun in hitting the talk-show circuit?

O'ROURKE: It's very tough on a writer to go on them. The time is so compressed on talk shows, the morning shows in particular. They go on at about the time the average author goes to bed. The average author's not real sober at the time *Good Morning America* is on. You have to get what you have to say out real quick. If you have some performance experience, maybe it's OK, but most of us don't.

GARNER: I practice before I go on tour. I've got my one-minute spiel, my three-minute spiel and my five-minute spiel. Because you're gonna get an anchor in the morning—a very apt term, I've just realized—and you've got to take control. My second interview ever was at five in the morning at ChicagoLand TV, a cable news thing in the burbs here. We sit down, and ten seconds before we go on air, the woman says, "I didn't get through your book as much as I would have liked." And I had a seventy-page book at the time. I learned then that you just have to run with it. You can't allow them to have their own say, because most of the time they're pretty dim.

LEYNER: I was on CNN and the woman said, "I've only had the chance to read the spine of your book." And I said, "Did you like the ISBN number?"

ESTEP: Charlie Rose confused me, scared me. That was the first thing I ever did, and I just froze. It was me and other writers, and he would ask us these incredibly long questions. And eventually we just started reciting poems and stuff because we were so confounded. Then of course my grandfather was watching and I did this sex poem. . . .

How has the market for humor writers changed since you got into it?

GARNER: It's always kind of sucked, I think.

LEYNER: That's why I'm quitting. No more books for me. And I'm only half-kidding about that. Since I have a family now, I think about these things a lot more. You have to work very hard to make a good living as a writer. And there are so many opportunities opening in television now, with all these cable operations, and the money is so much of an order of magnitude better, it's difficult not to give that some serious thought. The market for those who write humorous books is bad—just like the market for all people who write books is bad. The only place humor is respected now is television.

O'ROURKE: That's a huge change in the market. When *National Lampoon* started in 1970, and in its sort of salad years through the first half of the seventies, there was no other place to go. I don't know whether it was a good magazine or not, but it was certainly a magazine with a lot of talented people writing for it. And people say, "Why isn't there a magazine like that out now?" The very simple reason is you may pay a writer thirty thousand dollars or fifty thousand dollars at a magazine with a circulation of less than a million. But that same talent can go, as all the *Harvard Lampoon* kids have gone, out to Los Angeles and make a much better living. And that didn't happen until *Saturday Night Live* in 1975.

It's telling how humor writers are regarded as compared to performers of humor. Think about the big Saturday Night Live *curse that was posited when Phil Hartman was gunned down. Nobody mentioned Michael O'Donoghue as part of the* SNL *group that had fallen—yet he was one of the funniest writers to come out of the seventies.*

O'ROURKE: O'Donoghue was a good friend of mine. It was Michael who first pointed out to me that to learn how to write you have to take things apart. A parody is a really good method of learning how to write. He was an extremely sharp guy. You could never get him to write anything at length. He had these flashes of insight. But Phil Hartman . . . I'm a married guy, you know. I figure, that must have been a hell of a fight. He must have really said something wrong. It had to be a little worse than, "That skirt with those knees?" I'd like to know what he said, just to make sure I don't say it.

P.J. O'Rourke's and James Finn Garner's books are in the humor sections of the stores, and Maggie Estep's and Mark Leyner's are in the literature sections. Is that where you feel you should be?

O'ROURKE: I'm going to pout for the whole rest of the panel.

LEYNER: I think that's proper.

O'ROURKE: Cats vs. Keats. Who wins at the cash register? Garfield every time.

Frank Sennett is the editor of Newcity.com, an alternative-press portal site.

How to Write Funny

CHAPTER 4

The Six Basics of Writing

BY J. KEVIN WOLFE

Deep inside each of us lurks a Bozo. You may not be able to tell a joke. You may not have been the class clown. But you don't have to act funny to *write* funny. We were all born with the creative ability of a Woody Allen. We just have to unlock it.

You say you're mundane? That's probably what accountant Bob Newhart said before he became a comedian. That's probably what historian Terry Jones and the late Graham Chapman, M.D. said before they joined Monty Python's Flying Circus. All that's required to write comedy is a sense of humor. And you can write it without ever leaving the comfort of your own personality.

Many of today's geniuses of humor have never appeared on a stage. Their best performances are before the word processor. Those keys never hiss, boo or groan. Best of all, those mechanical critics say only what we want them to.

What's So Funny

Comedy dies quickly under the microscope, so analyzing it is difficult. Ultimately, comedy comes from within. Developing a strong sense of humor comes from examining what's funny in yourself. What are your quirks? Your own habits, biases and outlooks are a great source of material. What irritates you about others? Exaggerate their shortcomings, but also pull a reverse on yourself and examine your own hatred. What are the misfortunes in your life? Notice the tricks that fate has played on you recently. None of us is perfect; our flaws make us laughable. Write a few jokes about yourself. Humor is many times a painfully honest comment about ourselves, individually and as a species.

Many humorists make themselves the butt of their own jokes. After a great lovemaking session in *Love and Death*, Woody Allen's partner comments on what a great lover he is. Allen replies, "I practice a lot when

I'm alone." Mark Twain showed his disdain for physical labor when he commented: "Whenever I get the urge to exercise, I lie down and rest until it goes away." No doubt you've said things as funny as these, intentionally or not. Our lives are filled with events that can be translated into humorous stories and anecdotes. Look for them.

What topics do you know best? Computer programming? Hunting? Gardening? Each of us has some specialty we're best qualified to joke about. These topics become your trademark. For years Erma Bombeck joked about motherhood and never ran out of ideas.

Whether the humor you write grows from within you or comments on the world we live in, we can generalize to say that people laugh at two things: surprise and misfortune.

We laugh in *surprise* at the union of two things that don't fit together, such as the Pope skateboarding. Surprise humor leads you in one direction and then takes a sharp turn. If a skateboard goes flying past you, you'd expect to see a kid on it, not His Holy Eminence.

We also laugh at people's *misfortunes*: of the rich and famous, of the poor and ethnic, of living where you do, of being yourself. This type of humor has a butt. Think of jokes you've heard recently. Who did they slam? George W. Bush? The French? The person who is listening to the joke? There's usually an element of cruelty involved here, either verbal or physical, subtle or blatant.

In humor, surprise and misfortune often intermingle. The misfortune can be surprising. Joan Rivers is famous for humor of misfortune: "Elizabeth Taylor has more chins than a Chinese phone book." Stephen Wright mostly does surprise humor: "I'm not afraid of heights, I'm afraid of widths." Gary Larson's "The Far Side" has integrated both. A bull waking up in bed from a nightmare screams: "The golden arches! The golden arches got me!"

The Building Blocks of Humorous Writing

Your decision to introduce humor into your writing is more important than the precise sort of humor you are writing. An article or book with an occasional humorous moment will differ from a television sitcom or stand-up comedy routine in the *amount* of humor you build into the piece—as well as the humor's intensity and style—but the techniques for making the work funny will not. To produce laughs, use these elements.

As a budding humorist, you must be able to write *the joke*, just as a sprouting novelist must be able to write a sentence. The joke is the element that humor is built from.

The term "joke" may be confusing. For our purposes, it refers to anything that makes you laugh. It can be an involved dirty joke, a one-liner, a cute aside, an ironic observation, a funny concept. If you can pinpoint what made you laugh, you've found the joke.

Though a joke may seem complex, it comprises only two parts: The *setup* and the *punch line*. The setup introduces the elements necessary to get the joke. It creates its own little world in a bubble that the punch line will burst. Here's a simple two-liner:

SETUP: Ed McMahon sure has been getting political on those envelopes hawking magazines through the mail.

PUNCH LINE: The last one said: "Free cash! Free prizes! Free Wen Ho Lee!"

The setup introduces something we can relate to. The punch line delivers the surprise by showing that thing in an absurd light we haven't seen it in before.

Sometimes the setup presents a humorous concept. In this case the punch line comments on the concept:

SETUP: Mattel has a new doll—Biker Barbie.

PUNCH LINE: She's the girl next door, provided you live next door to a Harley-Davidson dealer.

Some humorists claim that they don't do jokes. Read some of Russell Baker's old columns, examine a Mark Twain story or watch Bill Cosby. You may not even notice the jokes. They may have implied setup lines. The punch line may have been seeded in the opening line; it wasn't funny then, but it grows into hilarious full bloom by the end of the story. The advantage of spotting these concealed jokes is that you also learn to hide them.

Look closely at a Cosby bit, for instance, and you'll see the setups and punch lines are there. Here's an early skit, paraphrased, from Cosby's club act: Noah is in the rec room, sawing wood for a home project, when the Lord calls Noah's name. Noah asks who's there. The Lord replies, "The Lord." Sarcastically Noah says, "Right!" The Lord tells him to build an ark. "Right!" Then gather two of every kind of animal on the earth. "Right! Who is this really?" The Lord identifies himself again and says he's going to destroy the earth. "Right!—Am I on *Candid Camera?*—How are you going to do it?" The Lord says by making it rain for a thousand days and nights. "Right! Do this, you'll save water. Let it rain for forty days and nights and wait for the sewers to back up." The Lord says, "Right!"

The main setup to this sketch lies in the concept: How would a common person react if God suddenly started talking to him or her? There are some spottable punch lines there: "Who is this really?" "Am I on *Candid Camera?*" and "Wait for the sewers to back up." But the funniest part of the skit is the repeated insincere "Right!" With each slightly harder-to-believe demand that the Lord makes on Noah, the "Right!" gets funnier. It also serves as a setup. Noah keeps repeating it until the Big Guy pulls a reverse by saying it to Noah. (Three other classic sketches that illustrate this technique of building humor are Abbott and Costello's "Who's on First," Stan Freberg's "Banana Boat" and Monty Python's "Argument Clinic.")

It is often said that effective humor lies in the *timing,* the second basic element of humor writing. The easiest way to explain timing is to compare it to music. When you tell a joke out loud, the setup establishes a rhythm. Because it sets up not only the punch line, but also the timing, it's important for the setup to establish a clean, solid rhythm. Staying on your topic is like staying on beat. If you get off the beat with a clever aside, you lose the momentum going into your punch line.

The timing of a verbal joke also depends on the beat in the rhythm that you skip before and after a punch line. The first pause gives the audience time to piece the setup together. It also clues them that the punch line is

UNRAVELING SOME YARNS:
HOW FOUR HUMORISTS SPIN THEIR TALES

Stories by Dave Barry, Russell Baker, Mark Twain and Garrison Keillor turn bland, everyday life into humorous events. What's their secret? Let's gut a few stories and see what they're made of. We'll discuss four elements of humorous storytelling:

A funny opening

Colorful narration

Colorful characters

A concise plot

Here are the opening lines from Dave Barry's "Bad Habits."

> My wife and I were both born without whatever brain part it is that enables people to decorate their homes. If we lived in the Neanderthal era, ours would be the only cave without little drawings of elk on the walls.

Barry's first sentence overstates his interior decorating awkwardness. It's funny and grabs your attention. The second sentence draws both an analogy and a vivid mental picture. Already his story is hard to put down. By the end of the second sentence, we already know something of Barry's personality. This brings up the second element: The narrator.

Whether the story is told by you or through a character, the teller's personality is revealed. The following is an excerpt from Mark Twain's "Accident Insurance—Etc."

> Ever since I have been a director in an accident insurance company I have felt that I have been a better man. Life has seemed more precious. Accidents have assumed a kindlier aspect. Distressing special providences have lost half their horror. I look upon a cripple now with affectionate interest—as an advertise-

Continued on page 41

next, but without a lot of fanfare. The second pause gives the audience time to "get it" and laugh before you continue. Those two pauses showcase the punch lines without flaunting them.

When you tell a joke aloud, the pause comes naturally. The writer's question is: How do you print a pause? If your punch line is short, sometimes a period is pause enough. Short sentences have intensity when placed between long ones. The comma followed by "and" or "or" can also break the rhythm:

> The sad thing about the sixties was that the three most remembered voices of the decade were those of John F. Kennedy, Walter Cronkite, and Mr. Ed.

The commas separate the three examples while the "and" provides the pause. The punch line should always be the last example. When writing a humorous story, try this method to skip a beat: Place some brief action in the dialogue between the setup and the punch line. Have a character spit, flinch or frown. Don't take too long with it, though. Even a "he said" or "she said" is sometimes all it takes to create the first pause. Ending a paragraph after a punch line provides an effective second pause.

Scripted humor—as in movies and speeches—needs a more obvious pause. You should clearly cue the readers how to deliver their lines. Some comedy writers use a dash—before and after the punch line. Others use an ellipsis . . . in both places. Some underline key words that should be emphasized. You may even see these marks in humorous prose, but be careful: They're powerful stoppers. In scripts it's also acceptable to write "pause" in parentheses. It's understood in acting or public speaking that anything in parentheses is an instruction and shouldn't be read out loud.

Internal logic is the third building block on which your humor writing will rest. Humor leans toward the absurd today, so it's important to understand how logic continues to be applied to humor. Even though your humor will regularly take situations—real or made up—to extremes, the logic of that situation must remain consistent.

John Cleese, the unofficial leader of Monty Python's Flying Circus, believes that the comedy troupe's strength is in its logic. You can see Python ment. I do not seem to care for poetry any more. I do not care for politics—even agriculture does not excite me. But to me now there is a charm about a railway collision that is unspeakable.

Twain maintained that the manner in which you tell the story is more important than the subject matter of the story itself. Though we've learned nothing of the character's physical appearance, we've learned quite a bit about how he thinks. You're set up to believe that running a life insurance company has made this guy a better man. Life is more precious to him. Then you find out the truth: He's saying the opposite of what he means. It's a reverse. The business has hardened the man. The final blow comes when he tells you of the charm of a railway collision.

The third element is the character in the story. Here's a description of Russell Baker's stepfather from his book *Growing Up*.

He was hopelessly addicted to the Senators, a team of monumental incompetence on the baseball diamond. A Senators victory lifted him to ecstasy, a defeat cast him into the pit of depression. For Senators fans there wasn't much ecstasy in life. Switching off the radio after the Senators had lost yet again, Herb looked like man who'd glimpsed the afterlife and seen that Heaven was a fraud.

In a few sentences, you've found that Herb was religious about baseball. As you can see, colorful characters, real or fictional, aren't always loud. The color is revealed through their quirks. If the character is a real person, emphasize what makes him or her unique. Exaggerate a little. Make comparisons that drive a point home, like Baker did.

If you're creating a character, you have the freedom to play God. Your characters can be believable with tiny, amusing quirks. They can be hard to believe, like Twain's insurance man. Or they can be outrageous parodies of extremists. For example, an adamant vegetable-rights activist who throws himself in front of a moving combine to save innocent ears of corn.

Continued on page 43

logic at work in this absurd premise: A college grad walks into an accounting office to apply for his first job. On entering, he's shocked to find everyone in the reception area is seated—on the ceiling. The other applicants are peacefully seated in chairs, upside-down. The receptionist is answering phones behind a desk, upside-down. Our grad, despite the fact that his gravity is different from everyone else's, must try to fit in.

From this point on, the humor stems from the applicant trying his best to be like everybody else. After receiving an application from the receptionist, he attempts to sit in a chair on the ceiling. First he jumps up and grabs the top of the chair. Then he lifts and contorts himself to sit in the chair, despite the gravity problems. With the application still in his teeth, he finally twists his legs around the chair legs to hold himself in. Meanwhile, the other applicants are trying to ignore him.

Once in the chair, our grad greets the people in the chairs next to him on the ceiling. He straightens his tie, pulls a pen from his pocket and promptly drops it on the floor. The boss, upside-down, too, then calls *his* name. With an obvious embarrassed smile, he pulls himself across the empty chairs on the ceiling to get to the boss's door. The boss meanwhile is impatiently looking at his watch.

See the logic there? The applicant's gravity was different from everyone else's, but the absurd premise remained constant. He accepted that he must conform to this odd gravity to fit in. Everybody else accepted the gravity as normal. Your humor must apply this same type of logic to any situation where something is out of the ordinary.

Somewhat related is the fourth element of humor writing: *internal consistency*. Logic also applies to mixing types of humor. Changing your focus from one type of humor to another in midpiece usually doesn't work. A biting satire can be cheapened by suddenly ending it with a slapstick riot. There are ways to incorporate other styles of humor, of course; if you're determined to use slapstick in your satire, use it as a subplot and not as a main punch line. But the general rule is if you start with satire (or whatever your style of writing), end with a solid satirical note. A character piece can be ruined by turning it into a pun-fest in the middle. If a character's flaw is that he constantly uses puns, keep them flowing all the way through. Then end with an unexpected pun.

It's important to breathe life into your characters. One way is to give them a humorous flaw. In *Roxanne*, it was Steve Martin's nose. In *Crocodile Dundee*, it was Paul Hogan's big-city virginity. You can use irony, perhaps a safety-conscious motorcycle daredevil who never quite jumps the buses because of the extra weight of his seat belts, airbags and emergency parachutes.

Look for character traits in yourself and those around you. Exploit your own quirks. Parody a current trend you've caught yourself following. Each of us *is* a humorous character.

The final element is a concise plot. Think of your story as an extended joke. And it's been long maintained that what makes a joke is the way you tell it. Here's how Garrison Keillor handles a boring topic: How the town got its name in *Lake Wobegon Days*.

> New Albion became Lake Wobegone in 1880, a change voted by the City Council to celebrate the fact that Norwegians had gained a 4-3 majority. Then the City Council voted to become the Town Council. The New Englanders bitterly opposed both changes, arguing . . . "Wobegone means dismal, unhappy, dilapidated, bedraggled!" . . . The Norwegians just sat and smiled. To them, Wobegone was the name of the lake they loved and nothing more. They liked the sound of it.
>
> In 1882, Lake Wobegone became New Albion again, Mr. Fjelde having lost his seat to Mr. Weeks by two votes. Mr. Fjelde got back on the Council two years later, and then it was Lake Wobegone again. State statute permits four name changes, after which a name is considered permanent . . . so Council changed it one more time, from Lake Wobegone to Lake Wobegon. Mr. Getchell resigned in protest . . ."

Keillor, in his subtle way, condensed more than four years of history into two paragraphs. The quick look at the long-standing petty squabble is what makes it funny.

Your audience expects you to be *unpredictable,* so it becomes the fifth building block of your humor writing. If you aren't unpredictable, they'll be surprised, but they won't be laughing. If your humor is always misdirected in the same direction, the audience can predict where you're headed. Perhaps they notice that you're always using "my spouse" as a punch line. If you notice your punch lines getting stale, try a different logic. Make your readers think you're doing another spouse joke and then pull a reverse on them.

Using old jokes in your work is very predictable. There's no surprise in hearing a joke for the second time. Use your own fresh material that comes from your own experiences.

A lot of humor is based on cliches. Verbal cliches, commonplace situations and stereotypes are important in humor. They're predictable and need little setup since everyone is familiar with them. They become unpredictable when you twist or parody them, but do so in a way that conforms to comedy logic. Still, many times you'll see them presented unmodified. Do these trite characters still strike you as funny: The country bumpkin? The dumb blonde? The lisping gay? Probably not, unless they have something incredibly funny to say.

Finally, the best humor is *concise.* Ask yourself: Is this line needed? Can I make this line shorter? Is this aside really that funny? Can I format this joke differently to make it move quicker? Here's an example of a lean joke:

George W. Bush's plan to gain environmentalists' support for his energy policy: solar-powered oil pumps.

Sometimes moving or deleting one word makes the difference between a solid joke and a weak one. In these fast-paced times, people become bored more quickly than they did thirty years ago. Compare an episode of *The Honeymooners* to an episode of *Friends*; you'll be amazed at how much faster the humor moves today. Today's humor is written in punch lines that set up other punch lines.

Exit Laughing

As I said, all humor begins with the joke, and so must you. Search out the humorous stories you have to tell. But tell them carefully; trust your audience *and* your writing ability. Be confident: If your writing is funny, the audience knows when to laugh.

J. Kevin Wolfe writes copy for a nationally respected advertising firm. He is the author of four cookbooks and until 1999 produced *The Gary Burbank Show* on Cincinnati's WLW radio, where Burbank was twice named the nation's top radio personality by *Billboard* magazine.

CHAPTER 5

Comedy Workshop

BY JENNIFER CRUSIE

Writing comedy is hard because "funny" is subjective. Tragedy is pretty much universal—Beth breathing her last as Meg, Jo and Amy weep; *Titanic*'s Jack Dawson turning into an ice cube in front of his horrified lover; Old Yeller traumatizing thousands of people who are now middle-aged but still can't forget—but comedy is all over the place. There are people who think Monty Python is brilliant, people who think Ovid is a real knee-slapper, people who think Jerry Lewis is a god, people who think Oscar Wilde has no peer and people who think Adam Sandler represents everything that is good and true about humor today. These are not, needless to say, the *same* people. It's hard to teach anybody to write funny when the vast teeming mass of readers out there can't even agree on what is funny.

Still, when you narrow the topic to writing comic stories, there are some universals:

- Humor begins in the writer's *voice.*
- Humor reveals more about *character* than anything else except action.
- Humor, like *plot*, is often couched in expectation and reversal.
- The best humor, the strongest and most thoughtful humor, comes from a serious *theme.*

Voice

Humor in fiction is based in voice, which is why humor is so different from writer to writer and why a strong voice is essential in writing comic fiction. The biggest mistake that beginning writers make is ignoring their own voices to try to sound more like Real Authors. The biggest mistake that beginning comedy writers make is ignoring their own senses of humor to try to sound more like Real Comedians. Voice and sense of humor are the most important hallmarks of the great comic writers, and they can't be copied or faked. Listen to these voices:

Was Edith here with you Thursday night? This place must be very becoming to her. Next to being in a coal mine, I can't think of anywhere she could go that the light would be more flattering to that pan of hers. Do you really know a lot of people that say she's good-looking? . . . Now to me, Edith looks like something that would eat her young. . . . — *Dorothy Parker*

The Middle Ages saw the breakdown of civilization in Western Europe—a severe decline in cultural values and standards; a rapid descent into chaos and near-barbarism. So it was a pretty good time for guys. They could spit pretty much whenever they wanted, and for entertainment, they could go to jousting tournaments and cheer for their favorite knights. ("Hey, Lancelot! You *suck!*") — *Dave Barry*

How long can we maintain, I wondered. How long before one of us starts raving and jabbering at this boy? . . . If so—well, we'll just have to cut his head off and bury him somewhere. Because it goes without saying that we can't turn him loose. He'll report us at once to some kind of outback nazi law enforcement agency, and they'll run us down like dogs. — *Hunter Thompson*

Nobody is more alive than I am to the fact that young Bingo Little is in many respects a sound old egg. . . . On the other hand, I'm bound to say that there are things about him that could be improved. . . . If you want shrinking reticence, don't go to Bingo, because he's got about as much as a soap advertisement. — *P.G. Wodehouse*

EXERCISE ONE: Write down something funny that happened to you. Put it aside for a day. The next day, tell the same story into a tape recorder, imagining an audience of your friends as you tell it. Transcribe the tape exactly when you're finished, and compare the two versions of the story:

How is the language different? Is your word choice more colloquial and relaxed in the transcribed story? That's your true voice, one you may have buried in an effort to sound authoritative or educated. (Authoritative and educated are rarely funny, or at least, rarely funny on purpose.)

Is the transcribed story longer? Spoken stories tend to feature a lot of unnecessary words—ums, ahs, likes, etc.—but they also tend to feature asides and verbal flourishes that make the story more fun to read in general and possibly funnier, too. Keep the good stuff that adds flavor and flourish, and cut the places where you buried your story in verbiage.

Does your sentence structure change from one version to the next? In particular, look at the rhythm of your spoken sentences. Where did you put the emphasis when you spoke the sentences that carried the comic freight? The pressure in telling a spoken story is that the audience is right there, so good storytellers tend to automatically phrase things for the greatest impact.

Chances are, the spoken story has the strongest voice, and is therefore more immediate and better paced, which also means it's probably funnier. That's why a good way to make sure your writing works is to read your finished drafts out loud. With a little practice, you'll hear the lines that clunk and be able to fix them.

Just as you must be true to your own voice as an author, you must be true to your characters' voices. You should know your major characters—protagonist, antagonist, major supporting players—so well that you can hear them distinct and different in your head, so well that if all you saw was an untagged line of dialogue, you'd know which character was speaking. The character dialogue in Richard Curtis's screenplay for *Four Weddings and a Funeral* is a good example of this. Look at the adeptly comic toast that Curtis's protagonist Charles gives at the first wedding and the terrible comic toast that Curtis's bungling but good-natured Tom gives at the next wedding to see how essentially the same speech will be vastly different depending on who delivers it.

EXERCISE TWO: To see how well you know your major characters' voices, write a short monologue for each of them telling the same joke. If your characters are truly individual, the three monologues will utilize different vocabularies and be phrased and paced differently, with different aspects stressed.

Character

Humor tells more about character than anything else except action. Many beginning writers think if they can just think up a funny situation, they'll have comic fiction, but the comedy or tragedy of any premise depends on the characters stuck in it.

Look at these premises:

A man who has lost his job, and because of that his marriage, is now about to lose his beloved son, too, because he can't pay his back child support. Tragic.

But that's also *The Full Monty*, a great story that's funny because of its characters, not because they are laughable but because they laugh.

An overweight, homely woman decides that since she will never be married, there's nothing left but suicide. Tragic.

But listen to her voice: "The first thing I did when I made the decision to kill myself was to stop dieting. Let them dig a wider hole." That's Sheila Levine from Gail Parent's *Sheila Levine Is Dead and Living in New York*, finding comic emancipation in anticipated death.

An addict whose life seems empty and hopeless overdoses. Tragic.

But Carrie Fisher's Suzanne in *Postcards From the Edge* opens her story with "Maybe I shouldn't have given the guy who pumped my stomach my phone number," and her tragedy becomes wry because she's wry.

A woman who is seven months pregnant discovers her husband is having an affair and is going to leave her. Tragic.

But Nora Ephron opens *Heartburn* with this and instantly makes her Rachel a sympathetic character coping with desperate humor: "The first day I did not think it was funny. I didn't think it was funny the third day, either, but I managed to make a little joke about it. 'The most unfair thing about this whole business,' I said, 'is that I can't even date.' Well, you had to be there." This is the voice of a character dealing with adversity through humor, and not just any humor but the humor of her own voice and values. She's not denying that the adultery happened or that it wasn't devastating, but she's telling the story on her terms, insisting that the story is about her not him—it's not that he betrayed her, it's that she can't find a replacement for him right away. Nobody believes this is true, not even Rachel, but the whistling-in-the-dark quality of the humor characterizes her spirit better than any other approach.

Humor is carried by character, not by action or plot. Comedy is not found in premise, it's found in the characters' reactions to premise.

EXERCISE THREE: Inherent in your story is probably at least one situation fraught with possible disaster. Go back to it, and rewrite it so that your protagonist uses wit to save herself or himself: He charms the antagonist; she recasts the reality of the situation to make it funny instead of insulting; he distracts the antagonist by making her laugh; she skews the power in the situation by setting up a context in which the antagonist will be a poor sport if he doesn't laugh, etc. (Note: The humor shouldn't be used as a form of denial; the humor should actually help the character control the situation.)

If you don't have any potential disasters in your story (and you should have; that's called conflict and it's necessary), try one of these examples:

Your protagonist is giving an important dinner party or business presentation at which everything has gone wrong and the person to be impressed has just gotten up to leave.

Your protagonist has just pulled a gun on a menacing thug only to find that the clip is empty.

Your protagonist has just proposed marriage only to learn that his or her significant other wants to end the relationship.

CHARACTER AND CONTEXT

There is another aspect of humor and character that good comic writers mine: context. Humor is subjective, so it often depends on the community in which it's offered; that is, humor depends not only on the character using it but also on the characters listening to it. And the way others respond and participate in the humor can demonstrate the health (or dis-ease) of the community or relationship.

There's a short conversation near the beginning of William Goldman's screenplay for *Butch Cassidy and the Sundance Kid* that conveys everything you need to know about the relationship among three men: Butch, Sundance and a man named Logan who has challenged Butch to a knife fight for the leadership of the gang. Logan calls to Sundance who is standing

How to Write Funny

beside Butch, and says, "When we're done, if he's dead, you're welcome to stay." Butch says to Sundance out of Logan's earshot, "Listen, I'm not a sore loser or anything, but when we're done, if I'm dead, kill him." Sundance then says loudly, "Love to." Logan thinks the answer is for him, the audience knows it's for Butch, which makes them part of the Butch/Sundance community; they're in with the in-crowd and Logan has lost before he's begun to fight. This kind of matter-of-fact exchange communicates loyalty and engages the audience much more strongly than any amount of on-the-nose "I love you, man" dialogue can.

One caveat: Don't become so enamored of banter that you lose sight of your characters. William Goldman was admirably honest about the flaws in his *Butch Cassidy* screenplay, but the only mistake he has said filled him with despair was that he had Butch and Sundance wisecrack as they died. His confession says it all: "How could I have done that? These are my *heroes*."

EXERCISE FOUR: Look at the community your protagonist lives and works in. Is he or she the insider (one of the good guys) or the outsider (the only functioning human being in a soulless environment)? If he or she is an insider, what in-jokes can you exploit as a writer to show the closeness (see any ensemble comedy for examples: *M*A*S*H* [scenes between the medical staff], *Friends*, *Seinfeld*, etc.) and to make the reader/viewer feel part of the group? If your protagonist is an outsider, what absurdity can you exploit to make the reader bond with the protagonist as outsiders together (see any anarchic comedy for examples: *Brazil*, *Head Office*, *M*A*S*H* [scenes against the military])? Rewrite the scene using humor to exploit the community already there.

CHARACTER AND RELATIONSHIPS

You can also use humor to cement individual relationships. The banter that has been part of romantic comedy since *His Girl Friday* is there not because it's funny but because it tells the reader that these are two people who understand each other so well that they can one-up each other without slowing down or missing a beat. In fact, they're so attuned to each other, they speak in the same rhythms. A lack of rhythm can have the reverse effect; antibanter underscores distance and dislike (see the conversation between Charles and John on page 55). This fusion-through-dialogue isn't only for lovers; it's also a staple in every buddy picture. See the *Lethal Weapon* scripts, the *Buffy the Vampire Slayer* television scripts, Rex Stout's Nero Wolfe novels and Robert Parker's Spencer books.

One caveat: Banter should never be insulting or hurtful; it's a demonstration of partnership, a friendly game of verbal ping pong, lobbing words lightly over a very small net. Another: Banter may be light, but the two partners are always communicating something important. No conversation belongs in a story just because it's funny, in the same way no scene belongs in a story just because it's funny.

For a classic banter exchange, look at the scene in Goldman's *Butch Cassidy* where Butch and Sundance have been trapped on a cliff high over roaring rapids, the one that begins with Butch saying "The next time I say let's go somewhere like Bolivia, let's go somewhere like Bolivia." It's done in fast-cut dialogue that works as shorthand to communicate the desperateness of their situation and their absolute bond with each other without ever mentioning either and ends with one of the best punch lines in comic narrative that also neatly nails both men's philosophy of life and the basis of their relationship.

EXERCISE FIVE: Choose a scene between your protagonist and another character who is involved in a close relationship with him or her, such as a best friend, lover or partner. What kind of in-jokes do they have, and what do those jokes say about their situation? What speech patterns and rhythms do they mimic (that is, how do they reflect each other)? How do they poke gentle fun at each other? How does their kidding demonstrate their loyalty and devotion? Rewrite the scene so the humor does double-duty by also characterizing their relationship and the context within which they function.

Plot

Humor is often couched in expectation and reversal, the surprise that makes laughter, as Hobbes said, that feeling of sudden glory. From the first sentence of your story, you set up an expectation; the reader immediately begins to guess what will happen, shaping that expectation as she or he reads on and gathers more information. This puts the author in a double bind: She has to meet that expectation or the reader will feel cheated of her promise, but if the expectation is met exactly, the reader will also feel cheated because that's what he thought would happen so there's no revelation or reversal, no sense of sudden glory in the outcome. Adding humor to this authorial catch-22 only amplifies the problem.

Dorothy Parker was a master at expectation and reversal, even in her dinner conversation. A man seated next to her at a party, knowing she was a great wit, challenged her to say something funny about horticulture. He'd actually given her a head start because "horticulture" is a ridiculous word, so her audience sat back, ready to hear something funny about a pompous term. If she'd said something wry about taking care of plants, people would have been disappointed because that's what they were expecting; if she'd refused or ducked the term, they'd also have been disappointed because she would have cheated. Instead, without pausing, Parker said, "You can lead a horticulture, but you cannot make her think." Expectation and reversal accomplished, and a smart remark made at a dinner seventy years ago still has the power to make people laugh.

Patricia Gaffney did much the same thing in narrative in the first chapter of her novel *Crooked Hearts*. The book opens on two hot, dusty people trapped in a stage coach, one a wealthy blind man, the other a poor nun. But as the book begins, the nun pulls up her skirt to adjust the gun that is digging into her thigh; she's not a holy sister, she's a con woman, collecting money for a nonexistent charity. Expectation: She's going to try to bilk the rich blind man but probably will end up taking care of him because she has a heart of gold. Then comes the reversal: The blind man's not blind; he's a con man, too, using his fake disability to scam the softhearted, and his next mark was going to be the nun toting around all that charity money until he saw her gun and her thigh.

Every scene you write sets up an expectation; every funny scene you write will be stronger if you use the reversal of that expectation to surprise the laughter out of the reader. (Caveat: William Goldman has said that one of the weaknesses of the *Butch Cassidy* screenplay is that there were too many reversals, to the point of setting the audiences' teeth on edge. You want to give your readers a ride, not whiplash.)

EXERCISE SIX: Write a scene that sets up a common expectation. The bigger the cliche, the better: Two men who are complete opposites are forced to be partners; a powerful and attractive man suddenly notices the spectacled secretary who has adored him for years; the most popular boy or girl in school decides to make the most unpopular student attractive and desirable. Then reverse the outcome in a new and different way so that the outcome is fresh, interesting and funny. (I never said it was going to be easy.)

PLOT AND SETTING

Setting can also use expectation and reversal to set up comedy. The fish-out-of-water story works because it reverses the reader's expectation of that setting: A man in a business suit carrying a briefcase isn't funny in New York City, but on a beach in the Bahamas he's odd enough to at least engender a smile. (Remember the movie poster for the classic comedy *Local Hero*? The image of Peter Riegert in a suit and tie, carrying a briefcase, standing in the ocean with his pants rolled up to his knees, telegraphed immediately that this was a comedy because it was visual expectation and reversal.) Like the context of community, the context of setting can heighten tension and create humor.

Example: Your protagonist is late to his or her own wedding rehearsal dinner and must placate a stuffy in-law.

If they're alone in the vestibule of a nice restaurant, there's the expected tension (blah) and no contrast.

If they're inside the restaurant with people watching and eavesdropping, the tension is stronger, but still pretty standard.

But if the protagonist made the reservations a year earlier and in the meantime the restaurant has changed hands and is now a theme eatery—everybody's wearing cowboy hats and calling the mother-in-law "filly," it's one of those horrible comic places where the waiters throw rolls, it's now a Hooters—your protagonist has a lot more to cope with, and the expectation/reversal possibilities are much stronger.

EXERCISE SEVEN: Look at the scenes in your story that need more humor and tension. Change the setting to heighten the comic pressure, rewriting so that the tension in the setting strips a layer of control from your characters and forces them to take new risks.

How to Write Funny

PLOT AND SCENE PATTERN

Look at the patterns you've established in your story. Even if you haven't worked with motif, metaphor or repetition on purpose, you probably have done it inadvertently. These are the places that you can make reversal work for you because they're intrinsic to the story. Chances are you've fulfilled the expectations set up by these repetitions, but when you deliberately shift the actions of the scene, you surprise the reader and fulfill the expectations.

Richard Curtis had to write four upper-class weddings for *Four Weddings and a Funeral.* That's the same expectation four times, with heightened demands for reversal each time. The first wedding sets up reader expectations: The protagonist, Charles, forgets the rings as best man, makes a roastlike toast of the bride and groom that comes off only because he's so awkwardly charming, ducks an ex-girlfriend and makes a fool of himself in front of a pretty girl named Carrie in a beat that has four reversals in five lines:

> Charles: So, John—how's that gorgeous girlfriend of yours?
>
> John: She's no longer my girlfriend.
>
> Charles: O dear—still I wouldn't get too gloomy—rumor has it she never stopped bonking old Toby de Lisle, just in case you didn't work out.
>
> John: She is now my wife.
>
> Charles: Excellent. Excellent. Congratulations. [Carrie excuses herself and Charles goes off to pound his head against a tent pole.]

This exchange is actually antibanter. John deliberately refuses to play conversational Ping-Pong with Charles, which heightens Charles's tension and underscores how out of sync the two of them are; they've never been and never will be friends.

Now Curtis has to do a second wedding. He brings in a comic vicar foreshadowed in the first wedding to botch the ceremony this time, has Charles's nice but not charming friend make a horrible toast as he tries to mimic Charles, sets Charles at a table full of his ex-girlfriends and then has Charles meet Carrie again only to find she's engaged.

With the third wedding, Curtis has set up a clear pattern of expectation: Something will go wrong during the ceremony, there will be an important-to-the-story toast/speech, Charles will have an ex-girlfriend encounter and Charles will lose Carrie. But if all these things happen, Curtis's story dies in its tracks because it's become predictable. So he reverses expectation while hitting all these aspects: The thing that's wrong with the third ceremony is that it's Carrie's, and Charles watches helplessly while she marries the wrong man. Later at the reception, one of Charles's closest friends tells him she's always loved him, and he's left even more miserable. And the toasts, a charming one by Carrie that emphasizes what Charles has lost followed by a clumsy speech by her clod of a husband, are given while another close friend dies of a heart attack. None of this is funny, but it provides the grave note that the best comedy needs while reversing and fulfilling expectation (see "Theme" on page 57).

Curtis's funeral scene is a complete reversal; a funeral is the opposite of a wedding and this one is the opposite of all the wedding scenes that preceded it: Everyone shows up on time, the toast/eulogy is beautiful, everyone (including Charles's ex-girlfriends) is united in their grief, and Carrie shows up alone.

The fourth and last wedding then becomes the scene with the highest expectations, and the reversal is just as high: This wedding is Charles's and he's marrying one of his exes; when Carrie shows up to tell him she's divorced, it's the ultimate ex-girlfriend encounter.

The reversals in your story must be unexpected and yet clearly motivated by the characters of the players. They must evoke a response from the reader that says, "I wasn't expecting that, but now I see that's the only possible way it could have happened." And if you're writing comic fiction, the reversals must surprise and delight in such a way as to provoke laughter. This is tough to pull off, but it's also powerful, so it's worth beating your head against the keyboard to master.

EXERCISE EIGHT: Find the patterns in your story and explore the reversals inherent there. Break the repeated scenes down into their different parts—e.g., Curtis's botched ceremonies, bad speeches, old girlfriends, losses of Carrie—and brainstorm the ways you can both heighten the repetition and reverse the expectation. Don't go with your first ideas; make a list of at least ten things that could change so that you find the freshest idea with the most comic potential, and then make sure the changes are things that the characters would do naturally.

Theme

Comedy is about pain because good comedy is about truth, and while the truth may set you free, it almost always inflicts a few wounds before letting you go. It is possible to write light comedy about superficial subjects—P.G. Wodehouse was a genius at it—but it's almost impossible to write comic stories about characters who feel real enough for the reader to care about without going to the dark places and showing the pain. Remember Goldman's despair over the wisecracking at the end of *Butch Cassidy*? Just as tragedy needs comic relief to keep readers from killing themselves in despair, so comedy needs some seriousness to ground it and make it meaningful.

Four Weddings and a Funeral desperately needs that funeral scene to bring the emptiness of Charles's lack of connection home, just as *The Full Monty* needs those heartbreaking father/son scenes to give the story depth and weight. Ephron's *Heartburn* is laugh-out-loud funny, but it's the fact that her heroine is always aware of the pit of despair that threatens to consume her that makes the comedy sharp and the ending a bittersweet triumph. And then there's Annie Bolles of Sally Mandel's *Out of the Blue*, who opens her story with, "I pictured God feeling a little bored one morning and sifting through his files until he found my name. Oh, yeah, that little jock, Annie Bolles. That flibbertigibbet who never sits still. Let's give her multiple sclerosis and see how she handles it." Mandel's novel is terrific romantic comedy in a large part because, although it is not a story about disease, it's a story weighted and freighted by the threat of disease.

Much of the power of comedy is that it is an explosion of relief; without a strong serious theme to bounce against, pure comedy can't offer relief from anything.

EXERCISE NINE: Your protagonist, if he or she is at all real, has flaws and fears, a dark side that isn't funny in the least. Go back through your story to find the serious theme under the laughter, the universal statement about the human condition that your story addresses in its subtext. Then see where the humor in the story reflects that theme. The places that remain, the scenes or the dialogue exchanges that are funny for the sake of being funny, are the ones to work on. If you can't make them meaningful, cut them. But if you can rewrite them to bounce off your theme, the laughter they evoke will be much deeper and much more satisfying.

And finally, a few don'ts:

• Don't try to add humor to a story. Humor in a story must come from character. Going back and adding a few snappy lines will only make your characters look shallow, like the guy at the party who keeps cracking inappropriate jokes until everybody hates him. Everything must be intrinsic to the story from the beginning. You can rewrite to heighten humor, but you can't just dump some in.

• Don't have your characters react to comedy in the stories if you can avoid it. If your characters laugh hysterically at something one of them says and your reader didn't think it was funny, that reader will think your characters are morons. Never supply your own laugh track.

• Avoid slapstick and complex physical humor in fiction. Slapstick is a visual shock, and you can't get the same impact by describing an action that you can by showing it. One of my favorite pieces of slapstick is from *Spaceballs*: Rick Moranis takes a sip of scalding coffee and spits it out just as somebody slaps him on the back, causing his helmet to fall forward just as he spits so that the coffee will ricochet back . . . Doesn't sound funny, does it? By the time you've visualized it, it's just a fancy spit take. But in the two seconds it takes to see it, it's a wonderful piece of physical comedy. The written story can't do action fast enough to pull off real slapstick.

Comedy is hard. In many ways, it's like singing: If you have perfect pitch, it's much easier. But you can still go a long way toward mastering the rudiments if you just trust your voice. Most of the mistakes I've seen people make in trying to write funny is that they don't trust their own senses of humor. They don't think they're funny, and they set out to write funny the way they've read other people being funny with a grim determination that pretty much precludes any chance that anybody is going to have fun. Relax, listen to your characters, exploit their fears and flaws, and mine their situations for places in which they can use their own brands of humor.

How to Write Funny

Then forget being funny to concentrate on your characters and tell the story they—and you—have to tell. Writing comedy is hard, writing *anything* is hard, but the rewards for both you and your reader make the struggle worthwhile. Good luck!

Jennifer Crusie is the author of *Tell Me Lies*; *Welcome to Temptation*; and, most recently, *Fast Women*. She has been named Best Series/Category Author by the Internet Romance Readers Anonymous listserv and received a Career Achievement Award in Romantic Comedy by *Romantic Times Magazine*. The RWA selected her *Crazy for You* as one of the top ten romances of 1999. She lives in Columbus, Ohio, with her three dogs, Bernie, Lucy and Rosie.

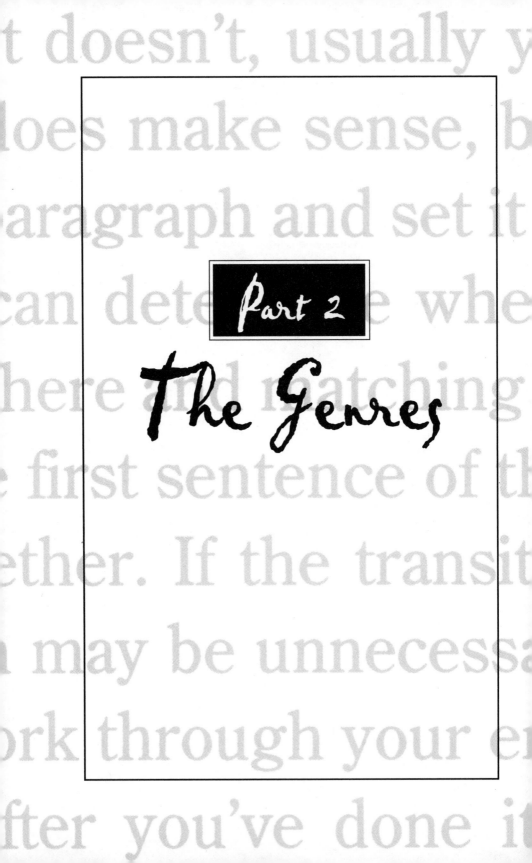

Part 2

The Genres

CHAPTER 6

The More and Less of Writing Humorous Fiction

BY CONNIE WILLIS

If you shy away from writing humorous stories, it's no wonder. They're tough to write. They're full of witty lines, sight gags and wordplay, as well as plots, characters, settings and everything else you're already struggling with. And to top it off, no one will tell you how to write funny. "Humor is unanalyzable," the experts intone, and "To dissect humor is to destroy it." Even Robert Benchley, a famous humorist who should have known better, declared, "Defining and analyzing humor is a pastime of humorless people."

The effect of all this is to surround humorous writing with a daunting air of mystery, to make you think it just comes naturally. (Trust me. *No* writing comes naturally.) And because it doesn't come naturally to you, *and* because Benchley said you're devoid of humor for even asking about it, you obviously have no business trying.

Balderdash! Humorous fiction has analyzable and learnable techniques. More than can be covered in a single article, in fact. But we can make a good start by looking at two of the most important techniques of humorous writing.

Exaggeration

To exaggerate is to enlarge or overstate the truth. It is the cornerstone of comedy and so pervasive that stand-up comics can't get halfway through "It was so hot last week," before the audience breaks in with, "*How hot was it?*"

Because of Johnny Carson and his peers, you might assume that exaggeration is a modern form of humor, but it's been around forever. Shakespeare called Bardolph's red nose a bonfire and said it was so bright it had saved "a thousand marks in lengths and torches." Samuel Coleridge described a night "so dark the cats ran against each other." And Americans have been telling tall tales for years about mosquitoes so big four of them could hold a man down, and places so cold that words freeze in midair and must be taken inside and thawed before you can hear them.

In *Roughing It*, Mark Twain, our national tall-tale teller, wrote about a horse so fast the wagon started thirty yards ahead of a cloudburst and made it home without getting a drop of rain on it—"But my dog was a-swimmin' behind the wagon all the way!" He also described the first time he ate a tamarind:

> They pursed my lips, till they resembled the stem-end of a to-mato, and I had to take my sustenance through a quill for twenty-four hours. They sharpened my teeth till I could have shaved with them, and gave them a "wire edge" that I was afraid would stay; but a citizen said, "No, it will come off when the enamel does"—which was comforting, at any rate.

Mark Twain called his exaggerations "stretchers," which is exactly the right word. Stretching the truth makes it funny, but don't yank it past the breaking point. Twain wouldn't have made his description of tamarinds funnier by writing, "And then they ate through my teeth and the insides of my mouth and my jawbone, and the whole lower half of my face fell off."

Those are definitely exaggerations, but not funny ones. It's not because we can't believe them—we don't believe Twain had to eat through a straw, either. It's that they don't have anything to do with how eating a tamarind feels. Exaggerating the literal truth, if it's done well, shows us the emotional truth of a situation.

When Twain writes, "they sharpened my teeth till I could have shaved with them," we laugh partly at the image it conjures, but mostly because we've eaten fruit that felt exactly that sour. The humor is already there. Exaggeration's purpose is to bring out that humor. It's like turning the volume up so we can hear better.

In the introduction to *Three Men in a Boat* (possibly the funniest book every written and a required primer for anyone interested in writing humorous fiction), Jerome K. Jerome says the book records "events that really happened. All that has been done is to color them, and, for this, no extra charge has been made." The events are all perfectly ordinary: trying to remember whether you packed your toothbrush, reading about diseases and convincing yourself you have them all, trying to open a can of pineapple when you forgot to bring the can opener:

> Then Harris tried to open the tin with a pocketknife, and broke the knife and cut himself badly; and George tried a pair of scissors, and the scissors flew up, and nearly put his eye out. While they were dressing their wounds, I tried to make a hole in the thing with the spiky end of the hitcher, and the hitcher slipped and jerked me out between the boat and the bank into two feet of muddy water, and the tin rolled over, uninjured, and broke a teacup.

This is exaggeration, but not by much. The truth has been colored only a little. And it feels more like the truth than a factual account of what happened. Jerome's exaggerations bring out the emotional truth of the situation.

So you must start with the truth when you write humor. You must think about how sour the tamarinds in your life are and how ridiculous you feel trying to open your cans of pineapple, and build from there. And you must know when to stop, because bigger and wilder and more ridiculous aren't necessarily funnier.

A classic example is the tall tale about the place in Texas so dry that during Noah's flood . . . You expect the punch line to be, "it didn't rain at all," which would be an exaggeration and fairly funny. But that's not how the story goes. It goes like this: "That part of Texas was so dry that during the flood it only got an inch and a half."

The story exaggerates well beyond the bounds of literal truth, but by stopping short, it somehow makes the whole thing seem almost plausible. (There *are* parts of Texas that seem that dry.) Sometimes less is definitely more.

Understatement

Understatement is less—much less. Instead of stretching or coloring the truth, understatement downplays it, describes it with restraint. Turns the volume down. Or off.

Mark Twain used understatement almost as much as exaggeration. "If at any time you find it necessary to correct your brother," he advised little girls, "do not correct him with mud." And he described an argument this way: "Then he rode over and began to rebuke the stranger with a six-shooter and the stranger began to explain with another." It's the exact opposite of exaggeration, and yet it makes you laugh because the description (or the language or the response) is so completely out of proportion to the situation. A gun battle becomes a "rebuke."

Don't get the idea you must choose one or the other. Humor is not a decision between More *or* Less. Twain often used understatement and exaggeration in the same sentence. After describing those tamarinds in hilarious overblown detail, he added laconically, "It seemed to me they were rather sour that year."

And Jerome combined exaggeration and understatement to wonderful effect in the episode of the pineapple:

> Then we all got mad. We took that tin out on the bank, and Harris went up into a field and got a big sharp stone, and I went back into the boat and brought out the mast, and George held the tin and Harris held the sharp end of his stone against the top of it, and I took the mast and poised it high up in the air, and gathered up all my strength and brought it down.

And just at the point when you're expecting Jerome to describe what happened in all its horrible, hilarious detail, he says instead:

> It was George's straw hat that saved his life that day. He keeps that hat now (what is left of it), and, on a winter's evening, when the pipes are lit and the boys are telling stretchers about the dangers they have passed through, George brings it down and shows it 'round, and the stirring tale is told anew, with fresh exaggerations every time.

But he doesn't tell us. All he says is, "Harris got off with merely a flesh wound." He leaves us to imagine the rest for ourselves, and the effect is funnier than anything he could have described.

Deciding when to use exaggeration and understatement is the problem, of course, and every author seems to have a different solution. Jerome sets up wildly slapstick situations and then, just at the critical moment, steps back and makes us imagine the outcome for ourselves. P.G. Wodehouse, on the other hand, never flinches at describing the ridiculous. It's his characters' responses that are understated, as in *The Return of Jeeves*. "Certainly a somewhat sharp crisis in our affairs would appear to have been precipitated, m'lord," Jeeves says when threatened with jail and a poke in the nose.

Twain uses understatement, as in his story of the ram standing at the top of a hill watching an old man bending down to pick up a dime, because the outcome is inevitable and no one has to tell us what will happen. And James Thurber exaggerates the content of his stories, but writes in a cool, understated style. There's obviously no set rule.

The best answer involves reading lots of Twain and Jerome. And Thurber and Wodehouse. And Calvin Trillin and Erma Bombeck and whoever you think is funny. Reading humorous fiction and trying to analyze it (no matter what Benchley says) will not only help you learn how and when to use understatement and exaggeration, it will show you those other techniques authors use to produce their unique comic styles.

Then you must practice those techniques. And read some more. And practice some more. Because writing humorous fiction is hard. ("*How hard is it?*") But at least you don't have to *make* things funny. Things are already funny; you're simply using exaggeration and understatement and whatever else to bring out the humor that was already there.

And you'll be More or Less on your way to being able to write humorous stories.

Connie Willis is a multiple Hugo Award- and Nebula Award-winning writer of science fiction. Her work includes the novel *Doomsday Book* and her comic short stories, "Even the Queen" and "At the Rialto." Her most recent works are *Passage*, a novel, and *Miracle and Other Christmas Stories*.

CHAPTER 7

Getting Laughs From Literature

BY JOSIP NOVAKOVICH

You've heard this before: "You're either funny or you're not." It's the defense claimed by those who say humor can't be taught; that it's a natural character trait. Or that analyzing humor is the best way to kill it.

Agreed: It's difficult to provide formulas for writing successful humor. But if you study such masters as Gogol and Wilde, you *can* learn from their unique styles.

Slapstick, Caricature, Exaggeration and Stereotype

Nikolai Gogol, one of the most versatile humorists in literature, used all kinds of humor. In *Dead Souls,* Gogol describes a giant: "He was seven feet tall, in other words, a born dentist."

This is a jab at Russian dentistry, a trade where strength to pull out teeth was the basic skill. The joke works through both exaggeration and the stereotyping of a profession. (Although perhaps it's not too much of an exaggeration. Once when I visited a dental clinic in Novi Sad in northern Serbia, three muscular dentists tied me to a chair and flexed their muscles on my jaws. I was reminded of the joke but did not laugh.)

Here's how Gogol used slapstick. When Chicikov, the hero of *Dead Souls,* runs into a landowner acquaintance, their meeting goes as follows:

> They immediately embraced each other and remained clasped in each other's arms for about five minutes. The kisses they exchanged were so powerful that their front teeth ached for the rest of the day. Manilov was so overjoyed that only his nose and his lips remained on his face, his eyes having completely disappeared.

Slapstick is perhaps the most common type of humor. It depends on exaggerating and, in this case, overdoing a simple social exchange. A hug with a greeting kiss becomes a major enterprise. Note Gogol's caricaturist skill. "Only his nose and his lips remained on his face, his eyes having completely disappeared." This wonderfully reductive image enhances the scene.

Gogol mostly uses typology, caricature and exaggeration in his humor. It isn't simple to reduce it to a formula, but seeing how a master does it provides writers with a model to follow.

Absurd and Cynical Humor

Here's a description of lovemaking from Samuel Beckett's novel *Molloy*. This excerpt may strike some as too dark to be humorous, but this is absurdist humor, and it depends on the author's voice and a peculiar logic working together. By peculiar logic, I mean a strange way of thinking. The strangeness will help surprise readers—and surprise is a necessity in most humor.

> And all I could see was her taut yellow nape which every now and then I set my teeth in, forgetting I had none, such is the power of instinct. . . . Anyway it was she who started it, in the rubbish dump, when she laid her hand upon my fly. More precisely, I was bent double over a heap of muck, in the hope of finding something to disgust me forever with eating, when she, undertaking me from behind, thrust her stick between my legs and began to titillate my privates. She gave me money after each session, to me who would have consented to know love, and probe it to the bottom, without charge. But she was an idealist. I would have preferred it seems to me an orifice less arid and roomy, that would have given me a higher opinion of love it seems to me. . . . The other thing that bothered me, in this connexion, is the indifference with which I learnt of her death, when one black night I was crawling towards her, an indifference softened indeed by the pain of losing a source of revenue. . . . What I do know for certain is that I never sought to repeat the experience, having I suppose the intuition that it

had been unique and perfect, of its kind. . . . Don't talk to me about the chambermaid, I should never have mentioned her, she was long before, I was sick, perhaps there was no chambermaid, ever, in my life. Molloy or life without a chambermaid.

The narrative voice undermines with indifference whatever it touches on. Beckett treats the first love and knowledge of love—traditionally topics of much sentiment—in a reductive manner, placing them in the context of a garbage dump. That reduction, in technique, is similar to cynicism; it portrays a higher level of human life in animalistic terms. People often resort to cynicism when writing humor. Twain's humorous description of prayer—"to tuck down her head and grumble a little over the victuals, though there wan't really anything the matter with them"—is a downshifting maneuver, bringing something in high regard (prayer) to something basic (grumbling).

To make cynicism come to humorous life requires wit and cleverness. Molloy's trying to get rid of his hunger by finding something disgusting in a dump of discarded foods is a clever twist. That the narrator calls the woman an idealist because she pays him for lovemaking is another. Paying strikes us as materialistic, but you can find some logic in this—paying for a service is an idea that she sticks to even though he'd do it for free. That he gets carried away and sinks his teeth in her neck forgetting he has none surprises you with its logical impossibility, and evokes an absurd picture of naked gums biting. In the statement, "Perhaps there was no chambermaid," the narrator's doubt continues where we don't expect it. Perhaps there was no narrator? No life without a chambermaid? As you reread the excerpt, look for the paradoxes, and sometimes logical impossibilities, laid out one after another, that serve to create an effect.

In this passage from *Molloy*, the narrator meets a man in the forest and asks him for a way out to his town.

A long dialogue ensued, interspersed with groans. I could not ask him the way to my town, the name of which escaped me still. I asked him the way to the nearest town, I found the necessary words, and accents. . . . When I made to go, he held

How to Write Funny

me back by the sleeve. So I smartly freed a crutch and dealt him a good dint on the skull. That calmed him. . . . I rested a moment, then got up, picked up my crutches, took up my position on the other side of the body and applied myself with method to the same exercise [kicking]. I always had a mania for symmetry.

Note how the dialogue is reduced to groans and mechanics—"I found necessary words, accents." To forget the name of your town—and to remember its neighboring town's name—is absurd, as is a cripple's whacking a forest man. Another inversion is created when the narrator applies methods of geometry (symmetry) to the irrational action of kicking a well-intentioned forester. So this is a truly twisted humor.

Gogol, too, was also a master at absurdist humor. Describing a shopping district in *Dead Souls*, Gogol writes:

One came across shop signboards with ring-shaped rolls or boots on them, almost washed away by the rain, and others with painted blue trousers and the name of some Warsaw tailor; in one place there was a shop with ordinary and service caps and a signboard inscribed: Vassily Fyodorov, Foreigner.

That there would be a shop, with "foreigner" treated as a trade, alongside the shops of bootmakers and tailors, is absurdly funny. Sometimes when I walk on Madison Avenue in New York, or on some other boutique-y street, I think this signboard would fit. This is a brilliant abstraction—and reduction, as abstractions usually are—about the boutique appeal.

Substitution Humor

Oscar Wilde's humor is like math; it is created through substitution of values: "The old-fashioned respect for the young is fast dying out," for instance. Or, "Divorces are made in heaven."

The technique is transparent yet effective. Wilde substitutes one element in a cliche to become something new, surprising, certainly funny.

"Even things that are true can be proved." That's a good response to the provability of false things. And along the same lines, "If one tells the truth, one is sure, sooner or later, to be found out." "Truth" is clearly substituted for "lies."

"Industry is the root of all ugliness," is a great response to "Sloth is the root of all evil."

"The ancient historians gave us delightful fiction in the form of fact; the modern novelist presents us with dull facts under the guise of fiction." Here Wilde uses simple role reversal. Historians, who should give us facts, give us fiction. Novelists, who should give us fiction, give us facts.

You can apply this technique not only in one-liners, but in two (or more) sentences, as does Wilde in *The Importance of Being Earnest*: "I hope you have not been leading a double life, pretending to be wicked and being really good all the time. That would be hypocrisy."

As though he's put a negative sign before a parenthesis, Wilde here switches good and wicked around. Everything else stays the same.

In the following Wilde example, you'll find a string of reversals:

> Many a young man starts in his life with a natural gift for exaggeration which, if nurtured in congenial and sympathetic surroundings, or by imitation of the best models, might grow into something really great and wonderful. But, as a rule, he comes to nothing. He either falls into careless habits of accuracy, or takes to frequenting the society of the aged and the well-informed. . . . In a short time he develops a morbid and unhealthy faculty of truth-telling, begins to verify all statements made in his presence, has no hesitation in contradicting people who are much younger than himself, and often ends by writing novels which are so lifelike that no one can possibly believe in their probability.

"Careless habit of accuracy"—usually "accuracy" strikes us as something "careful," and we accept the coupling of the two words quite mechanically. Wilde breaks the couplet, as he does with contradicting people much younger.

Now this is not all formula. Part of Wilde's humor is his voice, the stylishly and ironically highbrow way of putting words together. "Frequenting the society of the aged and the well-informed," for example, strikes a tone of leisure, of the English upper class. Wilde's comedy becomes one of manners, in addition to an example of the humor of inversion.

Wilde's substitution technique is not unique. Much of Beckett's humor conforms to this "formula." (I put "formula" in quotation marks because nothing guarantees that each line you write according to it will be funny. But some things will be.) Beckett's softening indifference with the thought of losing revenue in *Molloy* is a reversed phrase—we soften pain, in a cliche. He softens its near opposite, indifference.

George Bernard Shaw used the same technique: "A drama critic is a man who leaves no turn unstoned."

One element that makes the technique effective is that there's some truth in all of the statements, and our recognizing this catches us by surprise, enhancing the humor.

Situational Humor

Much situational humor depends on timing and confusion. Here's an example from Bernard Malamud's novel *The Fixer*, in which Yakov, on the way to Kiev, must abandon his horse to cross a river.

> The boatman untied the boat, dipped both oars into the water and they were off.
>
> The nag, tethered to a paling, watched from the moonlit shore.
>
> "Like an old Jew he looks" thought the fixer.
>
> The horse whinnied, and when that proved useless, farted loudly.
>
> "I don't recognize the accent you speak," said the boatman, pulling the oars. "It's Russian but from what province?"
>
> "I've lived in Latvia as well as other places," the fixer muttered.

The scene taking place is sad. Thus, the contrast, the fart in the solemn moment, cracks the solemnity, and it cracks up the readers. Take this phrase—"The horse whinnied, and when that proved useless, farted loudly"—and place it one line up or down, and you'll see that the joke doesn't work so well.

Timing, however, is not everything. Something high is brought low, human speech to a nag's fart. This downgrading results in humor. I don't think there's an absolute recipe for humor, but if you practice this down-shifting and timing so that one thing could be taken for another, you might create humor. (Of course, you can also upshift, as we have seen with Wilde's "Decay of the Art of Lying." There, an apparent vice, lying, is humorously elevated to the status of art and virtue.)

Notice one more point in Malamud's example. The protagonists don't laugh. They continue being serious. They don't notice the humor; the nag's fart has nothing to do with what they are doing. This increases the humor. If a protagonist in your story cracks a joke, don't have him and others roll on the floor holding their sides; this gives readers the impression that you're congratulating yourself. That's a bit like a laugh track in a sitcom. Deadpan humor is the best. If it's funny, your reader will laugh. If not, there was no promise of humor anyway. But if your reader encounters an orgy of laughter after a flat joke, she may resent not laughing. (Of course when it's important that a character laugh at a joke, let him laugh.)

Here's an example of situation humor from my story "The Eye of God." This scene precedes the rite of passage:

> Behind a partition in the room a naked peasant boy about my age looked toward my penis analytically.
>
> "A dog bit me," I explained the fresh scar on my thigh.
>
> "How long is it supposed to be?"
>
> "I don't know, at least a meter."
>
> "That long? Gee, we'll never make it."
>
> I realized that I was speaking about the dog and he about the normal penis size. I couldn't explain this because the deacon said "hush." The boy looked more and more worried until he yawned in resignation. He had probably decided that since his penis wouldn't be long enough, he might just as well become a Baptist.

How to Write Funny

The apparent misunderstanding in the conversation, set against the background of the solemn church atmosphere, works as humor. And as Malamud's text runs the risk of slighting Russians, mine runs the risk of slighting Baptists. (However, since I was brought up a Baptist, the joke's on me.)

I learned from Malamud's method how to make my situational comedy. You can learn how to make humorous passages: Analyze writings you find funny. In some of them, you'll find an applicable method.

Josip Novakovich is the author of *Apricots From Chernobyl: Narratives* and *Salvation and Other Disasters: Short Stories.* He teaches fiction writing at Penn State University. This article is excerpted from his book *Fiction Writer's Workshop.*

CHAPTER 8

Take My Wizard . . . Please!
The Serious Business of Writing
Funny Fantasy and Science Fiction

BY ESTHER M. FRIESNER

A centuries-old story tells that when a great Shakespearean actor lay on his deathbed, someone asked him how he was doing. The world is still full of people who insist on asking questions like that, and they need to have objects of middling weight flung at their heads at every possible opportunity or they will keep on doing it. Since the dying actor was too weak to perform the necessary public service of chucking a chamber pot at the busybody in question, he is instead reported to have settled for making the memorable quote: "Dying is easy. Comedy is hard." (The smart money claims that what the great actor really said was, "How am I doing? He wants to know how I'm doing? I'm dying, you moron, how do you think I'm doing?" But all experienced fiction writers—and most politicians—know better than to let the truth get in the way of a good story.)

The rules for writing effective funny fantasy and science fiction (both fields hereafter to be called collectively Speculative Fiction or SpecFic, in the interests of convenience, efficiency and because catchphrases are so cool) are only variations on the rules for writing effective comedy of any stripe. Taking it one step further, some of them are the same rules that apply to writing effective fiction, period. Let's begin with a few useful general guidelines.

Begin With a Character

In "The Rich Boy," F. Scott Fitzgerald wrote: "Begin with an individual, and before you know it you find that you have created a type; begin with a type and you find that you have created—nothing." A quote from the creator of *The Great Gatsby* is not as out of place in an article about funny SpecFic as you might think. Check out his story "The Diamond as Big as the Ritz" sometime. Besides, he's more than right: Always begin with a character.

The best characters are drawn from life. They are also recognizable and comprehendible to the reader. Even in SpecFic, where your characters can be ogres or aliens more often than not, they still need to be approachable ogres and aliens, with some vaguely human quality tucked in among all that Otherness.

Have a Little Sympathy

Readers tend to prefer characters who are at least somewhat sympathetic. In the case of villains, sympathetic is perhaps the wrong word: Understandable is better. Interesting is best of all. The bad guy whose sole reason for blowing up the galaxy is because that's what bad guys do won't be around for a sequel. Even Darth Vader needs motivation. It changes him from a cardboard cutout villain to a three-dimensional character, and three dimensions are far more interesting than two.

Interesting characters make for an interesting story. Whether they're rooting for the good guy to win or eager to see the villain get what's coming to him, readers must care about your characters. A writer's first task is to insure that his audience becomes interested in and involved with the story he has to tell, and the best way to do that is to make it a story about interesting people. Remember, part of your audience is the editor to whom you are trying to sell your story. Lose reader interest, lose sales.

Make the Joke Fit the Character

Unfortunately, one of the worst errors made in writing funny SpecFic is when the writer forgets to think of his characters as living beings and instead turns them into joke machines. Jokes come in many guises, but all kinds of jokes work best when presented by a believable character.

Taking this a step further, a joke or humorous situation works best when presented by a character whose traits either suit the gag or provide an element of sharp contrast that proves to be humorous, often on multiple levels. For example, when the bumbling apprentice magician has his cauldron blown up yet again, it's pretty much what the reader expects of him.

As far as comedy goes, an occurrence like that only works on the elementary level of slapstick.

However, when the character in question is an expert wizard, preferably one with an inflated self-image, the incident of the backfiring spell works not only as simple slapstick but also on the principle of upsetting audience expectations for the character involved. In addition, since we've already said that the hapless wizard has an unsuitably high opinion of himself, the reader can easily identify him with some real-world stuffed shirt (and don't tell me you can't name at least half a dozen of your own acquaintances!) and get lots of vicarious enjoyment out of seeing the high and mighty taken down a peg or two.

In brief, the more smug, snooty, self-satisfied and seemingly untouchable your character is, the more satisfying it is to see him get hit in the face with the proverbial cream pie.

Upset the Reader's Expectations

Now let's talk about characters specific to the realm of funny SpecFic. Despite F. Scott Fitzgerald's words of wisdom, sometimes you really do need to begin with a type. To speak about comedic characters in SpecFic, we must first speak about easily recognizable types (stock characters, if you will) found in the noncomedic side of the field. These include but are not limited to: the wizard, the witch, the dragon, the unicorn, the elf, the barbarian, the inept apprentice, the robot, the rogue, the scientific genius (mad or sane, with or without beautiful daughter), the alien (friendly or hungry), the swashbuckling hero, the evil galactic overlord, the overlord's toady, the all-purpose sidekick and so on.

The point is, these are all roles that are familiar to the reader of SpecFic, and in this case, familiarity breeds comedy, not contempt. When the reader encounters one of these types, certain expectations click into place: The robot will not understand human emotions; the elf will be beautiful and noble; the galactic overlord will be ruthless, etc. The writer of funny SpecFic often operates by taking these reader expectations and setting them on ear.

For this method to work, you must first be absolutely sure that your main characters can be matched to one of the genre's easily identifiable types. You can't make light of a subject with which you are not familiar, nor can your reader appreciate the humor in a situation if he doesn't understand the context. Someone who has never read any Conan the Barbarian stories won't see what's so funny about Terry Pratchett's creation, Cohen the Barbarian. As far as this hypothetical reader knows, all barbarian swordsmen are in the dotages, sick and tired of a life of high adventure, and plagued by the usual aches and pains of age. He also won't recognize the pun in the character's name. Cohen the Barbarian is funniest by comparison with Conan, so if the reader has no basis for this comparison, the humor won't work. (Luckily, the big, brawny barbarian has become such a standard image in fantasy that most readers are well acquainted with the Conan-type even if they haven't ever read an actual Conan story.)

Naturally this does not mean that your characters should be stereotypes. On the contrary, they must be easily recognizable types from the SpecFic lexicon while at the same time having distinct personal traits that make them believable, living people (or beings). What your characters are (wizard, robot, vampire) defines them for the purposes of comedy, but how they behave and why they behave that way makes them real.

Create the Illusion of Reality

You give a comedic character the illusion of reality by much the same means as you would apply to any fictional character. This is where our earlier advice about drawing characters from life comes in. Apply real-life attributes to your SpecFic type, and you will find you have created a living character. For example:

Give him a family and consider their influence on him. Give him a self-image and be ready to explain why he thinks of himself in one way and not another. Imagine his childhood, his upbringing, his environment, his desires, ambitions, fears, loves, hates and then . . . file it. File it well out of the way, too, or else you'll fall into one of a writer's most common pitfalls, namely: "I know all about this character and what makes him tick, and now, by golly, I'm going to put all of it into the story whether it has any bearing on the action or not, because I didn't do all that background work for nothing!"

Sorry, but no one likes a lecture. There's a word for stories where the author stops the action to make sure the reader realizes how hard he worked:

dull. You'll just have to have the personal satisfaction of knowing you did your homework. A character's job is to keep the story moving, not to bog it down. This is especially vital when writing comedy, because timing is as important as they say.

Flesh out your characters for your own reference, then only present as much of this information as is necessary for your audience to understand the action. If your reader can imagine your characters going on with their lives after the story ended (not merely "They lived happily ever after"), then you've done your job.

Give Them a Place to Go

There's nothing sadder than seeing a bunch of wonderfully fleshed-out, beautifully conceived characters all dressed up with nowhere to go. Writing funny SpecFic isn't the same as writing stand-up comedy: Jokes aren't enough. If you're writing a short story, you might be able to get away with making the whole piece nothing more than a setup for the punch line, but it had better be mighty short and with a mighty good punch line.

An effective comedic story is more than a series of setups, punch lines and rim shots. Few things are less likely to get a laugh than the author who interrupts his story just to tell a joke, particularly if the joke hasn't got much to do with the story itself and especially if the story remains stopped cold in its tracks while the author in effect demands, "Get it? Get it? Wasn't that funny? Ain't I a scream?" Well, he's right about the scream part.

Obey the Rules

To write a funny SpecFic story that works, first write a good story according to the usual rules: It should have a beginning, a middle and an end. The middle and the end should derive logically from the beginning. Remember all of those three-dimensional characters you developed? Their actions ought to remain in keeping with their established personalities, but as in life, these personalities may evolve in the course of the story. If so, you must account for it. When your cowardly squire suddenly becomes a fearless knight, you'd better show the reason why.

You know, sometimes the jokes don't all work. Sometimes you get one bunch of readers who think Scene A is hilarious while Scene B goes right over their heads, and sometimes you get a group for whom the reverse holds true. Not all situations are funny to all readers. If your funny stuff doesn't have the solid foundation of an interesting plot underpinning it, you're going to lose your audience's attention. Not good.

So where do you get your ideas for SpecFic stories that will both amuse and involve your readers? Schenectady. All right, I admit that Schenectady is the canonical wise-guy reply that most SpecFic writers have been trained to give whenever anyone asks us "Where do you get your ideas?" It's what you call an in-joke, and as such is a very good example of where not to shop for story ideas.

In-jokes are by their very definition exclusive. Exclusivity is all right for country clubs but death to comedy. If you present a funny situation to a large audience and only one person laughs while everyone else says, "I don't get it," something is gravely wrong. (It is all right to have one or two in-jokes if they are not intrusive. When Robert Asprin named a bunch of vampires after a group of well-known literary agents, those in the know had an additional giggle, but other readers didn't feel excluded because their enjoyment of the story itself did not depend on them getting this particular jibe.) It can't be said enough: To be accessible and understandable, humor must have some basis in the familiar.

Choose a Recognizable Plot . . .

In the case of funny SpecFic, the familiar includes not only recognizable character types from ordinary SpecFic, but recognizable plots as well. These include but are not limited to: The Quest; The Clash of Cultures; Saving the Universe/Kingdom by Blowing Up Something Bad; Saving the Universe/Kingdom by Not Blowing Up Something Good; Coming That Close to Blowing Up the Entire Universe/Kingdom (a subset of which is the Sorcerer's Incompetent Apprentice); Discovering That the Underdog Is Really the Royal Heir/Wizard/Messianic Figure; and of course, Boy Meets Girl/Dragon/Alien/Implanted Computer Chip.

. . . Then Make It Your Own

Once you have chosen a basic plot, you can make it your own. This is not stealing. Disney's animated *Cinderella* is as far removed from the movie

Pretty Woman as it is from the Brothers Grimm version in which one ugly stepsister chops off her own heel and toes to make her foot fit the glass slipper, but they're all the same story at bottom.

Each of the already mentioned basic plots has been retold so many times that it carries with it certain expectations. Humor relies on the upsetting of audience expectations. (Please be aware that cultural forces are constantly changing our expectations. We used to expect the brawny hero to save the princess, so when the princess saved the brawny hero instead it could be played for laughs. These days, most SpecFic princesses, elf or alien, are usually packing steel, so there went that gag.)

Verbal vs. Situational Humor

You have your characters, your basic plot and some idea of how you are going to retell that basic plot in your own unique way. Now what?

That all depends on how you choose to tell your story. Earlier on, we mentioned that jokes come in many guises. By jokes, we mean humor in general and not just "A troll, an elf and an orc walked into a bar. . . ." Before you choose your route, you'd better have an overview of the territory.

There are two main subsets of humor: verbal and situational. In a given piece of comedic writing it is possible for either to exist independently of the other, but you obtain better results by a judiciously balanced combination of the two. A pie-fight and a pun-fest are each funny in their own way, but only in small doses.

VERBAL HUMOR

Verbal humor includes puns, of course. Puns are the black sheep of verbal humor. This is because puns are fairly easy to come up with, and so certain writers tend to overuse them. If you do choose to include puns in your work, strive to avoid the rim-shot phenomenon. ("This must be the dragon's cave. I see the mark of his mighty tail in the dirt." "So that's what he's been draggin'!"—rim shot—author grins, says "Get it? Get it?" and bows to audience for being so clever. Audience leaves.) The less obvious a pun is, the better the effect. The deadly "stealth" pun works best. In Terry Pratchett's *Soul Music*, an aspiring rock band in search of leopard-skin trousers instead acquires a whole, live leopard, cheap. Why the bargain price? The beast can't hear. Deaf leopard. Def Leppard. This author's "Get it?" sounds in your ear as a whisper, not a shriek. He's made you work for it. You groan, but you really have no one but yourself to blame.

Double entendres are close kin to puns, since they, too, play with multiple levels of meaning contained in a word or phrase. In this case, the double meaning is sexually suggestive. Laughter is often a nervous reaction—we laugh because we don't know what else we can do in a given situation—and in our post-Victorian society the mere mention of sex still makes some people nervous. (This knowledge is a holdover from childhood, when we first discovered that using those words usually got one heck of a fun-to-watch reaction out of Mommy.) Sexual and scatalogical words in and of themselves will sometimes get you a laugh just by being there, but it will be a cheap laugh. If that's the effect you want, use them.

Another example of purely verbal humor is proper nouns. Names for characters and places can get an extra giggle from the reader. From my own work, *Majyk by Design*, I've had a number of compliments on my choice of names for the romance writer, Raptura Eglantine (overwrought and flowery enough to suit the reader's preconceived notion of what a romance writer's name ought to sound like), and her favorite cover-model Curio (not quite Fabio, but close enough for jazz). Sometimes names are also puns. Legolam the elf in *Bored of the Rings* is both a pun on and a parody of the elf Legolas from Tolkien's *Lord of the Rings*.

Finally, there are jokes, per se. It's perfectly all right to tell the one about the martian, the robot and the chopped liver; just don't stop the story to do it. Only tell those jokes that sound natural coming from a particular character at a specific time in the narrative. No fair cheating by having your characters lead off with the unprovoked remark, "That reminds me of a funny story."

SITUATIONAL HUMOR

Situational humor is a broader field. What makes a situation funny? Once more we return to the principle of upsetting reader expectation. We expect certain beings to act in certain ways in certain situations. We don't expect people to act like machines, which is why it's funny when they do. If there's a banana peel in our path, we adjust by picking it up and throwing it away. In comedy, we remain inflexible, keep going and take a pratfall.

In SpecFic, the inverse applies: We don't expect machines to act like people. We expect the computer/robot/android to process data or, in the case of superadvanced Artificial Intelligences, to try to eliminate imperfect, illogical humankind in favor of a more "perfect" machine-based civilization. In SpecFic comedy, the superadvanced AI exhibits distinctly human behavior, illogical, imperfect and as downright moody as it can get.

Apart from writing comedy by creating generally humorous situations, there are a few specific methods, including parody, satire and topical humor. All are interrelated and all have their advantages and disadvantages. It will be up to you as the writer to decide whether the pros outweigh the cons when you decide which and how many of these techniques to use in your work.

Parody upsets reader expectations by extremely strict imitation of a specific work of SpecFic. A funny story based on the legend of King Arthur can be set in New York City as easily as in Camelot (as Peter David did in *Knight Life*). A parody of the same legend must be set in Camelot, with the appropriate costumes, trappings and even speech patterns, but with the author inserting a series of changes that are close to the original but just different enough to ambush the reader's expectations. (The screenplay of *Monty Python and the Holy Grail* is rich with such examples.) If you are not deeply familiar with the original story in all its aspects, you can't write a parody of it. If the original story itself is too obscure, not enough readers will be familiar enough with it for your parody to work.

If you want to write satire, be prepared to write with bite. Satire's purpose is to point out what's wrong with the world—whether it's crooked politicians, the war between the sexes or yet another Spunky Teenagers Morph 'n' Mutate novel—and through ridicule, to encourage change for the better. (It doesn't always work, but at least you'll know you tried.) To write good satire, be sure that you choose a target that truly bothers you. If you're indifferent to something, you lack the motivation to make fun of it effectively.

Topical humor is the most risky. It involves parodying and/or satirizing a specific subject that is of current interest. If you wish, you can take Rush Limbaugh (please!), transform him into a SpecFic character (the king's personal wizard/advisor) and make fun of him within that context ("And another thing, Sire, it's a well-known fact that the reason your knights can't slay that dragon is because of all these Amazonazi swordswomen are taking their jobs away!").

How to Write Funny

However, things change. Future generations may well ask "Limbaugh? Isn't that some kind of weird dance with a stick?" There goes your audience accessibility, and with it your comedy. Today's topical humor can quickly become tomorrow's in-joke that only a scant audience of history buffs will appreciate. If you want your work to retain its comedic appeal over time, keep topical humor and satire to a minimum. Parody too only endures in value as long as people remain familiar with the subject parodied.

Get Serious

While we're on the subject of writing humor with staying power, remember this: Your story need not be one long laugh-fest. Humor is dead serious stuff. In fact, humor gains depth when it's about something more than just making the reader laugh. Food for thought—serious thought—goes down a lot more readily if it's coated with a little laughter. Humor observes, analyzes and comments on the human condition, which can sometimes be a pretty scary thing to face head-on. Humor helps us cope with some of life's harsher realities through laughter.

There's a very good reason that Death and Afterlife show up in so many funny SpecFic works: We need a handy way of dealing with our fears of mortality. When we laugh, we experience feelings of superiority to the object of our laughter. Humor lends us the conviction that we have a measure of control over beings and situations seemingly beyond our power to influence. Authority figures know this, which is why dictators whose rule most relies on Because I Say So (plus a lot of backup armed thugs) are also the ones who most fear laughter. Death is the ultimate authority figure from whose grim dominion none may escape. Dying is easy.

Fair enough. Where did I put my cream pie?

Award-winning author Esther M. Friesner, best known for funny fantasy and science fiction novels such as *Majyk by Accident* and *The Sherwood Game*, has previously penned (PC'd, actually) a number of articles about writing humor. However, she also writes on the serious side of the genre, with works such as *The Psalms of Herod* and *Child of the Eagle*. She lives in Connecticut and has a Ph.D. in Spanish from Yale University. This strikes her as pretty funny, too.

CHAPTER 9

Happily Ever Laughter: Writing Romantic Comedy for Women

BY JENNIFER CRUSIE

Women's humor is hot right now. As Birgit Davis-Todd, senior editor at Harlequin, says, funny romance writers are "laughing all the way to the bank." Harlequin's launch of the Love and Laughter line in fall of 1996 supports this; according to editor Malle Vallik, the line is in direct response to the growing demand by readers for laughter with their happily-ever-after. But along with the good news comes the bad: Women's humor is hard to write. It's not that women aren't naturally funny. Women laugh loud and long when we're together. But we've been told by a traditional society that women's humor is nonexistent and that our laughter is inappropriate, and so it's difficult for us to go beyond the traditional male humor, the joke and the put-down, to find the things that make women laugh and put them on the page.

The biggest barrier to writing women's humor is the intrinsic belief that Good Girls don't laugh. Ever hear a woman laugh out loud—really loud—in public? Chances are your first reaction was, "She's no lady." Although you can refer to women's humor and female humor, the term "ladies' humor" doesn't exist. It can't; it's an oxymoron because nice women don't laugh. Laughing out loud is powerful and sexual; it demands attention and announces knowledge, not innocence. As Regina Barreca notes in her outstanding work on women's humor, *They Used to Call Me Snow White . . . But I Drifted*, virgins don't laugh at small penis jokes. A woman's laughter not only tells the world she knows, it also communicates strength and confidence. A woman must be very sure of herself to make the joke, to tell the story and to laugh out loud knowing people will stare. She must be proud, strong and confident. No wonder modern romance readers love the heroine who can laugh and who invites them to laugh with her.

So how do you make that invitation? First you have to understand how women think, and how men's thinking—the thinking that fuels traditional humor—is different. One theory is that, generally speaking, most women think in patterns, using details and context, while most men think in straight lines, using cause and effect. This theory explains why women "can't" tell jokes; jokes are based on rigid, linear sequence. You can't tell the sentences of a joke out of order, and you can't add extra information to the joke or the clear line of cause and effect will be lost. To work, the joke must be told exactly the same every time. Women find this boring and ultimately frustrating because they're more interested in the experience and the context than they are in the trip to the punch line.

For example, a man may tell a woman, "There was a traveling salesman . . ." and she will ask "Traveling in what?" "It doesn't matter," he'll reply, exasperated, because it doesn't matter to the cause and effect of the joke. But it does matter to the woman because context creates understanding: Is he selling condoms or Bibles, miracle cures or pots and pans? The man may go on, "And he meets a farmer's daughter . . ." only to be interrupted with "How old is she?" "It doesn't make any difference," he'll reply, even more exasperated, and it doesn't matter to the progression of the joke, but it does to the understanding of the context: Is she sixteen and naive or forty and bitter; does she have experience with salesmen or is she going to be a victim? Women want to know the details, the world in which the story takes place, because that's where the humor lies for them.

Much Ado About Nothing

But while many women find traditional male humor lacking, many traditionalists reject women's humor because "nothing happens" in it. An example of female humor is Gilda Radner's story of dining in a very expensive restaurant after she became famous. The restaurant had ornate tapestry-covered chairs ("Who cares about the chairs?" male humor would demand, "Get to the point") and sometime during the meal, she began to menstruate. When she stood up to go, she noticed the stain on the tapestry, and she knew that everyone in the room would know that Gilda Radner had started her period. So she switched chairs with another table.

"That's it?" the traditionalist asks while women everywhere laugh, not at Radner because female humor does not laugh down, but with her because women have been in the same place and know how she felt. If those of us who are female were in the same room with her (with no males around), we'd immediately begin to contribute our own menstrual-disaster stories because we'd all have one. But the humor in Radner's story also goes beyond the immediate familiar situation to the context of the world at large and the absurdity of the way that world regards menstruation. The vast majority of women between puberty and menopause menstruate every month; it's normal, healthy and desirable. Yet the male world has such a phobia about menstruation that many traditional males would find Radner's story in bad taste (although finding Polish jokes and dumb blonde jokes perfectly acceptable). Women live in a world where men will take them to the movies to see heads ripped off and blood spurting but will refuse to buy tampons for them, even though the tampons are perfectly clean, wrapped in paper inside a cardboard box that is in turn wrapped in cellophane. It is this absurdity that makes women laugh at the contextual richness of Radner's tapestry chair story while men are lost, trying to make the humor work in terms of the joke, the punch line. In women's humor, if you're not part of the community, you're not part of the humor.

Which means that first and foremost in constructing women's humor, you need to understand women and women's communities. You need to understand how friendships between women work, how relationships between mothers and daughters work and how absurd the male world often appears to women. If you're a woman, this isn't hard: It's your daily life. And that's what you need to draw on to write women's humor. Forget slapstick unless it's drawn naturally from women's experiences, such as putting on panty hose in a hurry immediately after a shower while talking on the phone and trying to keep the baby's finger out of the light socket. Forget wisecracks and put-downs unless they're aimed up at those in positions of power over women—bosses, rotten husbands and lovers, Martha Stewart-types—who richly deserve it. Stick with relationships and community, drawing on the things that make women laugh in real life.

So how do you write humor specifically for women?

Base Your Humor on Shared Female Experiences

If you can put your heroine in a situation that most women have experienced or can sympathize with (she gets her period unexpectedly; her child

How to Write Funny

says the wrong thing at the wrong time; her shoulder pads come loose and move around her suit like small animals while she tries to make an impression) and have her deal with it using her sense of humor, women will laugh in recognition and support because they're part of her community of experiences. Think of the last time you were embarrassed, so embarrassed that you didn't know how you'd ever face the people around you again. There was the day I decided to become a blonde and bleached my hair out, changed my mind and dyed it black, and walked around with green hair for a month as the black washed out; I got a book called *Getting Rid of Bradley* out of that experience. Or there's my favorite moment of all time, the day I walked the entire length of the English department at Ohio State University with my skirt caught in my panty hose, wearing no underwear. And nobody I passed said a word.

I posted that on the GEnie computer bulletin board and within a day or so several other women had posted similar panty hose exposure experiences caused by static cling and other insidious forces. Some day in some book, one of my heroines is going to walk around with her skirt caught in her panty hose because that's something that happens to women, and my readers will sympathize and laugh with her because she's laughing, too. Nothing is a tragedy if you can laugh at it, and one of the things that women love most about their humor is that pointing out how ridiculous something is removes the sting. There's a lot of relief in "My God, you did that, too?" and it's not just comic relief.

Laughing With vs. Laughing At

But please note, you and the heroine are laughing at the absurdity of the situation, not at the heroine herself. Never, ever, ever make the reader laugh at your heroine. She can laugh with the heroine or at the heroine's mistakes, but she should never laugh down at the heroine, especially if it's because she's a cute little ditz. You want your reader to identify with your heroine, not sneer at her. This means no slapstick scenes where the heroine makes a fool of herself rolling around in the mud in a cat fight or trips on her dress and falls downstairs, spilling wine down her dress and breaking her nose. Women don't find misfortune funny. They will lose respect for the cat fighter and feel sorry for the tripper, and both of these are death to reader-heroine identification. On the other hand, you can use humor to show that your heroine is strong and confident in the face of disaster. If the heroine trips, spills the wine, picks herself up and announces that for her next trick she intends to do the same thing backwards in high heels, then she's used humor to take control of the situation without demeaning herself and is therefore admirable. However, she's still not very funny to women because they're sympathizing with her fall. Recovery humor is endearing, but it's not laugh-out-loud funny.

A classic example of a heroine who takes the sting out of a terrible situation occurs in Jayne Ann Krentz's *Perfect Partners*. The heroine, Letty, is telling the hero, Joel, how she walked in on her now ex-fiance only to find him with his pants around his ankles and another woman on her knees in front of him. At this point, she drops her face into her hands, and her shoulders begin to shake, and Joel tries to comfort her, assuming she's crying. But when she lifts her head, she's laughing. "Oh, I was shocked at first," she tells Joel. "But then I realized I had never seen anything so ludicrous in my entire life." Once Letty has laughed at her cheating ex, even though he's not there to see it, he can't hurt her again, and the situation has lost its pain. And the reader laughs along with her, delighted that she's strong and feisty and refusing to be a victim.

Arm Your Heroine With Humor as a Defensive Weapon

If you can show your heroine one-upping someone offensive (a mechanic patronizes her, her date is obnoxious, her boss treats her like a robot) with defensive humor, you can make women laugh out loud. One of the books I received the most oh-my-God-I've-been-there mail on was my first, *Manhunting*, because the heroine goes on a series of dates from hell and defeats them all physically, pushing one in a pool, stabbing another with a fork and generally fighting the good fight for women everywhere against men who deserve it while retaining her sense of humor throughout. A heroine in situations like these can get angry and complain, she can be noble and suffer through, she can get huffy and leave, but it's a lot more fun for the reader if she stays to turn her razor-sharp wit on the man who thought he was going to use her because she was too dumb to defend herself.

However, it's important to remember that women's humor is never offensive; it never makes fun of people who don't deserve it or laughs down at people who are less powerful. A woman who makes fun of a man who's trying to patronize her is wonderful; a woman who makes fun of a perfectly nice man who's trying to talk to her is not. Women's humor as a weapon should only be unleashed against powerful people who try to patronize women or use them in some way. Give your heroine enemies in situations that women can relate to and let her defeat them using her wit, and your reader will laugh with her.

Develop a Community for Your Heroine to Share Her Humor With

The power of community-based humor is evident in the success of shows like *Cheers, Frazier, Seinfeld, Mad About You* and *Friends.* Give your heroine an ensemble like these to work with, and your reader will feel part of that community the same way viewers feel that if they dropped by Cheers, they'd be welcomed right in. Solidify that community by giving its members common enemies and problems, and develop in-jokes for your characters that make the reader feel part of the community.

I did this deliberately in *Charlie All Night.* Charlie is set in a radio station and stars a producer-heroine and a disc jockey-hero who are surrounded by an ensemble that includes the station accountant and two other disc jockeys. Outside the group is the station's owner, a chronically grouchy patriarch, and the station's star, an ambitious but not-too-with-it morning show host who has dumped the heroine for a younger woman. This setup gave me all the dynamics I needed for women's humor: The in-group is a tight community that has shared experiences and problems; the boss and the arrogant host try to patronize and control the group which makes them acceptable targets for defensive humor; and the progress of the story gives me ample opportunity to create running jokes, the in-jokes of the community.

For example, as the hero's show gains in popularity, the morning show host panics and begins to make more and more ridiculous bids for the public's attention. By halfway through the book, all one of the characters has to say is, "Mark had a new idea this morning," and everyone in the in-group—including the reader—grins because everyone knows Mark has screwed up again. Community-based writing has several other advantages, not the least of which is that it's fun to write about a group of people who support and respect each other while having a very good time.

Georgette Heyer uses community-based humor beautifully in *The Grand Sophy*. Sophy comes to live with a large family of cousins, headed by her cousin Charles, a young man about to buckle under the weight of his familial responsibilities and his haughty fiancée, Eugenia. The rest of the cousins (and the reader) rally to Sophy, who, in the course of trying to bring some fun to the family, gives them a monkey that Eugenia loathes. In one scene the monkey becomes a symbol that the community of the family wants to retain and Eugenia wants to eject with Charles caught in the middle. Adding to the trauma is the fact that one of the brothers, Theodore, has just hit a ball through a neighbor's window and put the rest of the community in a weak position. As Eugenia runs down a list of reasons to get rid of the monkey, all of which Charles answers noncommittally, the rest of the family (and the reader) waits to see which side Charles will choose. Finally, Eugenia plays her trump card, "I believe a monkey's bite is poisonous," to which Charles says, "In that case, I hope he may bite Theodore." The rest of the family responds with relieved smiles—if Charles can joke about Theodore dying, he's not mad any more and he's not going to get rid of the monkey—but on a deeper level, their relief is really about saving Charles because he's with them, not Eugenia. And the entire scene is done without anyone "telling off" Eugenia or attacking her in any way. It's a wonderful example of women's humor.

Another community that is implicit in every romance novel is the community that the heroine and hero create by falling in love. One aspect that people find attractive in each other, placing high on wish lists compiled by both women and men, is a sense of humor. Everything listed previously that works in ensemble humor can be applied to the community of the hero and heroine alone (the in-joke works especially well here; there's nothing more seductive than meeting someone's eyes across a room and sharing a joke that no one else in the room gets), but the hero and heroine can also share something that the larger community can't: intimate banter. By intimate, I don't mean sexual, although that certainly can come into play.

I mean the trusting give-and-take of relaxed conversation with someone you're close to. Best friends often maintain this kind of mindless not-quite-arguing, and your heroine and hero should be nothing if not best friends by the time they've created a community or even while they're creating it. Their ability to respond to each other in a way that shows they're relating to each other without tension foreshadows their ability to establish the same kind of deeper relationship later. The following scene from my book *Anyone But You* foreshadows the relationship the heroine, Nina, and the hero, Alex, will have when they become lovers. In this scene, Nina has just rescued Alex from a Date From Hell:

Nina took her wine over to the table and sat down. "What happened in the middle of the entree?"

Alex sat down, too. "She smiled at me across the table, and said, 'I just want you to know where you stand.' Then she opened her purse and handed me two condoms."

"Oh." Nina blinked. "Well, she was just being prepared."

"Prepared?" Alex looked at her as if she were demented. "I wasn't even sure I wanted to yet, and she's handing me condoms. Don't you think that's a little presumptuous?"

Nina frowned at him. "So what are you saying here? You're mad at her because you're not That Kind of Guy?" She snorted. "Of course, you're That Kind of Guy."

"And two," Alex went on, ignoring her. "Two, for crissakes. Talk about pressure."

"Oh, right." Nina nodded wisely over her wine. "You are pushing thirty. I suppose the equipment is going soft."

"The equipment is fine, thank you," Alex said, glaring at her. "But there is such a thing as performance anxiety."

"You know, I've learned more about men in the past month with you than I did in fifteen years with Guy," Nina said. "I thought men just dove in whenever they got the chance. I would have assumed that you'd take that as a compliment."

"You would have assumed wrong," Alex said gloomily.

As in all other kinds of humor for women, however, the banter should never be insulting, hurtful or patronizing. Think of it as a verbal ping-pong match, not handball. Even if one of the shots hits home, nobody gets hurt. Writing humor for women, then, is nothing more than creating a heroine with whom the reader can identify; putting that heroine into a context and community that the reader finds familiar and comfortable; developing that community with in-jokes and relaxed, friendly banter; adding conflict that unites the community and provides a deserving outlet for the defensive humor of the in-group; and cementing the relationship between the heroine and her hero with a shared sense of humor. Do all this, and your reader will laugh with you all the way to the end of your story . . . and on to the beginning of your next one.

Jennifer Crusie is the author of *Tell Me Lies*; *Welcome to Temptation*; and, most recently, *Fast Women*. She has been named Best Series/Category Author by the Internet Romance Readers Anonymous listserv and received a Career Achievement Award in Romantic Comedy by *Romantic Times Magazine*. The RWA selected her *Crazy for You* as one of the top ten romances of 1999. She lives in Columbus, Ohio, with her three dogs, Bernie, Lucy and Rosie.

CHAPTER 10

Funny Business

BY DAVID A. FRYXELL

Telling a joke seems like the easiest thing in the world. You set up a situation or pose a loaded question and then—bam! You hit 'em with the punch line. Laughter ensues. But if telling a joke is so easy—and who hasn't cracked a few good ones?—why aren't we all Leno or Letterman or Seinfeld? What separates the casual wiseacre around the watercooler from the millionaire comedian?

You might wonder much the same thing about written humor. Again, it looks so easy, particularly compared to such vexing alternatives as the profile or the service piece. Skip that onerous research and interviewing, and just recollect the funniest moments of your life, or take some subject in the news and put a hilarious spin on it. A few thousand words later, you're the next S.J. Perelman or Dave Barry.

Though some jolt of common sense stops most of us short of open-mic night at the nearest comedy club, the apparent ease of being funny in print proves harder to resist. Just ask any editor swamped by submissions. You don't have to labor long with the blue-pencil brigade before developing a reflexive shudder at the cover letter that begins: "Enclosed please find my humorous reflections on motherhood, in honor of Mother's Day. . . ." (On certain holidays, everyone becomes Erma Bombeck!)

In fact, the visceral reaction to any writing that purports to be funny is more often a challenge than a chuckle: Go ahead, just try and make me laugh!

Writing From Scratch

Humor turns out to be among the most difficult nonfiction to write right. Liberated from most research and interviewing, humorous articles can, in effect, be about anything—so too often they wind up being about nothing. Because humor springs onto the page without any predefined external focus, because its organizational underpinnings are entirely up to the writer, it represents the purest example of the nonfiction writer working without a net. It's like the difference between baking a cake from a mix and whipping one up from scratch—including milling your own flour and snatching the eggs from under the chickens.

William Zenger once observed that "humor is not a separate organism that can survive on its own frail metabolism. It's a special angle of vision granted to certain writers who already write good English."

Still, it is possible to sharpen your humor articles so editors will chuckle instead of squirm. Just as a stand-up comedian can learn what gets guffaws, Bombeck and Barry wannabes can hone their senses of humor in print.

Paradoxically, one secret to mastering this wide-open form is developing the sort of discipline and architectural craftsmanship more associated with advanced magazine feature writing or "literary journalism." When your material is the least structured and predefined, as in humor, the organizational demands on the writer are the greatest. The spinning out of a humor piece must be as carefully calibrated as the cutting of a diamond—one wrong move and the whole thing can go to pieces.

So rhythm and pacing and tone and the other tools of the thoughtful writer are all essential to successful humor. But the writing fundamental that's most, well, fundamental to humor writing is unity—in particular, the unity that brings all the elements of a piece of writing together to create a sense of revelation.

Do You Get It?

You can see what I mean by *revelation* in the way the punch line of a joke operates. An effective joke appears to take you in one direction, then surprises you with the revelation that instead you've been led someplace unexpected. Yet what makes the joke funny rather than mere nonsense is that the place revealed by the punch line is not utterly unexpected: In the fresh light of the punch line's revelation, you can see that there were clues along the path you thought was heading someplace else. The punch line takes those clues, gives you a surprising way of looking at them and pulls together all that's gone before in a new—and humorous—whole.

This may sound like a highfalutin explanation of a phenomenon as basic and familiar as the yarn told at the watercooler or in *The Tonight Show* monologue. But it helps to understand what happens in a joke, because you want to achieve the same thing—in a much grander fashion, perhaps, or over a longer span of words—in your humorous articles.

Consider this joke that cruelly and unfairly humiliates the noble people of North Dakota (being from South Dakota, I know all about making fun of North Dakotans). The lead-up to the punch line starts your mind heading in one direction:

> Two North Dakotans were shoveling snow. One said to the other, "This is too much work. Let's just burn it."

Your reaction on hearing this front-end of the joke is, of course: "What an idiot. Doesn't he know you can't burn snow?" You picture this poor, stupid fellow futilely attempting to set snow ablaze—or snow, subjected to flames, turning messily into flame-dousing water.

The punch line takes this line of thought and gives it a sharp detour. To the other North Dakotan, the problem with burning snow isn't at all what you might expect:

> "No," replied the other North Dakotan. "What would we do with the ashes?"

Although this twist is surprising—and funny (at least to a South Dakotan)—it isn't as unexpected as it might seem. You've already been prepared for the notion that these are two awfully stupid fellas; the revelation that makes the joke work is that the second fella is far stupider (yet in an oddly logical way) than you imagined. The twist casts the pair's comical stupidity in a fresh light and forces you to reevaluate what you've already assumed—but it is not a cheat. You haven't fallen off a cliff that you didn't know was there; rather, your eyes have been opened to the revelation that what you thought was solid ground is actually thin air.

A good joke, like a successful piece of longer humor, finds its revelation within the material. That's the unity that makes it work, that leads the audience to chuckle rather than reach for the tomatoes.

Making Fun of a Family Feud

To see how this principle applies to a longer article, let's look at a light little back-of-the-book column I wrote for *Milwaukee Magazine*.

My focus was on how sports rivalries can cause disputes in even the happiest families; because our family had moved a lot, adopting new team loyalties each time, we'd had plenty of opportunities to spark fan friction with, in particular, my in-laws. On the surface, the point I pretended to make was that all these family sports feuds were the fault of my in-laws, not us. The revelation running throughout, however, was that we were as much to blame for "The Rooting of all Evil" (as the story was titled) as anybody—perhaps more so. And the fact that, as we'd moved, we'd switched our own fan loyalties willy-nilly underscored the ultimate insignificance of this subject that we were nonetheless willing to split the family over.

I set up the situation and telegraphed my self-deprecating subtext right from the start.

> I was always taught that the two subjects one never brings up in polite conversation are politics and religion. Nobody warned me about sports.
>
> In fact, our family can agree to disagree even about politics and religion. For example, I'll cheerfully agree that my in-laws are political troglodytes who make Genghis Khan look like Alan Alda. No problems there, unless you count a few drumsticks hurled at each other across the Thanksgiving table. No, it's sports that has brought our otherwise-civilized clan almost to blows. . . .

The exaggeration and irony of my "cheerful" barb against my in-laws signaled what was ahead: While seemingly pointing a finger at my relatives' sports craziness, I would in reality be making fun of my own fanaticism (and, by extension, overzealous sports rivalries in general).

It's worth noting here that the best target of a humorous article is almost always yourself. While you may make fun of the foolish and the faddish, it will go down much better if you wear the foolishness and faddishness yourself, rather than taking shots at others. Study the work of Dave Barry if you doubt this; the butt of Barry's humor, at least on the surface, is mostly Dave Barry.

In my sports-rivalry piece, for instance, I went on to explain why our family had so much trouble with this (our frequent moving) and doled out examples of sports-fueled squabbles. Throughout, the chief culprit always turned out to be me—despite my ironic take on the facts:

> My sister-in-law, whose boyfriend went to Georgetown and some-how infected her with that allegiance turned into the Hoya Fan from Hell when I worked at rival Pitt. . . . Please note that my wife and I are utterly blameless in all this unsportsmanlike conduct. Sewing a Pitt cheerleader outfit for our daughter and teaching her to spell out "H-O-Y-A-S S-T-I-N-K" doesn't count.

I described how even my daughter, born in Iowa as a Cubs fan, fell afoul of this mania when we moved to Pittsburgh, and she refused to switch her loyalties as I had done: "Not that we pressured her, except for that little incident when we tried to throw out all her clothes that weren't Pirates black-and-gold."

By upping the irony as the piece went along—going from my in-laws to my even more blameless child—I built up to the closing ironic exaggeration. In the ending, I took all that had gone before and blew it up like a balloon until it popped and I'd punctured the silliness of getting so worked up over a game. I concluded that these fan feuds boiled down to "the basic laws of the universe" and that my current teams were "simply morally superior to their foes." And then I added: "I defy anyone to argue with me on that—at least until I start rooting for some other team."

That last qualification was crucial to the "basic laws of the universe," and "moral superiority" took me right to the edge of the cliff; the final phrase pushed me off.

Focusing for Fun

What gave those words their pushing power, their ability to reveal the total foolishness of all I'd been spouting, was how they sprang from what came before. Why is my family's sports rivalry problem so acute? Because we've moved and thus switched teams so often. Why is my claim that my teams are superior so ridiculous? Because the reader knows that my loyalties last only until the next moving van pulls up. It was unity that gave my little punch line its punch.

Because I knew the ultimate effect I wanted to create, moreover, I was able to select just the anecdotes and more-or-less true events that would contribute. I've got plenty of funny stories I could tell—but unity demanded that only a handful fit my focus. That made my selection process much easier, of course, and gave me a clear standard for what to put in and what to leave out.

That's not as easy as it seems, but it's certainly easier than setting out to be funny without a focus. In the highwire act that is humor writing, you need as firm a net as you can find.

Now go ahead: Make me laugh!

David A. Fryxell is the Nonfiction columnist for *Writer's Digest*. He is also the author of *How to Write Fast (While Writing Well)*, *Structure and Flow* and *Double-Parked on Main Street*, a book of Midwestern humor.

CHAPTER 11

Print Humor: Columns, Articles and Fillers

BY MEL HELITZER

Newspaper Humor

Journalists call it the toy department—the editorial page of a newspaper. Reporters dream of getting there and doing their own columns. "If the editorial column is the land of Utopia," wrote Ed Cohen, "then the humor column is its capital city." While the political, medical, business and fashion columns are respected, studies show that a newspaper's two most popular editorial pieces are both humorous—the editorial cartoon and the humor column, in just that order.

Columns are soapboxes for clever writers to air their views. Humor permits them to take stands on issues of major and minor importance. Some of the most persuasive articles start out as humor pieces.

Bob Greene, a nationally syndicated humor columnist, was an avid Coca-Cola drinker. When Coca-Cola broke a ninety-nine year tradition and changed its recipe, Greene wrote an "outrageous" humor column demanding Coke bring back the old formula. He thought his temper in print would have no more sting than the usual political cartoon. Even he was surprised (and delighted) when his article helped snowball a national protest, and the public outcry encouraged Coca-Cola to bring back the old formula under the name "Classic Coke."

Most frequently humor columnists are discovered in some other area of the paper shuffling humor into their news articles.

None have a faster road to humor fame than the entertainment columnists who combine humor tidbits with celebrity gossip. They give the blue-collar workers a peek under the carnival tent of show biz, sports and the underworld. They are the most avid devotees of the celebrity wish-hunt. "I never name-drop myself," wrote Peter DeVries, "as I've said to Babe Ruth, Jack Dempsey and Bea Lillie."

Columnists need famous targets. Russell Baker claimed that President Reagan got rid of all the people on his staff who were funny. "I mean now we've lost James Watt. That's a real blow to my business. We've lost Alexander Haig. That was a terrible blow."

The average columnist works under the same daily deadline, but he doesn't have the excuse of general reporters that it was a slow day so there's no column today. On good days or bad days, approximately three times per week, their columns average 450 words, rarely exceeding 600. As a result they frequently concentrate on the beat they know best, themselves.

D.L. Stewart of the *Dayton Daily News* writes a column about ordinary things that happen at his house. One day his son, as a science project, had to observe the effect constant rock music has on house plants. "They're (the plants) all deaf and two of them are starting to grow zits. And last night our Boston fern's hair caught fire."

Some columnists work in rhyme, and nothing could be verse than that! This four-liner by Don Marquis, entitled "Nothing to It," refers to his humor column:

> I do not work in verse or prose,
> I merely lay out words in rows.
> The household words that Webster penned
> I merely lay them end to end.

Russell Baker once ridiculed the Internal Revenue Service with a "Taxpayer's Prayer" parody in Biblical form:

> O mighty Internal Revenue, who turneth the labor of man to ashes, we thank thee for the multitude of thy forms which thou hast set before us and for the infinite confusion of thy commandments which multiplieth the fortunes of lawyer and accountant alike. . . .

But verse or prose, column humor comes in only five forms:

1. The anecdote
2. The one-line joke
3. Overstatement
4. Understatement
5. Ironic truth

THE ANECDOTE

Humor in print demands a lighter touch than verbal humor. According to Roy Paul Nelson, in his book *Articles and Features*, a light touch simply means a relaxed writing style, but not so relaxed it ends up cute.

A light touch, for example, means peppering your manuscript with anecdotes, those short, short stories that are rarely more than a paragraph or two. Rejection slips from editors often mention that an article could have used anecdotes to illustrate adjectives like frugal, tough, fast-thinking and horny. Anecdotes breathe life into any article and can either precede or follow a generalization.

In nonfiction pieces they should be true. But, as in much humor, anecdotes have a unique permission to be fictional. Even after her three children were adults, in print Erma Bombeck's beat was still the problems of child raising and that thankless turf between the kitchen sink and the washing machine. "Housework, if you do it right, can kill you," she once wrote, but her children called her a fiction writer.

It's more important for anecdotes to be believable than to be true. Writers shade facts and edit true stories to save the punch line for last. When stories are made up, the readers should be clued with lines like "This story may be apocrypha, but. . . ." (Few readers know that word, anyway.)

Some anecdotes are obviously fictional; others may need a disclaimer. But if you start off with "One day, God, Jesus and Moses were playing golf," don't bother using a disclaimer. Keep 'em guessing.

Nels F.S. Ferre in *God's New Age* offers this anecdote to explain philosophical terms:

> Three baseball umpires were arguing. Said the first, "I call balls and strikes exactly the way they come." (This man was an objectivist.)

Said the second, "I can't do that. I call them balls or strikes the way I see them." (This man was a subjectivist.)

But the third had ideas of his own. "They are neither balls nor strikes until I call them." (He was an existentialist.)

The reader understands that Ferre did not happen upon three real-life umpires engaged in so convenient a conversation.

THE ONE-LINE JOKE

A joke is written differently for the verbal humorist than it would be for the printed page. Bill Cosby's monologues in script form are comparatively lifeless. Art Buchwald's columns could never be performed on stage.

Few do a printed joke better than Erma Bombeck did; she was the first to recommend that any husband who watches eight consecutive football games on New Year's weekend be declared legally dead. Her column "Wits End" was filled with one-liners like, "I don't think women outlive men, it only seems longer."

Columns and articles still use a high percentage of cliche-inspired aphorisms. The printed page permits more homonym reforming (puns), because they're easy to see in writing.

> *A pastor said to his congregation:* "To meet our budget deficit, I ask all of you to consider giving 10 percent of your income. Frankly, your church is fit to be tithed." — *Herm Albright*

> The Baseball Hall of Fame is known as the Cooperstown (NY) whacks museum. — *Antoni Tabak*

You'll find double entendre puns all over the editorial pages. These puns are also a basic tool of newspaper headlines and photo caption writers. Within hours after a humpback whale got lost and mistakenly swam sixty miles up the Sacramento River into the middle of California, editors and T-shirt designers were having "a whale of a time." And when a luxury car fell into a giant pothole in Columbus, Ohio, even the *South*

China Morning Post in Hong Kong ran the picture with the caption: "The hole truth—Mercedes bends."

OVERSTATEMENT—GOING FOR BAROQUE

Humor writers get more recognition in print than in any other medium. Pulitzer Prizes have been awarded to four syndicated columnists who are outstanding humorists: Russell Baker (1979), Ellen Goodman (1980), Art Buchwald (1982) and Dave Barry (1988). Even though there is no humor category, Pulitzer judges properly classify humor under "Commentary," and all four writers qualify.

Russell Baker is a master of literate humor. He is a natural cynic who sees the world as it is, instead of as it should be. In "An Idea That Must Be Unfolded Now," note how Baker used exaggeration to describe an early success of his "National Bumbershoot Academy":

> The pattern is familiar to us all. If you rise on a rainy morning and go to the closet for your umbrella, you find the umbrella gone. Usually it has gone to the office. If you go to the office on a clear morning, and it rains in the afternoon and you go to the closet for your umbrella, what do you find? Your umbrella is gone. Most cases it has gone home.
>
> From this pattern it was child's play to deduce what was happening. When an umbrella at home realized there would be rain by morning it went to the office. When it was loafing around the office and suddenly sensed an afternoon rain impending, it pulled itself together and went home.
>
> The reason for this behavior baffled men for twenty years, until Spitzstein (head of agency) explained it in his famous First Law of the Umbrella: "Umbrellas don't like to be wet."

Baker, a former Washington bureau chief for *The New York Times*, used humor to report hard news. He called the White House during President Dwight D. Eisenhower's term, "the tomb of the well-known soldier." In 1962 his first humor column was a widely acclaimed lampoon of President John F. Kennedy. Later, he turned his descriptive skill against President

Lyndon Johnson, whom he described as "a big, outsized, outlandish character out of some kind of medieval burlesque, a great bestriding colossus who ran every mood on the emotional gamut."

Another example of overstatement is Baker's attack on the Super Bowl, the Miss America pageant and the Academy Awards as three American religious rituals. He called them "utterly boring, meaningless, pointless and whatever happens doesn't make a goddam bit of difference to anything that is going to happen tomorrow. But when they run, the whole country comes together in some kind of great national town meeting."

Erma Bombeck also used a great deal of exaggeration, as when she described trying to pass her varicose veins off as textured stockings.

UNDERSTATEMENT

Art Buchwald's satirical humor is best when it's understated, so ironic that the uninitiated reader thinks Buchwald is deadly serious. In July of 1986, the Attorney General published the report of a commission formed to recommend action against pornography. Here are just a few paragraphs of Buchwald's column:

> The best thing about the report of Attorney General Meese's Commission on Pornography is its call for "Citizen Watch" groups to monitor what types of publications are sold in stores. If, in the view of the group, the material is pornographic, the citizen's group will organize a boycott, and God knows what else, to rid the store of the rot.
>
> . . . I'd like to volunteer my services. One of my greatest fantasies has been to censor magazines and send those who sell them to jail. . . . My qualifications? I've read many of the magazines the pornography commission finds objectionable. Secondly, I know exactly where in the store such reading materials are kept. I have done a lot of dry runs since the report was published. I know how to distinguish between literature with no redeeming value as opposed to magazines that are just trying to give me a cheap thrill.

If you elect me, I promise to go through every store in your neighborhood . . . You can trust me that no page will be left unturned without my stamp of approval. I'm not only talking about nudity, depravity and sexually obnoxious material, but also other stuff that might look offensive on the cover, but when you read between the lines can lead to crime too horrendous to mention.

Without wanting to brag, I think I'm the best man for the job. I've hung around newsstands all my life. I can spot a *Playboy* or *Penthouse* reader a mile away, and I know how to read any magazine sealed together with cellophane.

THE IRONIC TRUTH

Erma Bombeck once wrote, "Anybody can bring out your tears. That's a piece of cake. It is twenty times—no make that fifty times—easier to make people cry rather than laugh."

Jim Murray, a former columnist with the *Los Angeles Times* for more than thirty years, once wrote that the announcer at the Indy 500 had shouted, "Gentlemen, start your coffins." Murray campaigned for qualified black golfers to be invited to national tournaments. "It would be nice to have a black American at Augusta in something other than a coverall." And finally his observation: "Woody Hayes of Ohio State was a grouch, but Woody was consistent. He was graceless in victory and graceless in defeat."

Art Hoppe of the *San Francisco Chronicle* once wrote, "Writing a humor column beats honest work. It leaves mornings free for other projects, such as writing rare books. In my case, the books are extremely rare."

Humor columnists are introspective and fearful. I doubt there's a columnist who doesn't live in dread of drying up. Consider that Art Buchwald, Russell Baker and Erma Bombeck were the founders of the American Academy of Humor Columnists. They had a whopping membership of six, and they intended to keep it that way. Said Buchwald, "If a new young humor writer sends along some of his material—no matter how good it is—we write him back and say, 'You don't have it, kid. Go into advertising!' "

Magazine Articles

Magazine editors are demanding more, not less, levity. Even in serious nonfiction pieces, they're anxious to lighten the load with humor. They realize there are few new stories, so they're looking for new ways of telling the old story.

There's a fine distinction between being funny and being humorous. Writing jokes, you just want to be funny. When writing a humorous article, the object is to inform and educate in a humorous way. Humor is appropriate in either of the two following situations:

1. If the subject matter is a person known for humor, then humor becomes almost mandatory. The trick is to avoid trying to upstage the subject by forcing your own humor into the article. This is especially risky when you are writing about humor professionals who've spent many years perfecting their lines, while you've got only a few days to perfect *yours*. You're bound to come off looking second-rate. Make use of the great lines they've created. Don't compete.

2. If the subject is serious but can be made funny in the phrasing. For example, you can use out-of-character humor, someone who plays a role completely different from what you'd expect: an old lady who rides a motorcycle or a dog who sings along to rock music. And incongruous situations open up hundreds of possibilities.

Of the two possibilities, it's obviously easier to produce humor when the subject is humorous. The humor for the second subject must be gentle, reassuring, predictable. It celebrates ordinary events in a new way. It brings a smile of recognition rather than a hearty laugh. Its success is based upon genuineness of feeling and clarity of writing. These more serious subjects are researched like a regular piece, but then the humor is added to make it more memorable. Don't take extraneous jokes and try to bend them to fit the subject. Humor must come out of reality.

The key to a sale is the perfect marriage of quality humor with the magazine's special interest and audience. One team of comedy writers came up with "Hemorrhoids: They won't kill you—you just wish they would," and "The one sure cure of acne—old age."

They claim a fifteen hundred word article on a subject (like hospital-room etiquette) can contain up to eight humorous anecdotes or jokes and still be considered serious and informative. It isn't designed to keep the patient in stitches—he's probably already there.

The bible for selling magazine articles is the *Writer's Market*. Updated annually, it has a complete list of magazines, with names and addresses, that are looking for freelance material, including humor.

ANECDOTES AND FILLER

The *Courier-Journal* of Louisville, Kentucky, used to run "The Funny Bone," a joke column, in its Sunday magazine for more than thirty years. It used subscriber joke contributions exclusively. Readers not only liked the jokes, but also took great pride in seeing their names, and those of their friends, published. In articles, humor works best as a leadoff hitter. You can suck the reader into the story faster with a good anecdote. You'll find examples of that every day on the front page of the *Wall Street Journal.* A humor anecdote also works well as a sign-off.

Anecdotes and fillers are used more often by magazines than news-papers. And of all the publications that solicit public contributions, the *Reader's Digest* is the Super Bowl of humor achievement. It is, by far, the most rewarding market for freelancers. With over fifty million read-ers, they pay the highest rates for anecdotes, jokes and humorous quotes. To find the latest fees just turn to page four of the most recent *Digest* issue.

The term "filler" originated when type was set by hand or linotype. It refers to the one- or two-line tidbits printers used to quickly fill space at the end of a column or a page. Even though today's computerized typesetting has eliminated that need, fillers still appear in magazines—humorous ones, as leavening.

There is no precise formula for a filler. "A good filler," wrote Betty Johnston, a former *Digest* editor, "is one that the reader will want to quote or read aloud to a colleague." Because most magazines have four- and five-month editorial deadlines in advance of publication, fillers need a certain timeliness (or, better, timelessness) and relevance—a quote or anecdote from the past must have some special application for today.

Humor is integral. Regina Hersey of *Reader's Digest* has said that in the magazine's monthly reader's poll, humor sections are consistently ranked first, and humor articles are a consistently favorite format. This really comes as no big surprise, because *Reader's Digest* has at least nine different areas for salable humor: "Toward More Picturesque Speech," "Points to Ponder" and "Quotable Quotes" specialize in zany or inventive play-on-words phrasing; "Life in These United States" tries for true, previously unpublished anecdotes; "Laughter, the Best Medicine" is a joke department that includes puns, topical humor and celebrity quips. Humorous stories are reprinted in special sections: "Personal Glimpses," "All in a Day's Work," "Campus Comedy," "Humor in Uniform," "Tales Out of School" and "Virtual Hilarity." In addition, at the end of some articles, the magazine still uses miscellaneous anecdotes as old-fashioned filler.

There are twelve staff editors who do nothing but prepare the humor anecdotes and fillers. Humor is read by two editors before being rejected so that the bad mood of one editor won't automatically eliminate a marginal possibility. Then the magazine submits all material seriously being considered for publication to an "index" department where it's checked for originality. (Beginning writers can ruin their reputations with a magazine by trying to pass off someone else's material as their own.) Finally, a research department checks original sources for verification.

Anecdotes about yourself are acceptable, but anecdotes about famous people are particularly desired because names make news (or the other way around).

Many general publications have taboos against bathroom humor, vulgarity and stories that ridicule the handicapped. Put-down humor is acceptable when the joke is in the cleverness of the response. That's why, if the humor comes close to any of these areas, self-deprecating stories have a much greater chance of publication. Tell the story on yourself, don't make yourself the smart alec. The *Digest* is not above changing the point of view in these cases, but they'll always check with the writer.

A few magazines, like *Reader's Digest*, are also interested in reprinting good humor from other publications, and will pay readers handsomely for discovering it. *The New Yorker* delights in typos and short items with unintentionally weird or double entendre phrasing.

However, humor material in other major publications, like *Time, Newsweek* and *The New York Times,* is so thoroughly covered by *Digest* staff personnel that it's rare freelancers can get credit. Over eight hundred newspaper columnists regularly send their columns to *Reader's Digest* in the hope of editorial selection. Therefore, the magazine is looking for reprint material from remote areas like small regional magazines, corporate newsletters and local radio shows.

The winning combination for acceptability is a good sense of what's funny—and knowing how to present it. That gives the professional humor writer an advantage over the amateur contributor.

Stories must have a punch as well as a punch line. They should be written in less than three hundred words, thus they can't require long introductions or lots of background information. The best material has a sense of truthfulness, rather than a contrived setup. People in incongruous situations make the funniest stories because the reader identifies with the "It could have happened" possibility.

A filler, unlike a regular article, is paid for only on publication. *Reader's Digest* gets thousands of submissions each month, so they won't return material even if you include a self-addressed, stamped envelope (SASE). If your piece was intended for publication but omitted because of space, no check! If they like it you'll generally hear within three months. But sometimes they may take up to a year, so everyone's unhappy if you've given up on them and submitted the humor elsewhere. If you *have* sold the item elsewhere and the magazine's research department calls to verify, never lie. You'll win that game only once, but will be blackballed forever.

Material should be neatly typed, double-spaced, each item on a separate sheet of paper, with your name, address, telephone number and date of submission clearly identified.

LETTERS TO THE EDITOR

Even if you're just interested in writing a letter to the editor, you've got a better chance of being published if you use humor. The annual peekaboo swimsuit issue of *Sports Illustrated* prompts more letters to "The 19th Hole" than many other issues combined. It gets a lot of subscriptions "renude." An example of a letter that got published because of a basic reverse technique: "I was shocked at the display of flesh [that issue] contained: What legs! What chests! Where did you find those Sumo wrestlers?"

Mel Helitzer is a professor at the E.W. Scripps School of Journalism at Ohio University. He is the author of *Comedy Writing Secrets* and *Comedy Techniques for Writers and Performers*.

CHAPTER 12

Writing "Funny Bits" for Kids

BY PATRICIA CASE

"Do you think that all children's books ought to have funny bits
in them?" Miss Honey asked. "I do," Matilda said. "Children
are not so serious as grown-ups and they love to laugh."
—ROALD DAHL, *Matilda*

Matilda is absolutely right. Kids love to laugh, and authors who keep young
readers chuckling might make lifelong fans. What grown-up reader, for instance, can forget Roald Dahl's irreverently funny *James and the Giant Peach?*

Although Dahl's "funny bits" seemed to flow from his natural spring, he
used specific techniques to delight, amuse and tickle his young audience—
techniques you can employ, too.

To expose your funny bone, you must know how to observe humor,
use comic elements and know what type of humor works best for various
groups.

Observing Humor

Begin by collecting and tuning in to what amuses you. Dahl, for example,
collected odd names and incidents that later fed his young readers' laughs.
In his autobiography, *Boy: Tales of Childhood,* Dahl pulled a sidesplitting
anecdote from his collection about being chosen human defroster by his
boarding-school prefects. The school's unheated outhouse was located in
the bogs. As the "Boazers' " favorite "bog-warmer," young Dahl survived
the dreaded duties of sitting on the upper-classmen's toilet seat—to preheat
it by melting the ice—only because of his naturally hot bottom. A dubious
but hilarious honor. What experiences have you had—or simply heard
about—that you can use?

Tuning in is your funny-fitness exercise. When you awake each day,
remind yourself to look for life's light side. Focus on funny. When you
laugh, notice what struck you as funny. Why? If you provoke laughter, note

how you did it. Then jot these incidents in your notebook along with a few sentences about age groups that might find them appealing. Remember to include *humor*, not just jokes (more about the difference later).

In addition to informally observing humor, you can further tune in by delving into the growing body of formal humor research. The pragmatic joke analyses of comics such as Jack Benny and Johnny Carson have been joined by research in fields from medicine to television production. These humor studies contain a wealth of tips that are yours for the reading.

You'll be surprised at how quickly the practice of collecting and tuning in will improve your writing wit. The Cat in the Hat said it best. "It's fun to have fun but you have to know how."

Comic Elements

Once you've developed skills in observing humor, you're ready to use basic comic elements. Some old jokes are *really* old, tracing back to medieval times. Despite variations in individual funny bones, however, these jokes have survived for centuries because they work. Certain elements are almost *always* able to make people laugh.

Like basic plot structures, you can use the comic elements as dependable foundations for creative adaptation. As a children's *writer* rather than a performer, though, be sure to select elements adaptable to print. Here's a starting list: timing, mime, slapstick, repetition, switches, exaggeration, extremes, indecision, convention suspension and wordplay.

The first three, timing, mime and slapstick, are especially challenging for printed pages. Timing makes children laugh (ask anyone who's played peekaboo with a baby) but perfecting this element for print is difficult. It isn't impossible, though.

In her picture book *Scary, Scary Halloween*, Eve Bunting reveals that the unexplained scary noises and events were caused by a mother cat and her kittens. Bunting uses timing by waiting to solve the mystery until her wide-eyed young listeners are on the edge of their parents' laps. When she does, she provides comic relief—even though the words themselves aren't funny:

> It's quiet now, the monster's gone.
> The streets are ours until the dawn.

We're out, we prowlers of the night
Who snap and snarl and claw and
Bite.

The picture illustrating the page isn't funny either, but the timing in placing both together to solve the mystery brings smiles to young listeners.

Mime and slapstick are also tricky in print, although Mercer Mayer perfected the former in his wordless Frog books (check out Frog's facial expressions), and Don Madden achieved the latter with Miss Twig's boomeranging antics in his illustrated *Lemonade Serenade*. Fortunately, other elements on the list adapt to print more easily.

REPETITION
The Poky Little Puppy, Golden Book's all-time best-seller, is a prime example of repetition. Janette Sebring Lowrey wrote about the serious topics of puppyhood disobedience and discipline. But after the third repetition of Poky Little Puppy's mischievous behavior, every little audience member is giggling and clamoring to have the book read again.

SWITCHES
These can be both short and long. Dahl's *Matilda* delights middle-graders with her brief but jolly topsy-turvy switching of her mother's hair bleach for her father's hair oil. By contrast, in *Miss Nelson Is Missing*, Harry Allard shapes a longer comedy reverse when the ugly and mean substitute teacher Miss Swamp replaces the ladylike, gentle but unheeded teacher Miss Nelson. Prekindergarten through primary grades—any students newly familiar with school routines—gleefully greet the revelation of Miss Nelson's Viola Swamp disguise and the trick she played to teach her students polite behavior.

EXAGGERATION
In *James and the Giant Peach*, Dahl employs exaggeration to create the book's main vehicle of humorous escape, the huge blimplike fruit that carries James and assorted companions above the earth. In *George's Marvelous Medicine*, though, it's Dahl's exaggeration of individual story

components that draws chuckles from middle-graders: George's mixing of the medicine and its growth effect on his cantankerous granny. On the other hand, Dr. Seuss delights by minimizing (*reverse* exaggeration) the time it takes the Cat in the Hat to clean up a colossal mess.

EXTREMES

A.A. Milne successfully employs this element in his Pooh series. By the second volume (*The House at Pooh Corner*) Eeyore has become so extremely gloomy and churlish that even nursery-schoolers see him as a comic character. Similarly, in Shel Silverstein's *Where the Sidewalk Ends*, Lazy Jane shows such lethargy in getting herself a drink of water that giggling readers are soon lying down with their mouths open skyward to imitate her.

INDECISION

Perhaps because many youngsters agonize over choices, indecision is a ready element for children's humor. Children ages three to ten especially identify with characters who seesaw when faced with choosing. From the extended ambivalence of Kathryn Jackson's *Tawny Scrawny Lion* about eating Rabbit's fat brothers and sisters or settling for carrot stew, to Jocelyn Stevenson's *O'Diddy*'s frequent oscillations between giving up forever but then trying again, children laugh.

CONVENTION SUSPENSION

Whether by nonconformity, illogic or fantasy, suspending conventional controls amuses children of all ages. In numerous stories, both Dahl and Seuss quickly dispense with parents (the rule-makers) and then launch into frolicking fantasy worlds of nonconformity, illogic or silliness. Asked why she laughed over Matilda's parents leaving her behind while they escaped to Spain, one eight-year-old replied, "Real families don't act like that."

WORDPLAY

This element has many facets that tickle children. The fact that they get the humor shows them they've attained language proficiencies, which raises their self-esteem and creates camaraderie with their peers. Here's an example currently circling among kids:

"Have you heard about the disaster?"

"Where? What happened?"

"The lady next door backed into her lawn mower and it disaster."

Wordplay's popularity and comic possibilities are limitless. Puns, for example, are equally enjoyed by both punners and punnees of all ages. Jack Prelutsky's cuckoocloctopus (*The New Kid on the Block*) delights with its meaning, rhythm and sound.

Other wordplays such as malapropisms, nonsense phrases and made-up words (like "snozzcumber," "buzzburgers" and "humpcrimples") evoke laughs in Dahl's *The BFG*. In fact, "whizpopper," another of the Big Friendly Giant's concoctions, sparks great grins in kids. They've widely adopted it as an acceptable term for discussing a previously unmentionable but odorous bodily process.

Although not strictly a wordplay, one type of dialogue provides children so many laughs, probably in anxiety relief, that it deserves special mention here: frankly honest plain talk. It gets guffaws from middle grades to adolescence, even when statements are serious as when thirteen-year-old Anastasia says to her mother in Lois Lowry's *Anastasia, Ask Your Analyst,* "Mom, . . . I believe you are entering menopause."

While the previous examples illustrate the separate comic components of our list, many of them contain traces of several elements. Read each for yourself to appreciate the humor in context and to discern the subtle combinations employed by the authors.

For additional building blocks, read Melvin Helitzer's *Comedy Writing Secrets*. Although geared to general writing, the book's loaded with adaptable ideas and practice suggestions.

Know Your Readers

Kids themselves afford the best insight into what they like best. For example, a four-year-old on our block, in discussing a grocery shopping list, said, "And let's get some of those fruits I like. What are they, Mom, come-whats or go-whats?" When her mother laughed so hard she could barely answer "kumquats," the budding comedian lost no time telling the neighbors the funny bit she'd incidentally created.

In addition to listening to children of the ages you're writing for, study the work of those authors mentioned throughout this article. Paul E. Mc-Ghee, for example, has compiled the writings of thirteen researchers in *Humor and Children's Development: A Guide to Practical Applications*. Their findings brim with insights, from the clues youngsters need for recognizing humor to its uses in juvenile dentistry. Further, in her article "Let Laughter Ring!" (published in the February 1990 *Working Mother*) Eva Conrad explains the joking needs and satisfactions of age groups from toddlers through teens. Between these references and your own observations, you'll discover what amuses kids.

Remember the differences between humor and the less-evocative, but still useful, joke. Knowing which form works best in specific parts of your story will make your writing more effective.

Humor historian Mikhail Bakhtin (*Rabelais and His World*) provides guidelines. Humor grows out of the subject matter, situation and characters. At its best, humor evokes humane laughter at the universality of worldly frailties. Jokes, in contrast, function as self-contained capsules, introduced to get quick laughs at specific things or categories.

Jokes can be made entirely independent of the situation at hand. Those in *101 School Jokes*, by Sam Schultz, are particularly popular with elementary students. The category's well known, the jokes are short and they're acceptable for a laugh nearly any place or time. For example:

Where was the Declaration of Independence signed?
At the bottom.

Although jokes may not be appropriate in every story, it's always fitting for the innate humor to shine forth in any writing for children.

It also helps to know the difference between types of laughter. Bakhtin found that some eras reveled in joyous, accepting, enriching and renewing group laughter. Other periods—especially modern ones—have withdrawn into the satire of derision, rejection and often caustic individual laughter.

With humor's value clearly encompassing so much more than mere laughs, enhancing your witty writing skills is worthwhile. So practice observing humor, using its basic elements, and know your readers. You'll soon find yourself chuckling at your keyboard as funny bits flow into your stories. To paraphrase *The Cat in the Hat*, even if

> . . . it is wet
> And the sun is not sunny
> [You can write]
> Lots of good fun that is funny.

Patricia Case's credits include *How to Write Your Autobiography, Highlights for Children, Cape Cod Life, Genealogical Helper, Missouri Life, Teaching K-8, Wee Wisdom* and the *Society of Children's Book Writers & Illustrators Bulletin*.

CHAPTER 13

The Comfortable Chair:
Using Humor in Creative Nonfiction

BY DINTY MOORE

"You want a chair that makes you comfortable, isn't that right?"

My wife and I, blundering into a furniture showroom just slightly smaller than the state of Delaware, found ourselves ambushed by a chipmunk of a man. He was barely over five feet tall, stooped by age. His dark hair was thinning in patches, and his robin's egg-blue blazer was as unstylish and unattractive as any blazer I've ever seen. But he had clear, direct eyes, and quite the smile.

That was *my* initial assessment. What *he* saw, perhaps, were two shy, middle-class pigeons with "easy sale" tattooed on their foreheads.

The gentleman introduced himself as Howie, "your furniture consultant for today," pumped my hand and winked at my spouse. "You want a comfortable chair, yes? One you can sit in and relax?"

He was, it seemed, not just a furniture consultant but a mind reader as well, having intuited by my mere explanation "we're looking at chairs" that Renita and I had absolutely no interest in an uncomfortable chair that made us squirm and kept us endlessly tense.

"I'm going to take you around," he announced, a trace of Brooklyn in his voice. "We have over three thousand chairs in our showroom today. I'm going to show you all of them."

Later, after I had turned up my nose at the first few offerings, he really said this: "I only want to make you happy."

Even my wife has never said that to me. Howie did, however, and I began to believe him. He was pushy, slick, odd and yet it became somehow impossible not to like the little man. His gaze was warm and neighborly. He had that slow, spreading smile. I don't understand how it works, but within moments of entering Howie's magnetic field, I wanted to befriend him. I wanted him to be my grandfather, even though I suspected that if he *were* my grandfather, the piece of butterscotch candy he would pull for me from his pocket would be ten years old and lint-covered. I would love him anyway.

Howie told me he was top salesperson for the entire Mid-Atlantic region. I didn't doubt him for one second.

A little later still, when I rejected the whole category of chair that I call "marshmallow-puffy recliner," Howie turned, extended his hands palms upward and promised:

"I'm not going to make you buy something you don't want."

It didn't make sense to me at the time—why ever would I buy something I didn't want?—but after an hour with Howie, I understood that I might have done just that.

He had that certain power.

Humor and Nonfiction

The world of nonfiction has come a long way recently in letting down its hair, but the truth is, the genre of fact-based literary writing still stands awfully close at times to its cousin, journalism. With that proximity comes the latent baggage of objectivity, leading all too often to a dreadful, deadening seriousness.

This seriousness is not necessarily bad. As nonfiction writers, much of what we describe and illuminate is indeed grave—the ravages of disease, war or perfect storms, the inequities of society, the desolation of family—and in many cases it is entirely appropriate, maybe crucial, that our style and voice reflect this reality. But it needn't always, and often it is the case that a light touch of the pen can afford the reader a welcome breath of fresh air.

Novelists and short story writers have always known this. Even the most serious novel is helped along by a moment of levity; just as, of course, even the funniest work of fiction is infinitely stronger if there is a core of serious truth underlying the joke. In nonfiction, however, these two realms are often held separate.

But not always.

A loose tradition exists of American literary nonfiction humor, starting certainly as far back as Benjamin Franklin and including, of course, Mark

Twain. It was the latter gentleman who once said, "Get your facts first, and then you can distort them as much as you please."

What you make of that quote probably depends on your definition of "distort," because a fact is a fact, and if you change the facts, you aren't writing nonfiction anymore; you are writing something else. But maybe Twain was pulling our leg—he had that habit. Maybe what he meant was, "Get your facts first, and then you can present them however you wish."

The manner of presentation—the way a truth is packaged—is often all that differentiates what makes us wince from what makes us chortle. Every successful comic and humorist knows that the line between an uncomfortable truth and a good belly laugh is remarkably thin.

And then there are those occasions when even the most serious subjects seem to demand a comic presentation. In some cases, humor is perhaps the only sane way to really get at them.

Take Frank McCourt. His best-selling and widely praised memoir *Angela's Ashes* describes as bleak a childhood as any Dickens could imagine. McCourt's memoir presents a world of painful poverty, parental abandonment, infant death, alcoholism and class prejudice. These are not light subjects.

But McCourt's wonderful book is hilarious at points, simply wry at others, and if it had needed a subtitle (it didn't), that subtitle might be "grinning through the sadness."

McCourt could conceivably have presented his memoir without humor (hard to believe, actually, given McCourt himself, but let the premise ride for a moment), but it would have been a very different book. I'm convinced it would not have been as widely read, and in truth, I think it would have only been half the story. Humor was what brought McCourt and his siblings through their dismal early years. Humor is a large part of the tale.

And humor needn't be limited to memoir.

Any fan of Susan Orlean's *New Yorker* pieces or her classic nonfiction work *Saturday Night,* can see where a little levity, a sly wit, translates directly into style and voice. Yet Orlean is still, basically, a reporter.

Joan Didion, too, is a humorist by my definition, not because she presents knee-slapping frivolity or cracks conventional jokes, but because her writer's eye cannot help but to pick out the ironic detail.

Gay Talese's classic of literary nonfiction, *Fame and Obscurity*, is a serious book, dense with closely observed description, but full, too, of gently comic moments: the wig-bearing woman, for instance, in Talese's essay "Frank Sinatra Has a Cold."

Bill Bryson presents a broader style of humor in his travels across England, America and Australia, as do Ian Frazier in *Great Plains* and Jonathan Raban in *Hunting Mister Heartbreak*.

People are funny. For some of us, it is hard to write about them without pointing that out.

Why do these writers use humor, and why do we read their work?

Human nature. When I get together with my friends, one of the first things we do is to look across the coffee table and try to make one another laugh. That's what a lot of friends do, I think, and my favorite writers are no different. The experience of reading a writer like McCourt, Orleans, Bryson, Twain, is like spending time with a friend. A comfortable friend.

These friends keep me grinning through every page. We laugh, and we laugh, because it is all so true.

"You Need a Fence?"

Also true is that Howie tried to sell me his fence.

We passed through the giant circular showroom, rejecting chair after chair. "You like this one?" Howie would ask. He would pause then, study my face, and before I could form an answer, he would say, "Of course not, I knew you wouldn't!"

Along the way, my wife and I let it slip that we had just moved into town. Howie, it turned out, was about to leave our new town, for a better furniture consultant job down south. We mentioned our small, untrainable pup.

"You have a small dog? *I* have a small dog!"

Howie could not have been more delighted had I just revealed that I was his long lost son, orphaned at birth.

"You need a fence? I'm selling my fence."

I didn't need a fence, but had I needed one, or had Howie been just slightly more insistent, I would probably be in his backyard right now, taking his fence down, stuffing it into the back of my station wagon, instead of writing this essay.

What Makes a Story Funny?

Have you ever heard someone try to explain a joke? It seldom works. Explaining how to "write funny" may be just as futile an endeavor, but that is what I've been asked to do, so here goes.

There are a few basic elements that make a story funny—sometimes. They include:

JUXTAPOSITION

For some reason (probably because he had a book contract), Bill Bryson decided to hike the Appalachian Trail from Georgia to Maine, despite the fact that he was middle-aged, out of shape and not a seasoned hiker. That might have been funny enough, but Bryson lured a friend along—Stephen Katz.

Katz, as the following passage from *A Walk in the Woods* shows, was as improbable a companion as Bryson could likely have found, and that juxtaposition provides much of the engine of the ensuing story.

Here is how Bryson introduces his friend, exiting a plane at a small New England airport:

> Katz was arrestingly larger than when I had last seen him. He had always been kind of fleshy, but now he brought to mind Orson Welles after a very bad night. He was limping a little and breathing harder than one ought to after a walk of twenty yards.
>
> "Man, I'm hungry," he said without preamble, and let me take his carry-on bag, which instantly jerked my arm to the floor.
>
> "What have you got in there?" I gasped.
>
> "Ah, just some tapes and shit for the trail. There a Dunkin' Donuts anywhere around here? I haven't had anything to eat since Boston."

IRONY

Bryson's juxtaposition of Katz and the trail was intentional, but juxtaposition is often unintentional, and that we call irony.

Irony underlies countless good stories. Gay Talese's essay "Frank Sinatra Has a Cold" holds the central irony in the title itself—Sinatra's throat was worth millions, yet a simple germ could shut it all down. James Thurber's essays hold irony in every line. In his classic "The Night the Bed Fell," Thurber opens with this line: "I suppose that the high-water mark of my youth in Columbus, Ohio, was the night the bed fell on my father."

Thurber's father decided to sleep in the attic "to be away where he could think." The bed falls, no one sleeps, no one experiences any quiet at all.

That's ironic, and hilarious, at least the way Thurber tells it.

SATIRE

Frank McCourt's memoir is filled with irony, some of it tragic. But he is also a master of Dickensian satire—the skewering of the pompous man.

A case in point—the following passage. One damp Limerick morning, McCourt's mother takes young Frankie and his brother Malachy to the St. Vincent de Paul Society, in search of charity. There, they encounter the sarcastic, but effective, Nora Molloy.

> "The boots are all gone. Nothing I can do. What's this? Who's smoking?"
>
> Nora waves her cigarette. "I am," she says, "and enjoying it down to the last ash."
>
> "Every puff you take," he starts.
>
> "I know," she says, "I'm taking food out of the mouths of my children."
>
> "You're insolent, woman. You'll get no charity here."
>
> "Is that a fact? Well, Mr. Quinlivan, if I don't get it here I know where I will."
>
> "What are you talking about?"
>
> "I'll go to the Quakers. They'll give me charity."
>
> Mr. Quinlivan steps toward Nora and points a finger. "Do you know what we have here? We have a souper in our midst.

We had the soupers in the Famine. The Protestants went around telling good Catholics that if they gave up their faith and turned Protestant they'd get more soup than their bellies could hold and, God help us, some Catholics took the soup, and were ever after known as soupers and lost their immortal souls doomed to the deepest part of hell. And you, woman, if you go to the Quakers you'll lose your immortal soul and souls of your children."

"Then, Mr. Quinlivan, you'll have to save us, won't you?"

EXAGGERATION

Comic novelists have always used exaggeration to bring out the humorous in characters—think Dickens again.

But some people out there don't need to be exaggerated. Some people just seem to naturally exaggerate themselves. Howie the chair consultant was certainly one. He was the consummate salesman. He was, in all senses of the word, a perfect character.

So was Katz. And Nora Molloy.

All a writer had to do was capture the truth.

A FEW ADDITIONAL RECOMMENDATIONS

Juxtaposition, irony, satire and exaggeration are everywhere. Developing an eye for life's truly comic moments is part of what a writer must do to bring humor into the writing of nonfiction. If you find it honestly funny, then write it down.

But in truth, it is not *that* easy.

The trick is often in the presentation, the way in which the facts are packaged. Though there are no firm rules in this matter, there are some approaches I feel comfortable offering as suggestions.

The first is to avoid seeming to look down at the subjects of your writing. You can probably skewer a politician or personal injury lawyer with abandon, but you should be gentle when mocking the common man. If you seem mean-spirited, if you take cheap shots, we aren't so willing to laugh.

Secondly, you need a story. Just setting up a joke is not enough to keep the reader interested. If your goal is to write compelling nonfiction, the story always comes first—what is it you are meaning to show us, and why should the reader care? It is when the humor takes a back seat to the story being told that humor is most effective, and the finest writing is done.

Finally, there is nothing wrong with the occasional punch line, but remember that nothing kills a joke more than the joke-teller slamming a bony elbow into your ribs, winking, and saying, "Wait until you hear this joke, it is going to be hilarious."

The best humor sneaks up on you.

The Real Secret to Being Funny

The real secret is this: I believe that Howie really wanted me to have a comfortable chair. Putting my middle-aged bottom in a soft, commodious seat brought him a sort of pleasure. He wasn't *just* trying to sell me something, and as such, he could probably sell me the world.

Humor is like that. Don't ever try to tell a joke. Don't ever force humor. You have to be amused yourself, and you have to take honest pleasure in your amusement.

I want to tell my story of Howie, relay his dialogue, describe his person, because frankly, I am sitting here grinning just thinking about him. Really, truly, not sort of. Howie struck me as hilarious the moment I met him, and he still does. And I like him.

Humor has to be honest. Funny writers can make us smile, which is a good thing in and of itself, but the best comic writers make us smile, laugh, guffaw and then, maybe just for a moment, see something that is true, about ourselves, about our prejudices, about the silly world we inhabit. That is the power of humor, and the power of humor in the service of truth.

The Perfect Chair

"Tell me," Howie eventually asked, "when you think of a chair, what are your first thoughts?"

We were nearing the end of the showroom, and he was clearly worried. I had explained my stubborn dislike of busy fabric, my abhorrence of gratuitous puffiness, my disdain for Queen Anne, and we had come up empty.

"Wait. You'll like this one."

He pointed to a maroon recliner at the end of a row, not puffy in any way, a simple, understated pattern.

"Sit down, relax."

I did.

It was the perfect chair.

We left that day with a comfortable chair, and additionally, with orders for a new loveseat, and a home entertainment cabinet—one where you can close the doors and not look at your ugly television and stereo. We didn't know we needed this until Howie told us so.

My budget for the day was $700. Howie kept us within that budget, give or take an extra $1,800. The man could sell anything to anyone. We were in the presence of a true master.

Howie left town before the new furniture arrived, but it was delivered, as promised, and it fits perfectly in our new home.

I never bought his fence.

I never saw him again.

EXERCISES:

1. Think of someone who makes you laugh, not just because of what they say, but because of who they are, how they walk, the way they move their eyes, what they wear, the way they eat a piece of chicken. Try to describe this person in fewer than five hundred words, through simple observation. Try to make us believe that you love this person, despite the individual's comic attributes.

2. Use yourself as the subject. What is an entirely improbable thing for you to do, an improbable place for you to go, an improbable subject for you to encounter? Go there, try it and then write a first-person account of your (honest) experiences. Like Katz on the trail, the juxtaposition is bound to be funny.

Dinty Moore is the editor of *Brevity: A Journal of Concise Literary Nonfiction* and the online editor of *Creative Nonfiction*. He is the author of two books of nonfiction, *The Accidental Buddhist* and *The Emperor's Virtual Clothes*, and *Toothpick Men*, a collection of stories. Moore teaches writing at Penn State Altoona.

CHAPTER 14

The Seven Laws of Comedy Writing

BY DAVID EVANS

I'll give rule no. 1 right away:

1. Be Able to Throw Out Your Best Joke

Sounds strange, doesn't it? And yet, I've found it to be profoundly true. Time and again when writing a script for *The Monkees, Love American Style, The Bill Cosby Show* or any of the numerous animated films I've done, I'll come up with one joke that seems sensational and clearly eclipses all the other jokes in the piece—but that doesn't exactly fit. I want it to fit. It would be wonderful if it fit. But it doesn't.

The overwhelming temptation is to use it anyway. After all, it's such a terrific joke, it seems a shame not to use it. But that's what craft is all about. Everyone knows a comedy script involves jokes, but it also involves characters, scenes, situations, development, dialogue and story. A sensational joke in the wrong script can throw everything else off and ruin the rhythm and the flow. What you need is not necessarily *a lot* of jokes, but the *right* jokes in the right places.

Being able to throw out your best joke is so important that I consider it one of the fundamental laws of comedy writing. There are others. In fact, there are seven laws of comedy writing that I keep bumping into and rediscovering over and over again. Some are surprising; others are obvious. The Seven Laws of Comedy Writing apply throughout the wide spectrum of comedy. You've met the first one; here are the other six.

2. If You Don't Laugh, Nobody Else Will

When I first started writing for television, as a staff writer for *The Monkees*, I had an experience that dramatically influenced my life in comedy ever since. I was sitting at the typewriter, working on a script. Suddenly there was a knock at the door and one of the secretaries came in. With a perplexed look on her face, she said, "You're laughing! You're sitting here in a room all by yourself and you're laughing!" I shrugged and said, "Of course I'm laughing! I'm a comedy writer. I write funny things and they make me laugh!"

Bingo! I didn't realize how important that was then, but I've thought about it countless times since. In order to write comedy that makes other people laugh, you must be in close touch with your own comedy instincts. You must laugh. I have always been my own best audience. Fundamentally I write things that I myself laugh at. If I laugh at them, there's a good chance you might, too.

By contrast, a couple of years after I wrote for *The Monkees*, I was working on a script for a show that I didn't really like. It didn't seem like a funny show or even a potentially funny show. So I found myself sitting at the typewriter one day, trying to think of something that the producer would think was funny (since he was my employer). A bell went off in my head: I realized I was starting to short-circuit my own comedy instincts, trying to second-guess what somebody else would laugh at. I ended up leaving that project because I felt I needed to. (For the same reason, I left television altogether, and since then have focused on book projects and short, humorous, animated films. I'm having lots of laughs.)

As a professional comedy writer, you might become involved in a project that you don't find funny for any number of reasons: The money seems too good to turn down; your agent presses you to do it; it seems like a good "career move." But those are all dangerous reasons. You will start relying on "comedy writer's tricks," instead of your own sense of humor. If you're writing comedy and you're not genuinely, spontaneously laughing at what you're writing, something is radically wrong. You need to have fun with your own comedy, because your own true sense of humor is the single greatest asset any comedy writer can ever have.

3. Character Is 98 Percent of Comedy . . .

One of the most famous lines in the history of comedy is from *The Jack Benny Show*. Throughout his career, Benny developed the persona of the ultimate skinflint. On one show, a robber pulled a gun on Benny and threatened, "Your money or your life." Finally Benny spoke: "I'm thinking it over. . . ."

For the cheapskate Benny persona, this was a tough decision that required some real thought. And it is a perfect example of comedy derived from character. This was not a joke superimposed onto a situation; it grew organically out of the Benny character.

Another example from a different medium and a different era is the Woody Allen movie *Bullets Over Broadway* in which a young playwright seeks backing for his play, and the only place he can get the money is from a mobster. But the mobster will back the play only if his floozy girlfriend gets to play the lead. Since the mobster is insanely jealous, he sends along a thug bodyguard to watch the girlfriend. The bodyguard, who is constantly around the rehearsals, starts to have ideas about how to rewrite the script—and this complete thug turns out to have great writing talent, even more than the playwright. The comedy is completely driven by the character of the bodyguard. That's comedy—funny characters acting like themselves.

4. . . . *And Timing Is the Other 98 Percent*

Let's take another look at the Jack Benny segment. After the crook issues his ultimatum, there is a long silence. This is a beautiful example of timing—setting something up and then giving the humor the time it needs. It's important to write this silence into the script. Inexperienced or insecure writers often set up something that requires a reaction, but fail to write in the reaction. Silence is one of the most important parts of comedy, and it's an aspect of timing. It's like the white spaces of art or the musical silences of Miles Davis.

Consider *Bullets Over Broadway* again. The initial, superficial comedic hook is the incongruity between the worlds of the theater and of the mob. But the real comedy of the movie comes from the unfolding character of the bodyguard, and this is done gradually, throughout the whole film. If we knew the things about the bodyguard at the beginning that we know at the end, they would seem preposterous and unbelievable. But we don't. We learn only a little bit at a time, so that by the end of the movie we believe it totally. This movie is like a time-release capsule.

Another aspect of timing is repetition, and what comedy writers call "the rule of three"—the repetition of something three times, with a switch at the end of the sequence. Euclid and Aristotle loved the number three, and so did Oliver Hardy and Groucho Marx. For example, picture Oliver Hardy having to walk across a narrow patch of sidewalk covered with ice. He realizes that it's dangerous and studies the ice with great concern and apprehension before he even starts across. Then he crosses very slowly and carefully, fear in every step. Once across, he breathes a sigh of relief and puffs himself up with pride in his accomplishment. He goes back over the ice a second time, now with more confidence. Again he is successful. He is now very proud of himself. Jauntily, he walks across the ice a third time—and this time falls flat on his face!

What if he'd fallen the first time he crossed the ice, without any of the repetitions or the buildup? Not nearly as funny, is it? You need to build up to it. That's what the rule of three is all about.

5. The Power of the Step Sheet

When I first started in television I had a wonderful mentor, Jim Frizzel, one of the great, classic comedy writers, who'd written for everything from *Mr. Peepers* and *The Andy Griffith Show* to *M*A*S*H*. He showed me a powerful tool that I started using on *The Monkees* and have been using ever since—the "step sheet."

It's absurdly simple, but extremely helpful. You write down the sequence of scenes you're going to have in your comedy script. Then you write down in just a sentence or two what happens in each scene. You might have three or four sentences if a lot is happening in a particular scene. But the step sheet is not a listing of jokes or dialogue—just story points and character points. For example, a step sheet for *Bullets Over Broadway* would show only the progressive changes from scene to scene in the characterization of the thug bodyguard, as he becomes more and more involved in the writing process.

Remember the importance of character and timing in comedy? (You should; after all, you only read about them a minute or so ago.) The step sheet is the tool you use to make sure your characters and timing work with maximum effectiveness. It's one of the most powerful tools in comedy writing.

6. Hold the Jokes!

A common misconception in comedy is that the more jokes in a piece, the better. But I believe that the opposite is often true. I've written thousands of jokes, and a good joke can be truly wonderful. Yet the most satisfying comedy comes not from jokes but from a funny character, funny characters reacting to one another or a funny story. Again, *Bullets Over Broadway* is instructive: It's a very funny movie and it uses virtually no jokes.

A good test of whether a humorous piece is solid is if you can tell just the story, without any of the jokes, and still have it be funny. If so, you're in good shape. But if it requires jokes to make it funny, then you need to go back to the beginning and completely rethink it. Jokes are the horseradish sauce of comedy, not the roast beef.

7. Turn Off Your TV!

I've talked to many young people about comedy, and I've found that their projects relate to things that have already been on TV. Their work tends to be overwhelmingly derivative. Agents say the same thing. Prospective writers watch a lot of TV, and then when they write scripts, their scripts all look alike. My advice: Turn off your TV and keep it off!

Instead of getting your ideas from TV, develop your own comic vision. Consider Woody Allen: One of his greatest strengths is that he is authentic. He's not trying to be Jack Benny and he's not trying to be George Burns. He's Woody Allen. He is very Jewish, very New York, endlessly self-analytical and highly neurotic, and his comedy is an organic outgrowth of his persona. By contrast, I'm a preacher's kid from Kansas. Inevitably my comedy looks a lot different from Woody Allen's. It's supposed to. And recently I heard a young Latino comic named Chris Fonseca. He has cerebral palsy, has difficulty speaking and does his routine from a wheelchair. Much of his material deals with his comedic take on the stresses of living with his physical condition. He is wonderfully funny, because his comedy grows directly out of his own real life.

I believe that there is great power in being true to your comic vision and being in touch with your individual sources of comic inspiration. They might be obvious, as in the case of Chris Fonseca, or more subtle. It is because of the importance of comic authenticity that I urge you not to watch TV. I'm not saying never—it's good to know some of the things that are on. But don't derive your comic inspiration and models from TV. Read books; look at the Marx Brothers movies and the classic silent film comedies; look at print cartoons like the ones in *The New Yorker*; read children's books; look at the fabulous, comic theater pieces of Feydeau. Above all, look at yourself and the people around you! Real people and the absurdities and follies of everyday life are the richest sources of comedy.

These are the Seven Laws of Comedy Writing. They don't exhaust all the possible topics involved in comedy writing, but they cover the most important. If you follow these laws, they will guide you to write fun, funny comedy that will make you laugh—and make your audiences laugh along with you.

David Evans has applied his Seven Laws of Comedy Writing to numerous television shows, including writing the premiere episode of *The Bill Cosby Show*.

Part 3
The Interviews

CHAPTER 15

Lee K. Abbott Is Just Making Stories

I don't think of myself necessarily as a humorist, in the old-fashioned sense of the word. I do think of myself as a writer whose understanding of humor includes things that are funny; I laugh at something every day, and I'm convinced that most people do. I understand my characters to be self-deprecating in order to defend themselves, much as we all do, and there are ironies that go with that. We alleviate the tension by making a joke or by embarrassing ourselves in order to spare somebody else.

In one of my writing classes, I have the students use The Best American Short Stories anthologies, and we've discovered, as I've long suspected, very few funny stories in there. It's as if writing funny is somehow given less legitimacy than putatively serious work. Why is that? Why do all these people feel that it isn't art if it's not serious? Consequently, we get a lot of stuff that's just full of tears and heartbreak and the like. I'm not convinced the world's like that at all. For every Mark Twain there are ten thousand Theodore Dreisers. On one hand I can count the writers in America who are humorists, starting with Woody Allen. I am not convinced that it's in our best interest as a literary culture to suggest there is only one way to be sophisticated, one way to be important, one way to make meaning. People think of themselves as making art; I just think of myself as making stories.

I don't think of myself as a kind of knee-slapper. I think of myself as a kind of ironist. At times, irony is a necessary kind of defense strategy, and that's the way I use it. It goes without saying that you can't use irony unless you have a certain degree of self-awareness. Only the stupid are serious all the time, and I don't think of my characters as being particularly stupid. They may be ill-educated, they may be unsophisticated in a sense, but they are unspeakably self-aware, perhaps too self-aware.

Developing a Sense of Humor

My father was a very serious man, and my mother wasn't around for much of my life, so I don't see that either one of them had much to do with my sense of humor. I learned very early to be the class clown as a way of getting attention and to smooth the way in troublesome situations. I had a pretty ugly home life, so I used humor to take the pain out of it, I'm sure. That's what a therapist would tell you now. Then, of course, I was just making jokes, trying to impress the girls. I've also been a sucker for stellar comedians of our time like Lenny Bruce, David Steinberg, Robin Williams and Jim Carrey, people who have things to say about the world and understand it. Perhaps the message is best delivered with a smile.

My writing has been influenced by Eudora Welty's sense of humor, particularly as it shows up in those crotchety characters that she writes about in books like *The Ponder Heart* and short stories like "Why I Live at the P.O." Some of Cheever's stories are mildly amusing with a kind of bemused sensibility. Of course, there's Joseph Heller and *Catch-22*, Kurt Vonnegut and his work. A lot of the black humorists from the sixties I find very funny.

I think one can intend to write a funny story, but without a situation or a character that is funny, nobody's going to laugh. I also think beginning writers need to understand that writing funny is likewise an act of the imagination. They really need to exercise that. I find a lot of stories that are technically competent but are finally, sadly uninteresting because there doesn't seem to be an act of imagination at work. They seem so ordinary, typical, banal, predictable. One of the funny things about comedy is that you can throw the rules out the window and pretty much do anything you want. One of the things you should want to be is unpredictable.

Techniques That Work

Jimminy Christmas! I don't know if writing humor can be taught. A part of me wants to say of course not, but I don't know. It depends on the nature of the humor. I think it's easy for our tribe to make fun of other people, but it's another thing, and a more humane agenda, to make fun of one's self. I think we can actually do the former, but I don't know that I can teach you to do the latter.

For one thing, humor is subjective. The kind of writing you would write were you too sensitive would be of the most boring kind of stories. I'm convinced that I try to do my own job well, and if I do it well and somebody doesn't like it because it's not his cup of tea, that's fine. That's a legitimate complaint to register with a legitimate critical hack, but I don't want to give an artistic excuse not to do that. So if a joke needs to be told, I'll tell a joke. If you don't like the joke, OK, you don't like the joke. I'm not going to lose any sleep over it. What I lose sleep over is if you didn't understand the joke, if I were so clumsy a storyteller, you just didn't get it. At that point I get a little anxious.

There are ways in which young writers can develop their imaginations. As an example, imagine what's in the cupboard of a serial killer, what's in the refrigerator, then name the things in the refrigerator. Tell me what Madonna's last dream was. Name the books on Teddy Kennedy's bookshelf. What's in his desk drawer? Don't tell me pencils and pens, tell me things that distinguish that drawer from all other drawers. Give me the twenty-five-second version of *War and Peace*—ask somebody to do that. Establish a convention, establish something really crazy, stupid, absurd, unlikely, improbable, something anachronistic. The only two people on the Mayflower, for example. What you do is establish a situation with humor, if possible. You think about things that are incongruous, and you try to treat them as straight.

I start with a dramatic situation. I subordinate myself to whatever suffering there is to be suffered and see what happens. One of the reasons to subject yourself to this undertaking, which is so hard to do well, is more for the many surprises and delights you will discover on page 2 or page 4 that you didn't know were going to be there. I start off knowing what happens first and hope I can discover what happens second. I'm always thrilled to learn that what I thought might happen fifth doesn't need to happen at all. In fact, something else better happens. It's a surprise for me. That's why I don't understand people who outline, although I guess there are as many ways to write a story as there are writers of stories.

There are four things writers can do to add humor to their writing. First, unlikely metaphors: "He looked like a toolbox," something like that. That's one way of doing it. Another way is the absurd, like a character opens his wallet and what's in it but the *Encyclopedia Britannica* in miniature form or something like that. A malaprop—putting the wrong word in someplace, especially when it sounds similar to the right one—is a third good technique. I'm thinking of a ghetto version of the Lord's Prayer—"Deliver us not into Penn Station"—that kind of thing. Then of course there's always the spoonerism. That's where you mix up the syllables, so instead of "a group of peoples" you have "a grope of nipples." There are all kinds of exercises you can do.

A writer who writes things that are more serious needs to give his humor the most comprehensive license possible. Don't rule it out, and don't worry about the marketplace; it will take care of itself.

Lee K. Abbott's most recent work is *Living After Midnight: A Novella and Stories*. He is the author of several other books and has received many writing awards, including the O. Henry Award for Fiction in 1997. He is currently director of the creative writing program at The Ohio State University.

CHAPTER 16

Saying It Funny:
Gail Galloway Adams

There's a great quote from Sigmund Freud that says, "Only with misgivings do I venture to approach the problem of the comic itself." Here was Freud, who was not afraid to approach anything, saying this. It's a tough subject and a serious one. Every writer who uses humor has to contend with the other side of that, which is that if you work in the comic form, you can be considered lightweight. There's the worry that if you're making people laugh, you can't really be taken seriously. Saul Bellow said, "If I'm obliged to choose between complaint and comedy, I choose comedy as the more energetic, the wiser, and manlier."

In my own work, I don't think that I have a choice not to use humor. It's just part of the way I look at life, and therefore I'm writing out of my own particular philosophies, which tend to have a comic slant. I use humor to both reveal and deflect, and so as I write, even if the story is serious, I tend to have within it either comedic elements or a comedic tone. I became aware of it very early on. The things that seemed to happen right away as I wrote were comic in nature.

Influences

Both my parents are from the South, one from Alabama and the other from Texas, and both of them come from long traditions of oral storytellers. I also have a sister who's what I would call a cowgirl, and she is a tremendous storyteller. We were always encouraged to "make the funny story" about the world. Even if something tragic happened, you'd have to give it a spin so that we could laugh in the middle of all of it. My father is one of those people who always have a joke—sometimes the jokes are successful and sometimes you groan. During my childhood he always was trying to write things for *Reader's Digest* and giving us his salty take on the world. My mother is much more of a stand-up comic. When she tells a story, she takes on all of the personas of the people she's talking about.

Another important influence on my humor is Southern literature. I love it, and I read a lot of it, and I teach a course in it. I've come to appreciate the different traditions in Southern literature that combine the comic and the tragic. Maybe because of my Southwest connection, I've been influenced a little bit by the exaggeration of the tall tale. I don't much like that form, but it led me into an interest in its variance. Another influence is the urban Jewish sensibility, the ironic stance on life. I've always admired Mort Saul and Woody Allen and Lenny Bruce, those comics working from the anxiety personality, the self-deprecating, witty quality. So I'm truly schizophrenic in my humor influences.

I've always been drawn to the possibilities in humor. I've always loved the line "When in doubt, make a fool of yourself." Because it speaks to that point where you have to push beyond yourself and your limits and the story's limits. Most normal people would say, "Leave it alone now."

In my work I use a regional storyteller humor, in which someone is going to be giving the story from the outside, an outside narrator who can give it a comedic spin. The "I" ultimately is forgiving—it exposes those things that are foibles but presents them without a sharp edge. Also, I'm constantly looking in my fiction for those places where I can raise the comic quotient. Frequently that will come out in a dialogue exchange: two people facing off and saying things that will be funny. As I begin to write certain stories, I can see they're loping toward that. So then I let them go. I let the stories make fools out of themselves for a little bit. Then when I go back to revise, if it pleases me or makes my husband laugh, I decide I should work with this and make it a little stronger, maybe figure out how to work this opposition a little bit more. In some ways I see myself in the person who is the outside narrator/observer giving the story and making comments but probably on the characters' side, even while making fun of the character.

The Comedy Gene

There's a line in the movie *Funny Bones*, with Jerry Lewis and Oliver Pratt, in which a character says, "Some people are funny, and some people can say it funny." I recommend that my students see the movie to help them understand about writing comedy and being funny, and when I teach the workshops I have everybody say what they think that line means. I think it means that there are some people who seem innately able to make us laugh.

Does that mean that on the page their humor will hold up? Quite often, it wouldn't. You could transcribe everything that they said, and it would seem somewhat banal, and yet their presence gives it humor. And then there are other people who what they actually say is funny—they might not be able to present it, but on the page, if you read it, you would laugh. And so it's an interesting thing to me, how we can try to bring about that kind of fusion. Some people are writing the comic material for others, and other people are writing comic material for themselves, and then they become both performer and writer. Steve Martin moves back and forth between writing and performing. Garrison Keillor is a writer, but he's also a persona performer. Woody Allen has always been a writer of humor, then became a performer too.

Some people are simply funny on the page. I'm thinking of those writers I first stumbled into, like Peter DeVries. He was one of my heroes. I just loved his writing so much. I loved Thomas Berger. I loved all those domestic humorists—Jean Kerr, who is also a playwright, and Erma Bombeck, Peg Bracken and Shirley Jackson. They could write about their domestic situations.

In some ways, what I find funny has changed through the years. When I was younger, one of the things that I was very drawn to was black comedy, dark humor. So I see a lot of what drew me to Lenny Bruce and political satirists, who had a cynical take on the world—biting wit, the kind of political incisiveness we don't have now. As I mentioned earlier, Mort Saul to me was excellent, and I don't think he's ever had a replacement.

So I was much drawn to that bleaker vision of the world, a comedy as lifting the lid off the tragedy of life, and the kind of darker visions of comedy. I use Ionesco in my classes, and Ionesco has a wonderful quotation about the comic alone being able to give us strength to bear the tragedy of existence. My students seem to link to that idea immediately. But as I've grown older, I find that I'm more drawn to what I would call universal self-deprecation, in which people can make light of the tribulations of their lives, and there's a little more forgiveness for the foibles of mankind. Even though you might laugh at the pratfall, there would be an ameliorative statement after the pratfall. I guess in that way, I've sort of mellowed, so I don't have to see comedy as such a bleak vision as I did when I was young.

It's interesting to me to think about that and the subtleties that enter my vision. Many of my students love *One Flew Over the Cuckoo's Nest*. They've seen it first as a movie. They're very caught by it, and quite often come already with that clutched to them as a central comic text. There is a quotation in there that says, "None of this is really happening. It's all just a combination of Kafka and Twain." It's a really nice quotation because then we can lead into the difference between Kafka's wit and what we can call the dark comic that's in the tragic vein, and Twain's approach, which is to find the ridiculous in a thousand trivial things.

The Risks of Humor

There may be a certain risk with humor. Someone said it's not only ten times harder, it's fifty times harder to bring an audience to laughter than to bring it to tears. With humor, it's easier to bomb. I remember I wrote a story that I thought was quite funny, and I sent it off to a journal for their special humor issue. I got back a rejection that said, "This story is not funny. It's corny." My heart was stabbed. You don't want to be corny. Corny is something that's not funny. But I understood better when the issue came out that the editors had an aesthetic that wouldn't appreciate that story. Another editor might have seen it as something else.

How to Be Funnier

In my classes, I rely a lot on models. One model that I almost always use is Stanley Elkin's short story "A Poetics for Bullies." It has a comic voice, yet the subject is serious. It has dramatic elements that take it back all the way to classic traditions of humor. Another model I use all the time is a book called *The Book of Sequels*. My younger students are almost oriented totally to movie and television, and this book has things such as the drama "The Dry White Wines of Wrath," in which the next generation of Joads struggles to produce a reasonably priced, drinkable bottle of Chardonnay.

One of the questions I address in my class is, how much of the humor of a piece is innate to the style, and how can the humor of a piece be enhanced? We look at technical ways of enhancing the humor—making a name more interesting or using more vivid language. Also, the writer can look for unusual juxtapositions. Many times in my classes, a student will have a story that's anecdotal, but it doesn't have any of the concrete, specific and humorous detail that we need. The draft usually needs an exaggeration of some quality, perhaps in a character or in the accumulation of a particular device.

Some of humor's technical tricks can be taught. Timing is everything. If timing doesn't come naturally to someone, she can learn. In my workshops, we do small group work, and in each group I'll put someone who has a natural comedic ability. Sometimes that's evident very early. When you have someone who sees the world funny and "says the world funny," the others can pick up the timing. Also, to show someone, on the page, during revision, you can say, "Try to revise this to make it snappier," so that the pace moves briskly.

In some ways, the humor gene is innate, but if someone wants to write a humorous piece, you can brainstorm. That can be very effective. They might not be able to write a completely funny piece, but they could at least write a competent piece that moves briskly, like telling a joke second-hand. You can make the punch line and get a laugh.

One of the exercises we do is writing about an embarrassing memory. Those usually have comedic elements. To get over that embarrassment, you make it fictional and funny. Usually the student will write a bald narrative, and it's straightforward. Sometimes it's third person or there's a narrator. After the first draft, we begin to ask, "What is the core of the story?" Where can we place odd juxtapositions that will make the story funny? What exaggerations are needed? What can we do with the characters to make at least one of them funny, maybe give one of them a funny nickname? Or maybe there's a dog in the picture. If you insert an animal, a three-legged collie or a one-eyed cat, then suddenly it becomes a focus, especially for novel writers in comedy. It gets the burden off of the voice in question, and the writer can do more funny things with the animal. Or if there are going to be events, how exaggerated will they have to be and when will that exaggeration have to stop? That's when we have to use someone like

Dave Barry, who takes exaggeration to its utmost limits. Does the story have to be believable? If so, at what point is it realistic but still funny if you cut back a little bit? We need to think in specifics and use vivid language. What sounds funny? Make a list of ten foods you would eat that sound funny. Once they begin listing things that sound funny, they can use their list to replace the very generic details or just the details that aren't funny.

Be observant and seek out situations that might have humorous possibilities. As I said before, reading humor is important. I find my students often haven't read much humor. When they do, they will then find their own mentors. In class we do plays on words, and we always work with malaprops. We try to think about how jokes work as opposed to how a story works. Alice Munro said, "An anecdote is not a story, but sometimes an anecdote is the germ for a story."

In even the most serious stories, there is an opportunity for the protagonist or a secondary character to have some moment where they make an observation that's weird in terms of its juxtaposition to the larger story. There's always an opportunity to lighten a story with an occasional small turn, even if it's seen briefly in the narrative. That passing glance that you catch out of the side of your eye is something that lightens the narrative. I'm thinking of Ray Carver or Margaret Atwood, who are amazing writers in terms of the way the stories work. The stories seem so straightforward but are always infused with and enlivened by incongruities that ultimately deepen the stories. In some ways, humor will grow organically in the story if it's meant to be.

Gail Galloway Adams is a professor of English and creative writing at West Virginia University. Her short story collection, *The Purchase of Order*, was the winner of the Flannery O'Connor Award for Short Fiction. She lives in Morgantown, West Virginia.

CHAPTER 17

Burning With Sherman Alexie

I'm lucky in that I come from a number of different worlds. I grew up on a reservation, which has its own set of humor, and I grew up in a small white town, which has its own set of humor as well; I went to high school there. I went to college, and I'm something of an intellectual and scholar—there's a whole other set of influences there. And I've always been funny. I can make my friends cry with laughter, make my siblings squirt milk out of their noses.

I've lived such a varied life that I can tell all manners of jokes from the crudest, dirtiest joke in the world to the most esoteric and ultimately unfunny literary pun. The experiences of my life have enabled me to cross a lot of cultural boundaries and senses of humor. You know, I was funny in Spain and I don't speak Spanish. The night before I was scheduled to speak, I just picked up language cues and watched TV and repeated things and tried to work it. One of the biggest laughs I got in Spain was when I first got there, I turned on the TV and the Lone Ranger and Tonto were on. I didn't understand anything they were saying and made a joke about it the next day. I said, here in Spain I was watching Tonto, and instead of saying "How" like Indians are supposed to do, he raised his hand and said "Hola." It's just a surface examination of a culture and language, but even then you can find a joke. It's always about language. Jokes are poetry. It's about the manipulation of image, of language, the turn of phrase. I think great poets and great stand-up comedians have a lot in common.

Because I'm funny, my natural mode of communication is to tell a joke. This often gets in the way—it's often wildly inappropriate. My natural mode of communication is to go for the punch line, so when I sit down to write, my inclination is to go for the joke, for the irony or the pun. It's as natural to me as breathing by now.

I use everything from farce to what people call black humor. What's funny about the whole thing is that people equate humor with a lack of seriousness. I get that a lot, especially in regard to my public performances.

I find that when I call them literary readings—or I'm talking politics or any subject that's supposedly serious—and I tell jokes or am funny in the process, people equate it with a lack of seriousness. Often when I'm being funny in my books, people confuse political satire with broad farce, and they can't tell the difference between the two. The most effective joke is something that's funny about something that's *not* funny, something that's deadly serious.

I have an Indian character whose name is Tap Water. He says it used to be Spring Water but he changed it when he moved from the reservation to the city. For my money, that joke says a lot more about assimilation and the joys and losses of moving from the rez to the city than most people's essays could do. It's succinct; a joke is always succinct. Just because that thing is funny doesn't mean it can't also reveal a lot of pathos, a lot of the difficulties and the incredible change from Spring Water to Tap Water. It's a funny change with irony, but it's a huge personal change—the renaming of yourself and the whole redefinition of your identity contained in that little joke.

Finding the Joke

My generation is the situation comedy generation, and those comedies have influenced my sense of humor. I think we're the funniest generation in the history of the world. It's rare that I meet somebody of my generation who cannot tell a joke, who is not funny. We all have sitcom timing. We're a generation raised by television, more than any other before, so certainly that has a huge effect. That's just being an American kid. I learned timing by osmosis.

Also, within the tribal culture, in my tribe as well as in Native American culture in general, there's a lot of punning and wordplay. In the black community, it's called "doing the dozens," sort of "your mama" jokes. We have the equivalent, called "burning," where you burn somebody. It's a constant level of teasing that's really about keeping people humble. It's sort of a communistic endeavor. "Doing the dozens" and "burning" are really ways in which people are kept in their place.

I grew up in that environment; four years old, five years old, and you're in this complicated word game at school. The verbal skills of the average eleven-year-old in the inner city, a black kid, are amazing. You find the same on the reservation. There's a cousin of mine who can't read or spell, but she is amazingly adept at burning. I steal from her all the time. The humor happens all the time; for instance, we were at my uncle's funeral and there was this very attractive woman there. She was new in town and really beautiful, and all the boys had a crush on her. We were teasing my little brother about her, and she was right there. My cousin just looked and didn't say much. She doesn't talk a lot, she just comes up with these things. She looked at him and said, "Geez, James, your nipples are getting hard." That devastated him. He just fell over.

I don't know how much Native American oral tradition affects humor because you'd have to go back and look at European traditions as well. Look at the Germans—they're not funny. There's not a whole lot of German stand-up comedy. For myself, the most comparable culture I've been in and around is the Jewish culture. I strongly identify with the Jewish humor sensibility. In fact, I think in essence, when we're being funny, we're all Jewish. If you look at situation comedies and the art of comedy in the twentieth century, its genesis is in Jewish culture. The American sense of humor is Jewish. When I first walked into it and experienced Jewish culture firsthand, it was sort of like the circle becoming complete. Their masters of humor taught me to be funny, and now I'm walking among them.

I'm not such a great writer as much as I have great taste. My formula is: Read one thousand pages for every one you write. That's what I try to follow.

The funny writers I read now are mystery writers, like Carl Hiaasen. Lorrie Moore is a writer who has really influenced me lately and whose work has influenced my new book of short stories, *The Toughest Indian in the World*. She's so funny and clever, and her characters are so smart. It's a very literate humor, a very well-read humor. I went for that in my new book. I wanted to have these Indians be really smart and have this smart dialogue. There's this scene where a married couple is waiting to get to dinner, but they're not getting in. The guy says something along the lines of, "I knew they wouldn't let me in" and his wife says, "Well, it must be difficult to be both psychic and insecure." That sort of funny

How to Write Funny

dialogue was coming out of the mouths of Indians, that kind of sophisticated wordplay. There's another joke I make about "Emory" Dickinson. It's not necessarily funny, but it takes these Indian characters' intellects to a different level.

Sometimes people completely miss my humor. Some think *Reservation Blues* is a really depressing book. For me, the book is like this fantasy farce. I prefer to think of the book as my Marx brothers book, and people completely miss it. That always amazes me.

Often I think that people's preconceived notions about what Indians are or people thinking that we're not funny blinds them to the humor in the book. This happens to the point where, when I do public performances of the book and they're hilarious—the way they're supposed to be—people always come up to me and say, "I didn't know you were so funny." Or they say, "I didn't expect you to be so funny," or "I didn't think the book was this funny when I read it." It has to do with people's built-in stereotypes and biases about Indians.

It shocked me that people thought *Reservation Blues* was just despairing, that there was no hope. In fact, so much of the reaction to both *The Lone Ranger and Tonto Fistfight in Heaven* and *Reservation Blues* was about the depression and darkness in the books. That's one of the reasons why I wrote *Indian Killer*—to show people exactly how dark I could get.

Getting It Right

I've been surprised when things were funnier that I thought they were, or when I didn't even see the joke to begin with, but I've never felt that I've written something meant to be serious and had people laugh at it.

In some sense I've discovered that, even though I've written something I thought was completely serious, people would laugh all along, until the punch line ended up being something very moving and disturbing. I think that's always an effective use of humor, as a reverse; you go for the downer punch line.

Had I written *Reservation Blues* straight, it would have been cliched—the rock-and-roll band trying to make it big, dealing with the devil. The book was a series of cliches. Using humor elevated a familiar story to something eccentric and original.

The first draft of anything I write is usually completely funny and farcical. In my editing process and my rewriting process, I have to take jokes out so that the ones that remain have more power or are more thematically powerful. It's actually a reverse process for me. To create different paces and speeds and different emotional sections of work, I start taking away jokes.

It's like any good art. You get a good hunk of clay, and then you start shaping it. My hunk of clay is always funny.

If people are funny, I think you can teach them how to write funny, but I think that's the only way. When my books first started coming out, especially *Lone Ranger*, they made a huge impact on the Indian literary world. People went for the humor and were really influenced by it for a while. I read a lot of funny, vaguely Sherman Alexie types of poems written by a lot of different Indians. They said they'd been reading Sherman Alexie's work and appreciating the humor and thought they'd try to write some poems with more humor in them. But in some of them, I just didn't get the humor.

On teaching people how to write funny, my feeling is, make them sit in a room and watch *Duck Soup* a hundred times. I don't think sitcoms would help because I think you need to get a little more sophisticated use of language than you find in most sitcoms. Writers can learn a lot from movies with sophisticated language like *Mr. Deeds Goes to Town, The Apartment* and *Some Like It Hot*—movies that are much more literary than comedies are now. They could see the structure of the humor and how it's used to reveal character. This is blasphemy I know, but I think fiction writers can learn a lot about succinct character development from screenwriters, at least good screenwriters. A good comedy screenwriter can teach a novelist a lot about character development.

What I try to do in my humor is not to pick on people who have less power than I do. I'll pick on people who have the same amount of power and more power, but not on those who have less. I don't make fun of kids, and I don't make fun of the disabled because they can't fight back. Essentially, I don't make fun of people whose language skills prevent them from fighting back, but if there was some seven-year-old genius stand-up comic out there, I'd go after him.

How to Write Funny

Other advice for writers? Write naked—that will make you laugh.

Sherman Alexie is a Spokane/Coeur d'Alene Indian from Wellpinit, Washington, a town on the Spokane Indian Reservation. He is the award-winning author of several books of poetry, two novels and collections of short stories, including *The Lone Ranger and Tonto Fistfight in Heaven*, which was a citation winner for the 1994 PEN/Hemingway Award for Best First Fiction. His most recent book is *The Toughest Indian in the World*.

CHAPTER 18

Melissa Bank and
The Girls' Guide to Humor

For years my stories didn't have any humor in them because I was trying hard to be a great writer, that is, trying to be a writer unlike myself. I often wrote from an omniscient point of view, imitating writers who had religion or maturity to back them up. It was a long time before I figured out how to write in a way that was truer to my nature—questioning rather than knowing, irreverent and insecure—and my sense of humor followed. It came from respecting what was mine, even if that was ignorance. The trick, I think, is appreciating who you are and what's unique and true in the way you see the world. It's giving yourself the freedom to be yourself as a writer that will lead you to humor and anything else worth having. I consider myself a funny person, although I'm not funny with everyone all of the time. I find people who seem to take themselves very seriously or have a lot of pretensions or lack perspective are funny—or people who make jokes about taking themselves too seriously or having pretensions or lacking perspective.

I don't really get funny ideas, per se; I'll have an experience. When I was twenty-two, I went to dinner at a new boyfriend's ex-girlfriend's apartment, where I felt out of my depth and jealous. Then, in "Floating House," I sent Jane on vacation with her new boyfriend to the ex-girlfriend's house on an island for a week. It's taking an emotion and heightening and focusing and isolating it.

Whenever I hear something funny, I try to write it down, although I almost never use it in fiction. Usually, what happens is that I try to create a funny character, and then, joy of joys, that character surprises me with a great line. But my funny characters are often modeled after funny people. In *The Girls' Guide to Hunting and Fishing*, the brother, Henry, is modeled after my own brother Andy, who is hilarious.

Writing From the Outside

I think feeling like an outsider is key to establishing a sense of humor. Maybe being Jewish helped. I grew up in an assimilating Jewish family, which basically makes you feel outside of everything, even yourself, but the truth is I've always felt like an outsider, often for no discernible reason.

Being an outsider creates a certain tension. You can see what the inside is made of, which doesn't necessarily mean you don't want to be in there. There is a definite outsider perspective throughout *The Girls' Guide to Hunting and Fishing*. It begins in the first story, where Jane's family and her brother's new girlfriend discuss books they've all read or intend to read, except for Jane, which leads her to conclude that the girlfriend is the kind, helpful, articulate daughter her parents deserve. In "Floating House," when Jane notices that her boyfriend seems to have best friends all over the world, she remarks that all her best friends are from the tri-state area. And finally, in "Girls' Guide," Jane's observation that she is at a party Friday night and has a date Saturday, and that she's a dater, a snorkeler in the social swim, shows just how out of it she is.

I generally use humor to create intimacy between the narrator and a character, since often the reader is the only one who hears the joke. I think my humor works best when the stakes are high. It works to create or dispel tension. In "Floating House," for example, the tension increased when Jane mistakenly calls the ex-girlfriend "Belly." In "Worst Thing," when a neighbor arrives to housesit (to prevent a robbery) during the father's funeral, Henry says something like, "She seems nice—I hope they don't tie her up." Still, it's always tricky for me to come in with theories about how I do anything in writing, since my best work happens at a subconscious level.

My humor has also been influenced by what I read, mostly fiction, both classic and contemporary. I feel I ought to say that I was influenced by Shakespeare and Mark Twain, but that would be a lie. Pam Houston and Lorrie Moore—especially *Self Help*—made me feel like I could be funny because they were funny on the page in a way I had been only in life. Nick Hornby helped me understand how humor could make a story more moving; I loved *High Fidelity*. Other writers just make me want to be funny. I find David Sedaris's *Barrel Fever* and *Naked* really inspiring.

My sense of literary humor changed over the years. For a while, I always wanted the narrator to have the best lines and all the insight. Then I realized I was creating just one-character stories. The rest of the characters, the whole world, were the foil or my straight man. It seemed defensive and limited, like bad stand-up comedy, and doomed each story to be too simple, too similar. To overcome that, I began creating characters who had as much humor, insight and depth as the narrator.

I sometimes have to restrain my humor because I'm usually trying to do a balancing act between drama and humor. The humor is certainly intentional, but I don't want to write anything that would make a reader aware of me, the writer, which would take them outside of the story. What I'm trying for is a kind of realism, so that the jokes seem to arise from the real lives and minds of the characters. Even in the last story in *The Girls' Guide to Hunting and Fishing*, with the Rules-like authors coming to life, I wanted the jokes to seem to arise out of Jane's imagination rather than mine.

My style of humor is ironic, and sometimes I have to overcome the subjective nature of my humor. I think it's sort of the same as figuring out what's interesting; you test it out. I read almost everything I write aloud, and I can usually tell what's funny by what I'm eager to read. But not always.

I was sitting onstage at a luncheon in Detroit to benefit literacy when I realized that the section of *Girls' Guide* I was going to read had the word "fuckface" in it. I looked at the crowd, and saw that many of the women were upper middle-aged, and I wrote a note to the woman next to me, a librarian whom I loved on sight. "Dear Betty," I wrote, "I'm thinking I'll read a section that has some foul language in it. Will that be a disaster? Love, Your new friend, Melissa." She whispered that it was an educated crowd and would be fine. So, when I went up to read, I repeated our exchange to the crowd, and told them if they had any problems with my reading, they could speak to Betty. They laughed at that, but when I read the offending word, there was an audible gasp. They didn't forgive me. I was their daughter up there, and I'd dishonored the event.

Melissa Bank lives in New York City and East Hampton, New York. Her book, *The Girls' Guide to Hunting and Fishing*, spent fourteen weeks on *The New York Times* best-seller list and has been published in twenty-three languages.

CHAPTER 19

Inside Dave Barry's World

If you've read *Dave Barry's Complete Guide to Guys*, you have a head start on how this interview went. Pressed for time, interviewer and subject met in the cafeteria of the *Miami Herald* building, stabbing at salad, devouring a sandwich, talking with full mouths, spilling coffee and causing an avalanche of crumbs. Every word was carefully documented by a faulty tape recorder as a collection of useless scratches and pops.

In other words, it was a real *guy* interview.

Few writers can make fun of anything and everything with the jocular passion of Dave Barry. Besides the male condition, he's aimed his wit at Japan, the Olympics, getting old and, in his latest book, toilets (*Dave Barry Is Not Taking This Sitting Down!*).

Dave is an institution at the *Herald*, where he's plied his trade since 1983. In 1988 he amused enough people to win the Pulitzer Prize for Commentary. His Sunday *Herald* columns run not only in that paper but in two hundred fifty newspapers around the world, from Hong Kong to Israel. Life, if you're Dave Barry, is good. And funny.

Where do most writers go wrong in trying to write humor?

DAVE BARRY: The problem with most humor writing is that it's *not funny*. There are people who are funny. Those people make their friends and family members laugh all the time, so they think they can write humor. Often, they can't.

Why is that?

BARRY: The thing is, you have to know how to write. That takes years of practicing the craft, of honing your skills, rewriting—just like any writer, humorous or not. Rework the writing until it's funny. Test it out on some people before sending it off to get that big break. I've received stuff from people who think their work is hilarious, so they send it to me, and it's really not funny at all. Someone who's a funny person isn't necessarily qualified to write a humor book, the same way that a person who's been through incredible misfortunes isn't necessarily qualified to write the great tragic novel.

I think a humor writer has to keep his imagination limber. You've got to stay open to new things, new ways of writing and structuring sentences. The same methods don't always work for every topic or every idea. Calvin Trillin, for example, makes you laugh in many different ways. That's what you have to strive for.

How do you make sure the joke works?

BARRY: I spend a lot of time reading every sentence over and over, focusing on details. I mean small details, like word choice. Very often, that's what is going to determine whether an idea is funny. It can be as detailed as using the word "got" instead of "received," for example. I think it's important to try out as many variations of phrases and words as possible until you hit the right one. Even slight variances in punctuation can make a difference in the way humor is transmitted to the reader.

Do you ever have a first draft that you don't find very funny?

BARRY: Definitely. My first draft might be a lot like a photographer's 100 or 200 shots of his subject. He's got to pick out which ones are going to be in the layout. Certain ones are going to work, and most he'll never use. It's that way with writing too.

How do you handle the pressure to produce when you don't feel funny?

BARRY: That's every day! Really. Writing humor takes discipline and hard work. I have this theory. Here it is, My Theory About Writing: It's hard. The humor doesn't just flow as easily as people think. A funny idea has to be tooled and shaped so that it's funny to others when it's read. People think that because humor is light and easy to read that it's just as simple to write. Nothing could be more untrue. You have to work at it. Writer's block, for example. Here's My Theory About Writer's Block: People simply give up and don't want to put forth the effort to work through the barriers. No good writing is easy. It all has to do with overcoming the obstacles we find in the way of our creativity. You have to have the determination to do it.

Do you approach your books and your columns differently?

BARRY: It's pretty much the same, but with a book you can spread out more. You've got a lot of ground to cover and a lot of space to do it in, so you don't have to worry about being funny all the time. In fact, you want to break it up a lot with some straight stuff. You can't just have one gag after another. With the columns, you want to get as many jokes in there as you can.

Is the book audience different than for your columns?

BARRY: It's different in the sense that their options have changed. In the newspaper, they have lots of options. They could go to the comics, the sports, or, if they are really desperate, the front page. So I have to capture them and make them want to read what amounts to a very small portion of the newspaper. Books are a different story. The reader buys the book and specifically wants to read that type of writing, so it's really a captive audience.

Aside from Carl Hiaasen, whom you've cited as one of your favorite modern humor writers, what writers do you enjoy reading?

BARRY: Robert Benchley was the biggest influence. He wrote some great satire in the twenties, thirties and forties. I read all of his stuff. I still do. I also loved P.G. Wodehouse and Walt Kelly (creator of the "Pogo" comic strip). As far as modern writers, Roy Blount Jr., who is marvelously inventive and subtle, and P.J. O'Rourke, who will say anything, and Calvin Trillin, who is never too impressed. And, of course, all the works of Marcel Proust.

Where did you learn most of your techniques?

BARRY: Some from trial and error, and some from other writers. Mostly, though, from my mom.

Your mom?

BARRY: She was funny. She had a funny way of saying things, and she wrote great letters. Wonderful, funny letters.

Do you feel pressure in public to be a funny guy?

BARRY: I used to feel like I had to live up to that stereotype. Now I've come to understand that it's OK to be me. And I'm not the wild and crazy guy with a drink in his hand and a straw hanging out of his nose at parties. I can be funny when I'm lecturing because I know that's what I've been invited to do. But most of the time I'm pretty quiet.

Any last words of encouragement for humor writers?

BARRY: I think humor writers have a greater chance of getting published than most writers do. You don't have to be an expert on any particular subject to write the humorous side of it. You could publish a humor piece about cameras or your experience with photography and maybe get published in a photography magazine, whereas the rest of the writers with articles in there are probably experts in that field. So that opens up the market for humor writers.

Dave Barry's syndicated column and best-selling books such as *Dave Barry Slept Here* and *Dave Barry Turns Forty* have earned him a large and avid readership. His first job out of school was covering sewage and zoning issues for the *Daily Local News* in West Chester, Pennsylvania. "Sewage was even hotter than zoning when I was there," Barry says. He also worked for the Associated Press briefly in the mid seventies and as an instructor at business-writing seminars. He has written more than twenty books of humor. Interviewer Ramesh Nyberg is a Miami-based freelancer.

CHAPTER 20

Word Nerds and Butter Churns: Roy Blount Jr.

Everybody has some sense of humor, and everybody smiles from time to time; babies smile when they recognize somebody or when they understand something you said. Humor is a way of conveying something to somebody, making a kind of point, or at least establishing common ground between writer and reader.

For me, it's instinctive to look for the humor in things. I do not use humor exactly; I don't think of it in that utilitarian sense. I just try to make some kind of sense, and often I think humor is the principle of order or disorder that makes some sense. You have to simplify matters in order to make any kind of statement. There has to be some principle of organization; humor is a principle of organization.

As far as I know, humor is instinctive, on some level, for all writers. I don't think you can learn mechanically or by rote to be funny. If you don't have it in you, you go for something else. It's like, can writing be taught? I think anybody can be taught to write more clearly, and you can't be funny unless you can say what you want to say. You can't be funny unless you can write clearly, tightly and interestingly.

That is something you can learn by practice, by reading other funny writers and just by learning how to make sense. You can't be nonsensical unless you know how to make sense. It's a lifetime of trial and error, reading and emulation to learn how to write at all. There are lots of people who are funny orally but aren't funny on the page. Obviously, they have a sense of humor, but they don't know how to put it in writing.

I learned a lot from reading humor writers, but I also read humor writers because I love to read them. I have always been fascinated by humor since I can remember, way back when my mother was teaching me to read and reading to me. Back when I was listening to comedians on the radio as a little kid—I loved Bob & Ray—I was always fascinated by what was funny.

I also had a great high school English teacher in the tenth grade, Ann Lewis, who introduced me to the writings of S. J. Perelman, James Thurber, Robert Benchley, E.B. White and others.

I have lots of friends who are really funny writers: Garrison Keillor, Ian Frazier, the late Veronica Geng, Dave Barry, Calvin Trillin, Fran Lebowitz. Some other funny writers are Nora Ephron and Flann O'Brian, a great Irish humorist. I think Charles Dickens is very funny.

One of my favorite writers is somebody who is not appreciated enough, a humorist's humorist and a writer's writer—Charles Portis. He wrote *True Grit*, for which he is famous, and also the novels *The Dog of the South*, *Norwood, Gringos* and *Masters of Atlantis*, all of which have been reissued. I often cite him because, for one thing, I just love his writing, and another thing, he is a great example of the general truth that the funniest writers work though characters.

The funniest fiction involves characters who are not trying to be funny. They are really trying to be earnest and don't realize they are funny. I read things in which characters are laughing at each other's jokes, or the narrator quotes a character by saying, "he chuckled." The reader is supposed to chuckle, not the character. If you have to convey humor by invoking the character's laughter, you've lost the battle. In that example you're telling the reader it's funny, and the reader starts saying, "I'll be the judge of that." If "he chuckled" is a technique, then it's a technique to avoid.

Learning the Ropes

I don't think you can take a course in humor writing and learn to do it. I never learned anything except through trial and error, but you can teach people by making them try and by pointing out their errors.

I would hate for somebody to think of humor or writing humor as a technical matter. Grammar is technique, a sense of rhythm is a technique and looking words up in the dictionary to learn what they mean is a technique. You can't be funny unless you know exactly what you are trying to say.

Everybody knows that comic timing is important to oral humor, or stand-up humor, or for the screen or stage, but it's also important in humor on the page—humor that is just to be read but not read aloud.

How to Write Funny

You have to have a sense of how to write prose that changes speeds and jumps up and down and surprises you. The only way to develop that is by trying and by loving language and being tickled by the possibilities of the written word.

Trying to capture the sounds of things and feelings of things onto the page is a dying art, or at least a shrinking art. If you are writing for the movies, for instance, which I have done some of, they don't want you to write good dialogue, they just want you to construct a story and let the actors say it the way they want to say it. You are not really writing for the page, but for the screen.

If you are writing for TV or for the screen or for stand-up humor, it's different than writing for the page. Fewer and fewer do write for the page, but that's what I do and that's what I love to do. Furthermore, I think the only way to do that is to read people who have done it well and to keep trying to do it.

Bear in mind that writing clearly and well and precisely is just as important, maybe even more important, if you are trying to be funny than if you are just trying to transfer information. When you write funny you have to be clear enough not only to be informative but to be funny as well.

You can't be slapdash. Slapstick comedy in the movies requires intricate timing, intricate planning, and people like Buster Keaton and Charlie Chaplin, who were natural athletes for that kind of thing. But they also worked out those gags with all sorts of careful planning. Just trying to steal a railroad train on film was hard enough, but to steal one and make it funny was even harder.

Nobody should feel embarrassed about sweating and trying over and over and over. Some people may think if you are going to be funny, you should just be offhand. To sound offhand, you have to do all sorts of setting up and trying and tearing down and scaffolding and reworking and rewriting and chewing your fingernails.

You have to be a reader. You have to be able to read what you write. You have to have a reader in your head who is independent, insofar as possible, from the writer in your head. You have to have a reader, a writer and an editor in your head, and they must have different temperaments and levels of awareness. You can't write just for this internal writer or for this internal editor; the writer and the editor together have to deliver to the reader.

The great—and terrible—thing about writing is that you can always change it. So if you go too far or you write something that falls flat, you can let it sit for a while. You can look at it and decide if it falls flat or goes too far; if it's out of whack, you can change it.

On the other hand, the fact that you can change it means that you are never quite satisfied with it, and you may never turn it in. That's why it's good to have a deadline and to need the money, so you have to turn it in.

As for technique, Mark Twain said the difference between the right word and the almost right word is the difference between lightning and the lightning bug. There's a kind of technique in finding a single word, "lightning," to convey both similarity and dissimilarity, a kind of pun. Of course, Twain is making an abstract point by way of a concrete example. It's a metaphor, and it's a funny metaphor because, well, lightning bugs are funny. If you can't pick up on how that remark works without having it analyzed, then it's tough to explain. Notice that in trying to get technical about a funny remark, I am myself getting less and less funny.

The Language of Humor

Things pop into your head and that's what is funny; I don't know if that's a technique. That thing about the lightning and the lightning bug probably popped into Mark Twain's head, but it popped into his head after he heard lots of similar things.

That's the fun of it, I think—the things that pop into your head. Unfortunately, too often, perhaps even always, they pop into your head better than when you write them down. You think this is really going to be great, you are going to pop this right on the page, but then it gets on the page and the words are in the way, and you have to make it clearer to the reader in your head and the editor in your head, saying that's not going to work.

So you have to enjoy the fiddling. If you are not a bit of a word nerd, like a computer nerd, I don't see how you can stand to write. It's like trying

How to Write Funny

to stack up firewood. You have one piece that won't fit in. You love the piece, but it won't fit in the sentence one way or the other. You switch the sentence around, fool around with it back and forth, and you get sick and tired of it and go on to the next sentence. Meanwhile, you are looking at the last sentence and then you go back and work on it some more, but then when it does pop in, it's nice.

I think the American language is endlessly comical; all those different words and ways of hooking them together, all different inflections. Hooking American English together into sentences always presents all sorts of comic possibilities for me.

A lot of it is experience, and there are organizing principles, including what it says in the dictionary about what words mean. This is not to say you have to be absolutely bound by the dictionary, but you have to love the dictionary enough to work with it.

I enjoy being in the company of the American language. Words just seem funny to me, in the way people I like seem funny to me. I like hanging out with words and playing around with them and hearing the potential humor in them.

When I was a kid in high school, I started reading Benchley, Perelman, White, Thurber and various other *New Yorker* humorists. I wrote like Robert Benchley for quite a while and used a lot of his tricks and things. I was writing that stuff, and it didn't sound quite right when I did it; it would sound like someone else. It wasn't as good as Benchley did it because it was me trying to do what he was doing without realizing it.

The way you develop your own voice as a writer is to write like a lot of other people until you start writing like yourself. But meanwhile, you have all sorts of voices in your ears that mix into your own voice. Without consciously trying, I still every now and again write something that sounds like Mark Twain to me—just a little riff—and I will think it sounds derivative. That's part of the trial and error—that you sound like other people but not as good for a long time. It's a long time before you start sounding like yourself.

You have to like the process. If you don't, get somebody else to write your stories. As an act of enormous generosity toward future humor writers, I would admit to a lot of onerous labor, but it's less onerous than having to work for somebody in a corporation. There is a song sung by early rhythm-and-blues singer Wynonie Harris called "Keep on Churning Till the Butter Comes." You have to like to churn, and if you don't like churning milk, you're never going to get any butter.

Roy Blount Jr. is a humorist, novelist and journalist who has written over a dozen books in the past twenty-five years, including *Crackers*; *First Hubby*; *Be Sweet*; and *I Am Puppy, Hear Me Yap*. A contributing editor to *The Atlantic*, his articles, stories and essays have also appeared in more than 121 periodicals.

CHAPTER 21

Traveling the World of Humor With Bill Bryson

One of the things I most enjoy about humor and the thing that always makes it most successful, not just when I can do it, but just in humor generally, is the way a funny person notices something that we've all kind of noticed subliminally but never actually put our finger on. I mean, that's what a joke is really, it has to be that spark of recognition. I'm thinking of an Ellen DeGeneres stand-up routine I saw. She made a funny joke about people who write the letters "PTO" at the bottom of the page, like you're so stupid you couldn't figure out that because the sentence isn't finished, you had to turn the page over. It's something we've probably all noticed at one time or another but never dwelled on it in a way that would make a joke out of it. That seems to be the simple trick of humor, just to notice those things, to give voice to those things that everybody is aware of but doesn't particularly stop to reflect upon—the general absurdity of everyday life.

I can't tell a story to save my life. I'm the world's worst teller of stories. When I start relating an anecdote, a third of the way into it I'm saying, "No, no, no, he was riding a horse and he was coming from the west, not from the north." I don't, as a rule, make great jokes. The only time I can be funny is when I'm working at the keyboard, which suggests to me that it is, in a very large part, a kind of mechanical process.

My father was very funny. He was quite droll and very good at making puns, so I grew up in a household where a good joke was appreciated. We did laugh quite a bit. It was a diversion that was cultivated in our house, and it was something I grew up liking and admiring. My dad also collected quite a lot of funny books by people like P.G. Wodehouse, S.J. Perelman, Robert Benchley and lots of others, so I grew up with this extensive library of books that I could take down from the shelves and read. That was what captivated me when I was young and led me in that direction. I knew that

I wanted to write, and I was tickled by writers who made me laugh; I think I was sort of seduced in that direction.

Cultivating a Sense of Humor

Over the years, my own humor has become a lot milder and gentler, less acerbic. I think that's kind of inevitable as you get older. You see a broader picture and become more mature in your outlook, a little less sweeping in the things you're critical of or ready to mock. In addition, there is also the fact that I was strongly influenced by living twenty years in England; there was a completely different kind of sense of humor there. Their way of making jokes is really quite different from the American way of making jokes, so I learned a lot about new kinds of humor from living in England.

The differences in humor are very interesting because I write my books for people in different markets. I'm much better known in Britain, for instance, than I am in the United States, and it's not easy writing a joke that will be equally appreciated by people in the U.K., the U.S., Canada, Australia, Ireland and South Africa. The only thing I can do is write a joke that really amuses me and hope that other people will go along with it, that it will be humorous.

For instance, in my new book about Australia, *In a Sunburned Country*, there is quite a long passage that is sort of a satire on a cricket match. It's what it feels like to be listening to a cricket match on the radio in the car when you really don't understand cricket. I like to think that people in Britain, Australia and other cricket-playing nations will recognize my making fun of it, my teasing, whereas an American knows nothing about cricket. For all they know, this is actually a straightforward account. Humor is based entirely on recognition. You have to know what is being mocked for the joke to work. It just doesn't always translate to different readers, different cultural backgrounds.

In *A Walk in the Woods*, American-style humor was somewhat intentional in the sense that I knew I was writing the book for an American audience and I was dealing with an American subject. The people I was quoting and reacting to in the book are Americans. In that sense, the humor and everything else in the book is much more decidedly American than earlier books

I did about traveling around in Europe and Britain. Those are more full of British-type jokes, off-the-wall kinds of jokes and zany stuff. American humor tends to be built more around the one-liners and wisecracks and is very quick and snappy. British humor has a lot more elements of jokes that are off-the-wall, surreal. They are more subtle, so you hardly realize it's a joke until you start to reflect upon it.

Two things would have been different about *A Walk in the Woods* if I had written it as a serious work. One thing is that it would have been received much more respectfully in the hiking community. There were a lot of people who felt that making jokes about the hiking experience was somehow irreverent. It was almost as if I were insulting their religion. I wouldn't have had that problem if I hadn't made jokes.

The other thing, of course, is that the book would have lost a dimension that was fundamental to it. The book is made up of a lot of different components, including some quite serious editorializing about how we treat nature and the history of natural life in this country. There are all these different elements in there. I like to think humor is one thing that keeps the reader engaged with it. It keeps the reader sort of tolerant for the more boring parts, or the more worthy parts, and also acts as a mortar to hold it all together.

As a totally philosophical notion, I would say there are no subjects I couldn't consider as having potential for humor. As a practical notion, it's extremely unlikely that I would ever write a joke or think of a joke that involved someone's disabilities or someone's race or some sort of minority that was in some way being handicapped. It's possible that one day I would think of a joke about somebody in a wheelchair that would somehow pass muster, but as of yet, I don't see that happening. I can be very cruel, I can make fun of people, I can make fun of groups of people, too. In *A Walk in the Woods*, I did sort of play with the stereotype of Georgia backwoods people in a way that could be construed as cruel, but also I think it was clear that I was only joking and that it wasn't real. I think when you start talking about people's skin color or people who have some sort of terrible palsy or something like that, there's not much scope for jokes in that. There's none as far as I can see.

Crafting the Joke

The hardest part of the writing process, and I'm sure it's true for most writers, is just getting going. There's that formidable feeling of dread when you wake up in the morning that says, "Oh god, I've got to somehow fill all these empty pieces of paper with my words." My only real trick is that I don't mess around in the morning. I get up, I allow myself to have one cup of coffee quickly and take a quick look at the paper, and then with my second cup of coffee, when I'm still only half-awake, I go upstairs into my office, switch on the computer and actually try to start working. I force myself to sit down and start working, and then this miraculous transformation happens. This activity that I was dreading, this hard work, I get into it and then find I don't want to stop. It's more or less the same mental activity you use in going through a crossword puzzle or something that is somehow gripping. You've got this kind of challenge that you're really engaged by. So, once I start working, I'm very happy to keep on working. Very often, I work too long, to the point where I'm sort of burnt out for the day. My one failing is that I will keep working throughout the day and the next day realize the whole last three or four hours of writing the day before were a waste of time.

The thing I've learned about humor is less is usually better. Don't push the joke too far or too hard. It's very easy to tip over the edge and go too far with a joke. It's much better to err on the side of caution with jokes. Even in the most capable hands, it becomes very tedious to be inundated with jokes, one joke after another. There are a lot of very funny writers whose stuff I think works much better in small doses. The greatest humorist ever, S.J. Perelman, is about as funny as a person can get. If you read his shorter pieces, after six or seven or eight pieces, you begin to get kind of wearied by them. I think the tip I would give to aspiring humorists is to hold back. Don't feel as though you've got to fire off a joke every two lines.

To me it's just instinctive somehow, this question of timing. When I'm constructing a joke or a humorous passage, I work on it over and over and over again until I just have a sense that I've got it right. You know in your heart when it's still not quite right, that something's wrong here, something missing, some element.

It's sort of like asking someone to teach you to improvise jazz; you just have to have a feel for it. The way to get a feel for it is to do it so much, for so long, that it actually becomes second nature to you.

Humor is a very strange thing. There is a process that happens to me almost every time I write a book. Before I go on a book tour, I decide which readings, which passages, I will read and so obviously, I choose the ones I think will get the biggest laughs. I get onstage and I start to read, and very often what I think are the best jokes don't particularly enliven the audience. And then something I thought was a much more feeble joke is the one that gets the biggest laughs. Partly that's because things work differently on the written page than they do spoken aloud, but it's also just the fact that everybody's sense of humor is slightly different from everyone else's. I come away from doing a book tour feeling as if I'm less of an expert than before I went on the book tour because people are laughing at different things than I expected them to, laughing in different measures than I would have predicted. It's kind of a worry, when your best jokes aren't working as well as you think.

The whole dynamics of audience reaction are very strange because people all want to laugh together. Skills are required, I think, to be a performer in a public forum when it comes to humor, and those skills are really quite different from the skills that work best on the written page. There are some people who are very gifted in both—Steve Martin, for example. He can get up and perform and be hysterically funny, and he can write on the page and be funny, but he's actually two completely different people when he's doing that. His writings aren't anything at all like his performances. I think very often when you read a book written by some stand-up comic, the jokes aren't all that good. They might be great if he delivered them or if you could see him acting them out, but on the page suddenly they don't work.

If I had to get up in front of a class of aspiring writers, I wouldn't know what exercises to give them to help them become funnier writers. All I can tell you is that for me, getting the joke right is a very complicated and involved process. It's so dependent upon timing and getting everything to build up just right so the punch line comes at exactly the right moment. It's a question of just feeling your way through it. I've learned from experience, from having the experience of reading some of my earlier books, rereading them much later after they were written. It was almost like reading them for the first time and seeing that some of these jokes were either telegraphed much too clearly beforehand or weren't good enough, and I should have rejected them.

In some of my earlier books, there was much too much of this feeling that I had to constantly keep up this sort of machine-gun fire of jokes. In fact, in a book-length work, that usually works against you. Jokes should be much more selective; they should be sprinkled throughout the work. You should come across them little by little rather than be inundated by them. They should be a gentle spring shower rather than a deluge. I learned that over the years by writing books; there's a reason why stand-up comics only do sixty minutes or whatever it is they do. It's because people can only laugh so long. You get tired of laughing. Even if you're really enjoying it, the idea of spending five hours listening to even the funniest comedian in the world begins to feel like torment. You don't want to keep on laughing, you want to relax. Everybody's heard of comic relief, but actually you need a straightforward relief from comedy. It took me awhile to realize that, but I think it not only gives the readers a relief, it also makes the jokes, when they come, that much more effective.

Bill Bryson has recently returned to live in the United States after almost twenty years living in England, where he worked for the *Times* and the *Independent*. He is the author of several books on language and travel memoirs, including *The Lost Continent, A Walk in the Woods* and most recently, *In a Sunburned Country*.

CHAPTER 22

Tom Bodett and the Interstate 5 Cow Rollover

It has never been a tactical decision of mine to be humorous. It just started out that way. I suppose I'm aware of being able to make people laugh, but the comment I hear the most from people who first meet me is that I'm more serious than they figured I'd be.

I appreciate the absurdity of life and am entertained by it daily. When I'm writing about something I find particularly absurd or heartbreakingly unfortunate, I always end up joking about it. It's more pleasing to the palate than anger and sadness most days. Without humor my novel *The Free Fall of Webster Cummings* would be a very dull story about a bunch of Americans thrashing around trying to find some meaning in their lives. If people wanted that kind of story they could always go visit their relatives. The novel works because it is about a bunch of Americans looking for meaning in their lives and pretty well screwing it up every inch of the way. That's life. That's us. That's funny.

Basic human nature is a virtual comedy cornucopia. We take ourselves so seriously, yet we are to greater and lesser degrees incompetent at almost every single thing we do at one time or another. A while back I packed this huge rolled-up mattress straight up a hill from my boat to my cabin across the bay from Homer, Alaska. I heaved it off my back on the steps of the porch, and it bounced and started rolling right back toward the bay. I chased it right to the cliff and was laughing before it hit the water. Maybe in his mercy the creator gave us the ability to laugh because he didn't make us all that damn smart.

Growing Up With Cows

Being a white guy from the Midwest apparently doesn't hurt in the humor business—Mark Twain, Ring Lardner, Garrison Keillor, David Letterman—to name just a few. We either all have a lot of repressed hostility we mask with good humor, or it is very advantageous to a young humorist to grow up around cows. Worthy of further study, I'm sure. My father also influenced my sense of humor. An engineer by trade, he could be a very funny fellow when he was in the mood. His wit was dryer than a popcorn fart and quite clever.

I don't tend to read a lot of humorists. I find it a disorienting experience. I either compare myself unfavorably to what I'm reading, or worse yet, I find a subject addressed that I had thought of doing myself. Once I see that, I scrap the idea as being unoriginal. Of course, there's not much in the world that hasn't been handled by one humorist or another, so I find the less I know about them the better.

Stylistically, I'm not aware of any direct influences from other writers that I've incorporated into my work. In matters of integrity, I'd have to point to Tobias Wolff. He shows an exceptionally courageous personal honesty in the memoirs he has written—*This Boy's Life* and *In Pharaoh's Army*. His work points out how one man's life can be interesting to a mass audience when told from a place of humility and with rigorous honesty.

Another author who impresses me in this way is Richard Ford—*The Sportswriter, Independence Day, Women With Men*. While not autobiographical in presentation, all men's internal lives bear resemblance to one another, and Ford looks at that in excruciating detail. He also writes the most perfect paragraphs of any author I've read.

Over the years, my sense of humor has changed. It may be a part of my own maturity or simply that writing for a national audience requires more sensitivity than what I got away with around the job sites in Alaska all those years. I find it increasingly difficult to leave a funny line in something if I think it has the potential to be offensive to a reasonable person of one stripe or another. I won't allow myself to knowingly offend people or publicly make light of somebody else's troubles. I have enough of my own foibles to lampoon without having to import anyone else's. I don't mind offending the stuffed shirts, charlatans and zealots of the world, but my struggling brethren don't need my grief on top of the doses they get from their regular suppliers.

Still, I don't think a writer can overcome the subjective nature of humor. There are always going to be people who don't get it. There are always going to be people who send money to those paste wax preachers on cable, too. What can you do? I'm fortunate in that I am pretty much the "National Average" in virtually every aspect of my life. I am the guy that airline seats are designed for. I am the guy Al Gore was trying to reach. Everything I try to buy from a catalog is back-ordered. I am the generic American. I want what everybody seems to want. My life is so ordinary that when I make fun of it, it tends to entertain a good many other people, too.

If you asked me what my favorite humor piece was, I'd have to say "The Best Sauna Story So Far" from my book *The End of the Road.* It's just a silly farce about two couples who burn up a sauna along with their clothes on a remote trail and have to ski naked in the dark in subzero weather back to their car. I've had more people tell me they about peed themselves with that story than any other. Second only to that is the one where Argus Winslow's dog catches on fire. Don't ask me why. I've written more sophisticated tomes, but those are the ones that have held up over time.

Just Be Yourself

I have no specific writing process regarding humor. Either something is funny to me, or it isn't. I've never tried to plan humor in a piece of work; I'm not sure how a person could. Once I did work on a television sitcom pilot where I was advised to write "two laughs per page." It was very strange, but not impossible to do. I could see where a writer could develop that rhythm with some practice, but I don't think the humor would ever rise much above garden-variety comedy. Real humor, the kind that sneaks up and captures you, takes some time to deliver.

In detail, my humor is not at all intentional. In general, I can decide to be funny, if you will, but I look at it more as you might "turn on the charm" before entering a room rather than deciding in advance what witty things you might say when you get there.

As for my writing process in general—I sit at a word processor and stare off into space for 90 percent of a working day thinking of every single thing under the sun except what I'm supposed to be thinking about. Then on the eleventh hour of the eleventh day, so to speak, I write the damn thing.

So, where do I get my ideas? Earth, mostly, although auguring two multimillion dollar space probes in a row into the surface of Mars is showing some great potential for that planet as well.

I don't develop a given idea into a humorous piece. I develop a humorous idea into a piece of writing. If you gave me the subject of cancer and told me to develop it into a humorous piece, I would not know where to begin. I don't, at this point, think cancer is funny. However, if I had cancer or had recently recovered from cancer, I might find humor in some of the ways it affected me. I might laugh at the deals I made with Providence or at all the hair in the bathtub drain, or I might have fun with radioactivity. But, I could in no way do that without having the experience, and maybe not then.

I don't think I could develop door hinges into a humorous essay, either. Slamming my fingers in doors, however, would be easily executed. It's funny to me, or it isn't. I can't say it enough: If a subject doesn't evoke some kind of honest humorous reflex, don't try to force it. The world does not need any more two-dimensional puns.

Occasionally, my humor bombs. I recently wrote a tongue-in-cheek tribute to read at the twentieth anniversary concert celebration of our local public radio station. I filled it with cheap, sappy metaphors that became increasingly turgid as the piece reached its climactic and ridiculously sentimental conclusion. It was intended as a parody of my own tendency to be cloying and to overwrite. Halfway through it, I could see the rapt and confused faces of my friends and neighbors, and scarcely a chuckle could be heard. The night before I'd read it for two close friends, and we'd howled over it. To my knowledge, not one single person in that crowd of a thousand people understood I was kidding. Several thanked me for "putting words to their feelings." I fled to my cabin and read it for the eagles, who also sat deadpan.

On the other hand, readers sometimes think something I write is funny when it isn't meant to be. Actually, that happens all the time with live audiences. I'm always billed as a "humorist," which gives people the expectation that everything I say is going to be funny. I've written a lot of sad stuff, and I've spoken at some pretty serious events where people laugh at the first thing I say. It's an awkward moment or two, but it passes. I'm not aware of that same thing ever happening in print.

I don't think you can write funny unless you think life is funny. If you don't think life is funny, then give it up and write poetry if you're able, or point-of-view columns on landfill issues if you're not. Maybe humor can be taught, but I wouldn't know how to do it. I do think you can learn to laugh at yourself, though, and that's a good place to start. A way to do that would be to hitchhike around the world by yourself. Do odd jobs along the way, get arrested, escape, lose a limb, fall in love, learn to fix a motorcycle, be caught outdoors in the rain in women's underwear. This would all take no longer than would an associate's degree in creative writing at an accredited junior college, but it would teach you how to laugh a lot sooner.

Parody, I imagine, could be learned with practice. Those faux Hemingway contests are hysterical. Just pick any serious prose or even a newspaper story, and try to write something that sounds just like it about some goofy thing, like a cow, for example. (There's that Midwestern upbringing again.) No matter what you do, it will be funny: A cow rollover on Interstate 5 backed up the morning commute for several hours on Tuesday. . . . It's not great humor, but you might learn to write good humor this way.

There are three things I think writers can do to add humor to their work:

1. Lighten up. Look for the funny side of things. As an exercise: Refuse to take seriously anything your spouse or partner says to you for one entire month. If he or she asks you to do the dishes, laugh and say, "Sorry, too busy." If he or she says "I love you," laugh and say, "I've heard that line before." You'll certainly be thrown out of the house in a few weeks. Then, while you're living at the Y trying to sort out your wasted life, you can reflect on the absurdity of your existence and the ironies of relationships, and you'll be well on your way to becoming a humorist.

2. Be yourself. More to the point—be true to yourself. Don't pretend to be rankled about something you're not. I've always had the suspicion that Andy Rooney could really not give a rat's behind about the stuff he's been complaining about all these years. Mostly, he seems to be searching for things he figures other people are complaining about. Maybe that works for him to some degree, but real humor has to come from the same place your passion, your fear and your obsessions come from: your parents. Seriously, it has to come from your guts.

3. Stop trying to be funny. If you want to craft clever one-liners, that's fine. There's plenty of work for that kind of writer in TV and comedy clubs, and it's good work if you can get it. Humor is a different deal. It has to come from who you are. Some people have no sense of humor at all, and they should not be writing it, or anything if you ask me. Some people have a good sense of humor, and they can all learn to express that on a page just by learning how to write well. If they learn to write, and they have a sense of humor, they'll learn to write humor. And some people have a great sense of humor. These are rare gems, and they need no help from anybody.

I think, and I'm willing to be wrong about this, that if writers don't know how to add humor to their work, then they shouldn't try. There is nothing wrong with being a writer of serious prose, and there's nothing right about humorous writing if it's done badly. If you can make people laugh in your everyday life, then you'll probably figure out how to do it in your work. If you don't, then you'll be better off not trying to fake it.

Tom Bodett is the author of six books and fifteen audio programs. He has been a commentator on National Public Radio's *All Things Considered*, host of the PBS series *Travels on America's Historic Trails* and spokesman for Motel 6. He currently hosts *Loose Leaf Book Company*, a weekly public radio program for adults about children's literature.

CHAPTER 23

A Dash of Levity: Peg Bracken

I think humor is very evanescent, but I am not sure that's the right word. It reminds me of when I was in college and went to the infirmary because I had a bad cold. They put me to bed. My boyfriend was coming over to see me, and I wanted to impress him with how sick I was, so I held a match to the thermometer the nurse had given me, and it broke and mercury was running all over the sheets. Did you ever try to catch mercury on a bed sheet? It's impossible. That's the way humor is. Wasn't it E.B. White who said, "If you try to analyze humor, the patient dies on the dissecting table"?

Humor is more important and deserves more respect than it is often given. People will say to a humor writer, "When are you going to write something serious?" It's a lot easier to write something serious than it is to write something funny. Also, I don't think you can write humor to order. I believe it was *McCall's* that thought there was a funny idea in an article about how all women are supposedly kleptomaniacs, which becomes clear in hotels and motels: We just can't leave that dandy little washcloth, so we take it home with us. That example made me question what kind of person the editor was, because as it happens, I do not steal anything from hotels— doesn't match my bathroom. But, I wrote the piece anyway, and it turned out to be quite unfunny. I tried my best, but it never quite gelled, and *McCall's* got a lot of hate mail on account of it.

I had a syndicated column for several years, a newspaper column, and it was funny. It had a light approach to things, and I used to envy the people who were doing solemn pieces on the structure of the Democratic Party or the state of the American Medical Association or something like that. That was easier to do than to make people laugh.

Norm Cousins certainly understood that. He was a great proponent of humor being actually good for you—a healing force. When Cousins was in the hospital after a serious operation, he watched nothing but Marx brothers tapes because he always enjoyed them; he laughed, and they made him feel good. I think laughing does have a definite physical reaction on the human body. It increases serotonin levels or something of the sort. I was really pleased to learn some years after *I Hate to Housekeep* had come out that the Sloan Kettering Clinic in New York would give a copy of the book to women patients as a kind of graduation present.

Shaping a Sense of Humor

I think my sense of humor is genetic. My mother was a funny woman, and I think there is sort of a gene for humor. My mother—this is when I was a little girl, way before the day of the dishwasher—would wash dishes and I would wipe them, and we would make up funny poems and just laugh hysterically. We thought we were awfully funny. Some people are born solemn—I think the phrase is "They are born one drink behind"—and some people are not.

My sense of humor has also been influenced by different writers; I think there are more flavors in humor than Baskin Robbins. Calvin Trillin has a lovely, delicate touch, and Molly Ivins has a very forthright touch. The all-time master is Mark Twain because he remains funny after all these years. I suppose my favorite Twain piece would be that wonderful criticism he did of the early American writer James Fenimore Cooper. In Twain's mind, Cooper should have been digging ditches or something. It was extremely funny. I also love his *Life on the Mississippi.* Anything he wrote had little glints of humor, if not an all-out laugh.

I started out writing verse and have been a verse writer all my life. Once in a while, I have written what I consider a real poem, but mostly line verse. I realized you couldn't be funny in verse. You can be clever, but Ogden Nash is the only verse writer I ever came across who is funny. So I switched to prose. In prose I could be funny, yet in verse I could only make a cynical remark or a sly observation.

I was selling a lot of stuff to the *Saturday Evening Post* in those days, to the PostScript Page. I was selling so much that the editor asked me to choose a pen name because my stuff was piling up, and the staff didn't want to have a page that was half me. So, I chose Pat McQuesten, which was my mother's maiden name.

Humor is like poetry in that one word can make all the difference. That's why humor has to be written and rewritten and rewritten and revised. It was Michael Frame, the British humorist, who said it was a fact that anything easy to write is a pain in the ass to read. That's really true. You can write something, dash it off and oh boy, it just tickles you to death—then look at it the next day, and you may lose your breakfast.

If I had written *The I Hate to Cook Book* without humor, it would have dropped like a snowflake on a blanket. It was the humor that sold that book, that and the title. People had treated cooking as a fairly solemn subject, and they were reverent about it. Six publishers turned down the idea when my agent showed it to them, because they said that no, it would never go, women felt that cooking was a little too sacred a subject to kick around. But then it took a woman editor—Jeanette Hopkins, bless her heart, at Harcourt—who said, "Hey, we have to do this." Being a woman, she could understand.

Oddly enough, I don't think I'm a good cook. I like to bake, but I don't like to cook, and I just hate the idea of having that on my mind every day. My husband is awfully good about saying, "Let's eat out." Those are the three little words every woman wants to hear, you know.

Learning From Rejection

Ideas occur to me at four in the morning. I always have a little flashlight and notebook by my bedside. My husband sometimes wishes I didn't, but that is the way it is. It may be a word I have heard that is out of the ordinary from my usual vocabulary that makes me think, that starts me out on some kind of funny little detour. I sharpen my skills by just writing a lot, and I keep fairly comprehensive journals, all of which got burned up [in a house fire]. I had them for about thirty or thirty-five years. They were these fat notebooks—all of them gone now. If you're going to keep a journal, keep a copy of it somewhere else.

I don't think humor can be taught in school, but it is taught by editors who send things back. Every rejection slip is a lesson really, and that's the only way people can learn. It's very foolish, I think, to write something, then show it to your mother or Aunt Bessie or your husband, because they're not judges. The only person who can judge is an editor or agent, and they certainly make enough mistakes. When you show your writing to somebody, you are asking for compliments, and when people have shown me manuscripts, I've learned the hard way that I lose a friend every time.

A form rejection slip just tells you that you haven't made it yet. You try to study as objectively as you can what that magazine is printing, what it considers good, and then edit your own stuff and ask, "Where am I falling short?" The one thing I would tell any writer is to rewrite. Again and again. I think reading widely is a help, too, because how are you going to know that some idea is a cliche unless you read a lot and find that this topic has been handled a lot of times?

If there is a magazine you like a lot, go ahead and be a copycat. Try really hard to write something that a particular magazine would like. That's not a very popular viewpoint; everybody says to be yourself. I don't agree with that. It's been my experience that to get something in *The New Yorker*, you just better damn well read *The New Yorker*, unless you are absolutely a one-of-a-kind genius, whose work is burning so brightly, no editor could miss it. But who of us can make that statement?

I am not sure that a writer can overcome the subjective nature of humor. I think people are people, and we are all of us pretty much alike in a number of fundamental ways. Did you ever read Aristophanes? I was really astounded at how I was laughing at this old Greek, as I read either *The Frogs* or *The Birds*, I forget which, but he was funny. An old Greek was still telling fundamental stuff that made me laugh today.

There are some constraints I put upon my published stuff. I don't like four-letter words. I think that sometimes in telling jokes an occasional expletive is necessary, but I don't care for that in published stuff. I was disappointed when *The New Yorker* started sounding like a truck driver.

Right now, I'm working on sort of a commonplace book that, so far, seems to consist of a verse with some explanatory material or a news item with verse that may develop into prose, too. As you can see, it's a very loose thing. I've always wanted to write a commonplace book, and this is sort of a different thing. W.H. Auden had a commonplace book, and I bought that thinking I would like it, but I didn't. It didn't tell me anything about him. It was just a collection of things he had read and liked. Longish paragraphs and so forth, but no exposition by him. Mine is not going to be like that. So much of it burned that, in a way, I'm back to square one. However, I feel OK about it. I use a computer, and after the fire, I hustled out and bought a typewriter. Boy, I tell you—it feels like walking instead of flying. I don't see how we did anything before computers. I have a computer on order, and when it comes, I may just toss the typewriter out the window.

Peg Bracken's first book, *The I Hate to Cook Book,* was published in 1960, has sold millions of copies around the world and is still in print. It was followed by *I Hate to Housekeep* and other humorous books. She is also well-known as a television spokesperson for Birds Eye.

CHAPTER 24

The Absurd World of Andrei Codrescu

I come from Romania, where the absurd is a fact of life. This is why we invented the theater of the absurd through Ionesco. The founder of the Dada movement, Tristan Tzara, was a Romanian. The Balkans have had a history that doesn't make much sense, so people defended themselves against it by finding expressions for it, and the absurd is a very good way to understand it.

My first favorite writers were actually writers who wrote in English. I read all of Mark Twain when I was about thirteen. I think one of the funniest books I ever read was *Three Men in a Boat* by Jerome K. Jerome, a totally wonderful book. Another influence was the Russian satirists and humorists, people like Evgeni Petrov, who wrote *The Twelve Chairs*. It was a rich tradition of literary humor, so by age sixteen, I was pretty much conversant. These were the books I enjoyed tremendously, to the expense of the more serious, psychological, tormented epics like Dostoyevsky's stories.

Almost everything that smacked of what the Communist Party called decadence was forbidden, so that was a great source of interest to us, the so-called forbidden. Since we didn't really have any access to it, we had to sort of invent it or imagine it, but it became a great source of material and inspiration.

I am really not a humorist; I just find the world funny because I'm an observer and I also try to stay amused. Because of those two things, occasionally my writing is funny to whoever reads it, not because I employ humor on purpose, but because people laugh when they have the shock of recognizing the familiar under an unexpected light.

Coping Through Humor

I find things equally funny and tragic. I guess one defense against the terrible tragedy of being born and living in a world that is not always to our liking is to see what can be redeemed from it and made funny.

It's another approach to the grim things of life. It's a way to have a longer perspective on the world and say, "Well, things seem grim right now, but if you look at them from a different angle, they are actually funny because this restaurant I'm sitting in, having a terrible meal, has been around for about 150 years or so and someone has sat in this same chair and died, so things really aren't so bad for me, from the perspective of time."

My mother's view of life was invariably tragic. She reminded me of the line from John Ashberry, the American poet who said, "All things are tragic when a mother watches." She had such an exaggerated, pessimistic view of the world that I guess just by contrast I developed the opposite.

Where I come from was a rich oral culture. People told stories all the time. Families never quite chased the children away at bedtime; they'd sit under the table and listen to the adults talk. There was a rich verbal world all around. People told stories and they talked a lot. They talked a lot for pleasure, not for efficiency. One thing about this familial environment, not just in my own family, but in the entire country of Transylvania in the late fifties and early sixties, was that people talked because they couldn't do very much else—everything was controlled. But they took great pleasure in things like innuendo and double meanings and puns and word games to pass the time. They were, in fact, a form of resistance to the rigid official culture.

Now I'm a U.S. citizen, and I have the same normal outrages of the average citizen against what sometimes seems an impossible system or systems. Big companies with voice mail piss me off, the personality of service that emanates from the corporate states, bureaucracies of every kind—these kinds of things really get me. I've been sensitive to them since living in Romania. From the point of view of the average citizen, I feel outrage, and I feel the most efficient way to speak about it is using humor rather than vitriol or polemic, which just raises the blood pressure.

I think writers are people who use themselves as an instrument for understanding the world. I don't think there's any other way to do it. All writers do that, no matter what degree of objectivity they possess. If you are a writer, you're a kind of writer from the very beginning. Personally, I don't think there are any great books, for instance, that are not also books of comedy in some ways.

I don't believe in tragic writing. I think the greatest books are books like *The Good Soldier Svejk* and Milan Kundera's *The Unbearable Lightness of Being*. Even Dostoyevsky is quite funny in the better translations. I think most of the truly terrific masterpieces, beginning with the earliest novels, *Don Quixote* and Francois Rabelais's *Gargantua and Pantagruel* have humor in them. People laugh when they have the shock of discovery, and that's what the greatest writers do. They force you to see with new eyes, and that's shocking. The shock is there absolutely for the writer as well as the reader. That's what's so terrific about discovering things in the process of writing; you're writing, then suddenly find something that's totally exciting.

Satire and Humor

I think there's a big difference between satire and humor. Satire is much more deliberate because you're going after something, and you're going to destroy it by making fun of it. Then there is humor, which is more benevolent in some ways, because it reveals the absurdity in a situation. I think for the most part, my humor is involuntary. It's just how I see things. I don't think there's any difference between my personality and my writing. I talk the way I write pretty much, but I also write satire. That's quite a different thing because then the object is to criticize or critique something by using humor deliberately to discredit it.

The best way for a beginning writer to approach satire is to read the great satirists. Certainly the American literature has great writers like Twain, H.L. Mencken, Ambrose Bierce and some of the best columnists writing today. There are quite a few contemporaries who write satire very well, and I think beginning writers simply should delight by immersing themselves in the great satirists. That's one way to do it. I've never really believed in a set of rules for doing this sort of thing although, if pushed, I could write *10 Ways to Demolish an Object*.

There is definitely a bias on the part of big publishers and mainstream media against humor. Big publishers don't believe that if you write a satire, you should call it a satire. My novel *Messiah* is a satire of every apocalyptic strain I could find. My publisher just resisted having the word "satire" anywhere near the cover because, in his opinion or the market research opinion, satire and humor don't sell—which is simply not true.

I say it's not true because if you look at cable television, there's an explosion of comedy and satire all over the place, and people obviously love it. It's really the so-called serious culture establishment that has got a stick up its ass. It is actually preventing some of the best stuff from doing what it does in the market. I think it's a kind of insecurity, really, a taste that's been created and promoted particularly in New York for a sort of sentimental fiction.

I think that about the midseventies, maybe earlier, we started to come out of the high-minded seriousness of high modernism, and a lot of what the critics call postmodernism now is really forms of humor. Quite a bit of this writing had the writer in it as self-referential. It's kitsch and comedy and slapstick and schtick. I think most so-called serious writing is in fact comedic; it's just that there is a commercial reason for pushing sentimentality and schlock. I don't agree that there is a kind of high-art seriousness; it's just a hangover from modernism, which really hasn't been around since the late sixties. High art has been funny—I mean everything in pop art is funny. Andy Warhol actually played an enormous joke on people. Quite a bit of that is really funny, but there is a mainstream kind of faux seriousness that is really sentimentality and kitsch.

Learning Humor

One of the most pathetic things I've ever seen was one of those inspirational speakers talking at a company meeting trying to teach them humor. He was juggling balls, and he had different props on the table, and he had the audience turning around to each other and saying things like, "Shit, I'm sick of it," stuff like that. I had to walk out of the room because I was totally nauseated by it.

I think you can teach people how to relax. I don't think you can teach them how to be really funny, but if you teach them how to take it easy and see that something that really entertains them is in fact quite hilarious, then you're half there. But there are people who just cannot do that. For instance, I think people constrained for years by rules and regulations at work and in their environment probably need dynamite to get them to express themselves publicly in a way that's not sounding so terrible.

You can't teach humor to a grim person, not to somebody who has an essentially tragic disposition. I think the ancients used to divide temperament into different categories. I think the choleric temperament, for example, couldn't be taught humor because the first reaction of a choleric person was anger. I think humor can be taught to people who have a fairly gentle disposition, who can create a kind of distance between themselves and the world. In that case, maybe it's just a matter of teaching writing, not humor really, but teaching how to express something in some way that's funny.

I try to stay awake. I have a notebook, and I jot down impressions all the time of things I find interesting, some of them funny, some of them just plain interesting or weird. Then I use my notebook as sort of a mulch to write longer pieces when I actually sit down formally at my laptop and think about how to put them together.

And I don't worry about how subjective my humor is. It's not a problem for me. I don't even attempt to hide the fact that it's one person writing it. In fact, I probably exaggerate the fact that it's me. There's kind of a self-deprecation that goes with some of the better humorists who are actually able to laugh at themselves first before they laugh at others.

I apply some constraints to my radio pieces because you can't say the seven words forbidden by the FCC. But I found very creative ways to say them that sound a lot worse. I'm never quite satisfied with how far I've gone. I want to go a little further. You get your third or fourth wind, and then you can get wilder and nastier if you keep pushing.

Sometimes, my humor is misunderstood. Quite a few people have said they don't get it. I have a friend who told me that whenever he meets people, he asks them if they know my stuff. If they like it, he know he's going to be friends with them; if they don't, he knows he won't. People don't say anymore that they don't get it. They lie now, but I'm sure it happens. I know people that I've outraged, but they couldn't quite respond because the humor got in the way. They didn't want to seem like fools by responding seriously to something that was satirical. It's extremely hard to respond to something that includes a dose of humor.

How to Write Funny

I think the best advice I could give young writers is to dress like buffoons, and walk naked down the main street of their hometowns, and whatever happens to them write down as soon as they get home. The first rule is really not to take yourself too seriously.

Andrei Codrescu has written fiction, poetry, memoirs and essays, including *Road Scholar*, which was also made into a Peabody Award-winning movie. He teaches writing at Louisiana State University in Baton Rouge and is a regular contributor to National Public Radio. His most recent book is *The Devil Never Sleeps and Other Essays*.

CHAPTER 25

Provoked by the World: John Dufresne

I grew up in a big extended family. Nobody ever moved from the town. My grandfather was one of nineteen children, so I had relatives everywhere. They got together every week and told stories they could laugh about, and I would listen to the stories. That's how I really got interested in telling stories.

You could see how humor bonded people; sitting around the table drinking their beers, smoking their cigarettes, laughing with each other, tapping each other on the shoulder. The stories and the humor made people feel good about themselves and the community, whatever community they were in. It was an antidote to loneliness as well and made connections to other folks. I was more an audience than a teller of jokes and funny stories, but humor can get you attention, of course. People pay attention to somebody who's telling a joke. I guess in that way humor can be sort of a call or plea for love and attention.

I think I'm more serious than funny, but I consider myself to be an appreciator of humor. I enjoy laughing and I like humor. I'm usually the person who's laughing in the room, rather than the person who's telling the jokes. I can't remember jokes. I take to writing them down and telling them, trying to memorize jokes.

There's a connection that's made in humor between you as the author of the joke, as it were, and you as the author of the book with the reader. Laughter is a physical response. It's a behavior as well as a thought, an emotion. It's how you change somebody, to make a connection. I can appreciate that. I feel close to the characters—not as a writer when I do that, but as a reader.

What's funny is something that is surprising or unexpected, and there's a moment of recognition like, "Oh yeah, this happened to me." It's like Emerson said when he was talking about genius: "In the words of genius, we recognize our own rejected thoughts." There's some of that recognition when we hear a joke as well. It's something that amuses us. We say, "Yeah, that's right," and that creates sort of a bond between you and the person telling the joke.

I like intelligent humor. I appreciate the cleverness of puns and I admire them, but there is also something about people who make puns. You know they're not paying attention all the time. They're sort of distant from the conversation, so it's a little bit off-putting. I guess I don't like silliness, and I prefer humor that causes you to reflect a little bit.

Movies were a big influence on my sense of humor, starting with the Marx brothers. Groucho Marx is probably the funniest person in the world. Growing up, I had a lot of friends, just kids in the neighborhood, who were funny. I realized that I was attracted to, not people who told jokes, but people who had a funny take on things and could make you laugh or tell a story. The best jokes to me are the jokes that are narrative.

There are some things I wouldn't joke about. I don't like pointing out people and making fun of them to laugh at them, but to try and humanize them, I guess. I try not to point fingers at people in that way. There are things I wouldn't write about, whether they're funny or not. There are things I'm just not interested in—pornography, for example, or sentimentality—so if the humor were taking me in that direction, I wouldn't go there. My humor is sort of a response to the world rather than creating the world. I'm just trying to see what's humorous out there.

I take my own life seriously, probably too seriously. Sometimes, I don't think things are funny, but if I step back a little bit, I realize they are. Humor gives you that kind of distance. It puts you at a distance from the event, as you are looking back on it a year from now, and you can think, "Oh, wasn't that funny, what happened? The way that happened, how stressed out I was and how I couldn't sleep? That was so funny." Then humor puts things into perspective.

I think humor sustains your life. It helps make life worth living and helps put life into perspective—I'm not the most important person in the world, we're all here together, and we're all going to the same place. We should help each other and cheer each other up along the way.

I was on a panel last year in New Orleans at a conference on humor. I was thinking, "Boy, as soon as we start talking about humor, how is it going to be funny? It's going to be deadly." So, I prepared a couple of jokes to tell—I thought if nothing else, I'll tell a joke, because I don't know if I can talk about humor—and it turned out fine. People in the audience were telling jokes, the panel was telling jokes. Everyone was there to laugh and not really to learn anything about humor.

I like to laugh and like to make myself laugh. I gave the character in *Love Warps the Mind a Little* the name Laf, and part of that was meant to be a bit of a pun. It's a way to break the ice—you meet people and tell them a joke, tell them an amusing story, and then they tell you one back. It's sort of bonding together. That's what you are trying to do with the reader.

For some people, when they say somebody is a humorist or a humorous writer, it's kind of a pejorative term. It's a term meant to confine you to a certain area. It's like saying somebody is a Southern writer or a regional writer of any kind. It's meant to limit you in some way, which is ridiculous. Humor confronts the human condition rather than trying to avoid it, rather than trying escapism. It's the literature that explores the human condition. That's what I'm trying to do.

Part of what you're always doing is entertaining. You've got a plot there for two reasons, one of which is to engage the reader in the story, and one way to keep the reader around until the end of the story is to make the reader laugh, make the reader think about life through humor. It's just another tool that a writer has and should use. When I read fiction, stories and novels, I don't need to laugh, but I'm hoping there is something fun there somewhere. When it comes I always appreciate it. It makes me think more highly of the book.

Humor as a Character Builder

There's a kind of humor that's an expression of tenderness. When I'm writing, when I'm using humor in a novel, I'm feeling tender toward a character, and I'm hoping the reader will, too. There's another kind of humor that's more malicious, like satire, which can be dangerous for a fiction writer. I read satire, I appreciate it, but I'm not interested in writing it. I think, because of the maliciousness, you need to be careful of it.

For example, in *Love Warps the Mind a Little*, there are a number of letters written by this rejected writer to editors and from editors to him. There's maliciousness there, but it's on the part of the characters. I think the reader appreciates that. If the reader senses that it's the writer being malicious, then I think you'll lose the reader.

It's the stance of a satirist to be morally superior, to say I'm going to point out what's wrong with this because I'm better than these people, and that's not something a fiction writer can endure for very long. You have to love the truth more than you hate the wrong, the error.

In *Love Warps the Mind a Little*, you have this guy, Lafayette Proulx, who is not a completely nice guy, although he was very nice in the beginning. How long will readers put up with this guy and see him evolve hopefully, and change, and mature and all of that kind of stuff? If he's nasty for too long, they're not going to. So, my strategy was to make him funny in a self-deprecating way so readers understand he does know what he's doing and that he's distanced from himself a bit. He'll tell a joke, or he'll have some funny observations—all efforts to save himself. I felt that might hold people, keep them around for a while.

I also gave him the dog, and anyone who loves a dog can't be all that bad. Because he could love the dog, we realize he's capable of loving something, and the dog loves him. The dog became comic relief in a way. When people needed an emotional break from the very serious business of cancer and all that, the dog comes through and everyone could smile, take a breath and go on. If you're laughing, you forgive a lot of sins. Laf's aware of himself and he'll be OK.

Laf's sense of humor is his way of saving his self, like giving himself something he won, that kind of wiseassed humor. In writing, I get to be a wiseass with people in a way that I don't necessarily want to be in my life. You get to mouth off. It's sort of like a little fantasy. You get to be funny in kind of a cruel way, as long as the reader doesn't think it's you, but coming from the character.

Writing fiction makes you honest. While you're writing fiction anyway, you're more honest than you are in the rest of your life because that's your job, just to find out a truth about something. You don't let yourself get away with what you might in your life. In life perhaps, you might be cruel to somebody or say something to hurt somebody, but the purpose of a book is never to hurt anybody. So you don't use your humor cruelly or hurtfully. Not everyone agrees, of course. Satirists would not agree with that, but I'm after a different thing, I guess. I'm not smart enough to be a satirist. I don't have any answers; all I have are questions.

There's a term Flannery O'Connor used in one of her letters. She said a writer has to develop anagogical vision, which means seeing the world on many levels at the same time, or looking at something and seeing that it's many different things. I think there's an element of that kind of vision in humor; if you look at the world with humorous eyes, you see it on many levels. You see what's surprising, what's not logical, what doesn't seem to fit but really does fit.

Always ask yourself, What else can it be? It can be this, but it can also be that. It can mean this, but can also mean that. Think hard about whatever it is you're writing about, whether it's a character, a piece of furniture or an incident. Think about how you can use it and exploit it elsewhere. I like things to resonate through the story, so set down a theme early and hit that note somewhere later on. Repeat it incrementally. You look at a character and say, he drives a cab, but what else does he do? Well, he's a socialist. Oh, a socialist cab driver, that's funny. He's trying to organize himself in the union or something like that. How can I play that out?

Getting It on the Page

I generally write in the morning. I get up, drink some coffee, read the paper and sit down to write. I'm often working on more than one thing at a time, but usually there's a big project, a novel let's say, and I'll just be working on that all morning. I write until noon or so, then I have lunch, take a break. Depending on the rest of the day, I'll either write more, if I don't have to teach, or prepare class. I write longhand on a legal pad with a fountain pen, and I write draft after draft after draft. I go over and over and over it again. I like going slow, I like rewriting.

When I'm writing a novel, I work in chapters, sort of. I revise the chapter to the point where I like it, which may be that I have written it ten to twenty times, at least the early part of it, because when I revise I go back to the first line and revise it all over again. I know it's going to get better if I do that. Every time I rewrite a page, it's a better page. It's not an efficient way to write, but it's the way I write. When I get a chapter done, I'll go to the computer and type it in. I type with three fingers, so it takes a while. I type it in and make a hard copy of it because I don't trust computers. I also revise in hard copy. I'll get a chapter and revise it, and when I get the whole novel done, I'll go through the whole book several times revising.

When I stop for the day, and I think this was Hemingway's advice, I know what the next thing I'm going to write is. I might make a note, "Write this scene," or "This line comes next" or something like that. What I usually do is sit down at my table and read over what I wrote yesterday to get the voice back and the rhythm and the prose and all that. I also usually read some poetry before I write, and that reminds me how important language is and how effective it can be. Sometimes it gives you things to write about, completely unplanned.

Everything I know at this given moment in my life I try to put into a novel, everything that I'm learning myself. So, I'm always reading all kinds of things to get me thinking in an unaccustomed way. I take notes all the time. I'm low-tech, so I just need a little memo pad and I go around and write things down. When I come home at night, I put them into a notebook I keep on my desk. It's very unsystematic.

Get yourself used to being in chaos, being in clutter and messy for a long time. That's one thing writers need to learn, that you can't keep it ordered. It's disorder that's the fount of creativity. It's what you don't know that's important, not what you know, because what you don't know makes you want to find out. That's that assertive curiosity that makes writers wonder about things. Get used to that and sort of relax. On the other hand, you try to keep your life disciplined in a way; I write every day at set times. Keep order in your life, so you can be crazy in your writing.

It would have been very difficult for me to have written *Love Warps the Mind a Little* without humor. It would have been dreadful to write. It's very serious business I think, the illness and all that, and some of the questions I was trying to address and ask. I think you just have to lighten the tone. For example, when I thought of cancer in the book, I gave Judi ovarian cancer because I couldn't get it myself. I'm a bit of a hypochondriac, I guess, but really it was that I didn't want to be distracted by thinking,

"Oh, Christ, I better go to the doctor." That's how seriously I take this stuff. I've got to deal with all my personal feelings about what it's like to be dying.

I guess the humor in the book was also to cheer me up as I was writing. At the center of our existence is death and loss. It's the sadness that we all deal with; we can't hold on to anything, can't hold on to what we love, everything's going to vanish, we're going to die and that's not fair. The beauty and nobility of our lives consists of refusing to crumble in the face of that knowledge, to go on and try to find love with people and have intimate relationships and try, in fact, to hold on to what's going to vanish. It's really hard, without humor.

If you believe that, as I do, it would be hard to even live if you didn't have a sense of humor. If you took it too seriously, I don't know what you would do. You'd be like Dostoyevsky and crawl into a corner and shoot yourself. I think it's that kind of wanting to love, wanting to feel good about people and life while we're here, that gives us something bright and cheering.

Humor can be cultivated. I think it's got to be part of your life, not something artificial. It's got to be in the way you look at the world and the way you think about the world. People always tell me I'm funny. When I'm talking or doing writers workshops and conferences, people always tell me how entertaining I am and all that. I use humor to make that personal connection. It's not the prepared stuff, it's in what comes spontaneously that I look for the humor in what I said, or what's going on in the room around me, things like that. I think at some point I had to tell myself, after years of reading Faulkner and Tolstoy and others, that I could be funny. Lighten up. Great literature doesn't need to be tremendously serious all the time. There's Tolstoy, but there's also Chekhov, who, though serious, had moments of brightness and humor in his work. You can bring that into literature and use it. I think the humor always needs to be in the service of the plot and the characters. You can't have a joke just for itself, just to show off that you're clever.

You learn to be funny by paying attention to humor in the world and trying to be funny yourself. You just sort of cultivate it. You work from what you appreciate, work from your strengths. If you go for a certain kind

How to Write Funny

of humor, do a lot of that. It does seem like an odd notion, doesn't it, trying to teach people to be funny?

I think you can probably teach people to be aware of humor, to see different levels, to say, "This can be serious, but it can also be funny." A lot of times in my books, when I think of minor characters or supporting characters, I'm looking for some hook that they might have and it's always humorous. It's some eccentricity that I can exploit or explore. Minor characters come in to be funny sometimes, but I always give them serious moments as well. I think if they're going to be funny, they've earned the right to have a lyrical moment or two in the book.

I guess being funny is all about making metaphors that are so surprising they cheer you up. As a reader you just marvel at them. The question is, can you teach metaphorical thinking? I'm not sure that you can teach it, but you can cultivate it, make people aware of it. You're always looking for metaphors. Fiction writers have to read everything in the world and pay attention to everything because they're looking for metaphors. Some of them are going to be funny if you can make the connection.

The creative mind makes associations. That's what it does best. I always tell people you can't be logical or analytical and write fiction, at least not in the composing process. You need to later on, but first do the unexpected, be arbitrary in your thinking, to provoke your brain into doing something unexpected. It's why people write sonnets, because they think in a different way when they have fourteen lines and five beats in a line and have to rhyme certain ways. You can say things in a sonnet that can't be said any other way because the syntax and the form make you think differently, in a way your brain is not used to. I think screenplays can do that because they're so paradigmatic.

If I were to do that in class, I would take ten or twelve words at random, write them on the board and say, "Make these into four even groups of three," and we would talk about the groups and why people group them as they do. The brain makes connections. You make leaps in your thinking if you're just completely arbitrary. Just say, these three things are going to happen in this chapter and I'm going to connect them somehow. Then your brain immediately begins to make associations—you can't even stop it. Some of these associations are funny because you've got things that are far-fetched. You have to leap toward them.

Open yourself up to the creative and the humorous. Don't be rational, logical, analytical. Look at things and try to see what else they can be. How are they connected to other things? Just make those funny connections. Part of why I write is to be surprised, to find out what my characters are going to do today. It's got to be a complete surprise to me, and I know it's not going to be the first thing I think about because everybody else would have thought the same thing. What sort of provocative element can I bring in here that will make the characters do something different?

When you are a writer, you look at the world, and you try to be susceptible to everything that's out there, knowing that a story could begin anywhere, that everything might be important, that one image by itself may not work but when you combine it with another they ignite a spark. It's like the neurons in your brain; they're not as important as the space between them. You're going to have to leap, have to fire across that chasm. You try to be provoked by the world. Sometimes you bring those provocations in. Your brain will do the job if you let it, if you don't interfere by being critical of yourself. Any idea can be stupid. It's in the execution, and it's after the fact that you know if it worked or not. You can't judge it while you're doing it. Just go with it and take chances. Lighten up. Loosen yourself up and rattle your brain. That leads to humor.

John Dufresne has worked as a cab driver, bartender, house painter, blueberry picker, draft counselor, teacher and writer. The award-winning writer has written three chapbooks, a short story collection and two novels, *Louisiana Power and Light* and *Love Warps the Mind a Little*. His new novel, *Deep in the Heart of Paradise*, will be published in 2001.

CHAPTER 26

A Cynical Idealist: Denise Duhamel

Humor has always come naturally to me, but I became aware of it in a whole new way while I was working on my collection of poems *Kinky*, a book about Barbie dolls. Using the potentially silly nature of Barbies, I was able to write political satire. I felt that when I tried to write about issues of gender and race, seriously, often I would become didactic. Barbie helped me avoid that impulse.

Nevertheless, I almost never work a joke into a poem. I would never try to force a poem to be funny if it's not meant to be. Humor, to me, is all about the unexpected, the twist. Why do we laugh when someone falls down? Not because we're delighting in their clumsiness, but because we don't anticipate what's coming.

I'm less articulate orally than I am in writing. I think of a lot of good comebacks on the way home from the party. I guess writing gives you an advantage—you get to edit and sharpen the joke. In person, I think my humor is less political and broader. The humor that goes from my brain to my hand is different from the humor that goes from my brain to my mouth. It's the same with language in general. I've kept a tape recorder by the bed to record dreams, but I just mumbled incoherently into the mouthpiece. I've had much better luck keeping a notebook by my bed. My brain sends better signals to my hand.

Because I'm a poet, I read a lot of contemporary poetry. I'd say about a third of the books I read strive to include "funny" poems. Tim Seibles writes about the politics of race and gender through characters like the Roadrunner, Bugs Bunny and Little Red Riding Hood. His poems are extremely poignant in their humor—many could be considered political satire.

Billy Collins is downright goofy, and I mean that in the best sort of way. He sees the absurdity in everyday life, which is reflected in poems like "The Willies," in which he describes what the willies are, as in having to use public bathrooms.

Nin Andrews's *The Book of Orgasms* is an underground classic. Each prose poem in the collection is about a different kind of orgasm, complete with an appendix that describes page after page of words in terms of orgasms. The book was out of print for years but has been re-released from Cleveland State University Press. Andrews takes a joke and pushes it to its limits.

I'm also influenced by Erma Bombeck (the use of the domestic in her writing) and poets Ron Koertge (his biting edge) and Bill Knott (especially the way he performs his poems). David Sedaris is wonderful because he is completely self-effacing and writes about taboo subjects, such as going to the bathroom on Thanksgiving to find someone else hasn't flushed. When *he* tries to flush, it doesn't go down and he's afraid to be blamed for it. His irreverence and his self-mockery, especially the essay about his lisp, are irresistible.

I don't think poets are obliged to use humor. Even so, I like coming across funny poems in the middle of a serious book of poetry because it lets me know the poet is not taking himself or herself too seriously. In other words, they're trying to use humor to forge an alliance with the reader.

The Role of Gender and Politics in Humorous Poetry

I remember reading *No More Masks!*, the famous women's literary anthology. I was struck to find that there were hardly any belly laughs in those hundreds of pages. Perhaps only recently do women feel distanced or detached enough from their situation to address it through humor.

Generally, I find women's humor is a lot more self-deprecating. Even when Woody Allen is down on himself, he still winds up with the pretty girl. I think most readers who appreciate women's humor are interested in women as people as opposed to glossy images in magazines or fulfilling some specific female role, such as mothering.

I'm very interested in political and social satire, although now I may be more willing to write something silly, something that's funny because of wordplay. That could be because of my recent rereading of the New York School poets. I taught a graduate literature class on the New York School poets (Kenneth Koch, James Schuyler, John Ashbery, Frank O'Hara and

Barbara Guest). In David Lehman's book *The Last Avant-Garde*, he argues that none of the New York School poets wrote political poems (as opposed to the poems by Beats.) Of course, many would say that at least O'Hara wrote about race and homosexuality. But still, their poems did not reflect their personal politics.

I found this really interesting—the humor in their poems is instead often derived from wordplay or pun or absurdity. I was drawn into their techniques, writing poems with various constraints, just to see what would happen. The methods took the pressure off to always have a "message." But, I don't think I'll ever fully let go of the political. I'm part cynic and part idealist, and I just have too much to say. I really want everything in the world to be OK, and I'm too smart/hyper/depressed to accept that some things maybe are the way they should be.

Can Humor Be Taught?

I think humor can definitely be taught, but only to those with an inclination for it in the first place. The Oulipo (Ouvroir de Littérature Potentielle/ Workshop for Potential Literature, 1960), a Paris-based writers group founded on the premise that games and formal constraints lead to artistic liberation, came up with a device called N+7. In N+7, a writer takes all the nouns in a chosen text, looks them up in the dictionary, and replaces them with the seventh noun after the original. You can also play V+7, instead replacing the verbs, or W+7 and replace random words. This method can be a wacky way to alter political speeches, recipes, or even early drafts of your own poems that seem to be going nowhere.

For me, humor can fail if it's "mean," if a poem is vengeful or sexist or defensive. Instead, using rhyme and internal rhyme can heighten a poet's chance of coming off funny. Surrealistic techniques such as exquisite corpse can also be useful. And, most important, don't be afraid to poke fun at yourself.

The weird thing about writing humor in poetry is that sometimes you don't know whether your writing is funny until you read your poem before an audience. You may read your poem and people laugh at the parts you didn't think were funny, or you pause waiting for a laugh after the line you think is hysterical and there's silence. Some audiences laugh at different lines or different poems.

The same goes for stand-up comics. I think poets should watch HBO comedy specials. I'm serious. Poets especially can learn a lot about timing, which can translate into how to break lines for the most comic effect. I was drawn to Roseanne Barr as a standup comedienne and then became a total devotee of her show. She took feminist rage to a whole new level. She was big and loud and lovable. My favorite lines of hers are (when talking about men's power mowers) "I'm not going to vacuum until they invent one I can ride" and (when a cute guy comes into her restaurant) "I'm married, but it's not like I'm a fanatic or anything!"

Denise Duhamel is the recipient of a 2001 National Endowment for the Arts Fellowship in Poetry. Her latest poetry collection is *Queen for a Day: Selected and New Poems*. She is also the author of *The Star-Spangled Banner*, which won the Crab Orchard Poetry Prize, *Exquisite Politics* (with Maureen Seaton), *Kinky* and *How the Sky Fell*. She teaches creative writing at Florida International University.

CHAPTER 27

Whistling in the Dark With Joe R. Lansdale

I recall growing up that my father wasn't what I would call a humorist, and he wasn't always cracking jokes. He was not that way at all, but he was a great storyteller and had sort of a dry, Twain way of telling a story. He wasn't setting out to be funny. He didn't say, "This is funny," but it was just the way he told the story. He could pick up on minutiae and little details that made it funny. He could just see this particular little thing that you would never think of and never realize was funny.

Strictly speaking, I don't consider myself a funny person. I know that I can be, and I know that sometimes my books are, so I think I have a sense of humor. A lot of people tend to think that I do, but there are friends of mine who are naturally much funnier, so I certainly don't think of myself as a comedian. I've done some stand-up talks that were funny, and purposely funny, but I don't think of myself as a humorist per se, although I think I use humor as one of my tools.

I guess that's the distinction—if people think their main purpose is to convey humor, then they think of themselves as humorists. In my case, I tend to see humor as just one of the tools in my toolbox.

Humor has a lot of different functions in my work. One thing it does, and this is the obvious one, is relieve tension at times when you've gotten too serious or you've gotten too dark. You can let off a little bit of steam with humor so people aren't so engulfed in this darkness that they become overwhelmed by it. On the other hand, it also works as a two-edged sword because humor, if used properly, makes darkness darker, sometimes makes things worse because you think, my God, this is a horrible thing, and yet here I am feeling the urge to laugh at it, yet all these horrible things are happening. It makes you realize that the darkness and the humor are two sides of the same coin; it's just how you turn the eye.

There was a horror movie called *The Changeling* that I think was very good. There was one scene where this wheelchair comes bounding down the stairs, and it is very frightening. If you look at it in another movie, it's hilarious—but it's the same scene. Your reaction, depending on how it strikes you at that moment, can be totally different.

Robert Bloch, who wrote *Psycho* and many other fine works, was a master of this and he was, in many ways, one of my mentors from reading him. He would take a situation that was just horrible, and he would chuckle along and be gleeful about all these horrible things. It was no wonder Alfred Hitchcock was attracted to *Psycho*. He had sort of the same kind of sense of humor.

An example of using humor to heighten horror is a short story I wrote called "Drive-In Movie" that I believe was one of the most horrifying stories I've ever written, and I've written a few things that were just unrelenting. It was about two serial killers who got dates by kidnapping and murdering and then raping the dead corpse, but it was told from the killers' perspectives and it was humorous. It was horrible, yet it was humorous because these two people are so unaware of their own evil, so unaware of their own horror, because no one, or very few, people generally think of themselves as evil people. To me, using the humor made it far more horrible. It might have been more disgusting, more upsetting, to some people, which is exactly what I wanted. I wanted you to look at these people with a clear eye, knowing these are the same kind of guys who go home, put a pizza in the oven, have a beer, watch television, maybe have a dog they like, yet there is something slightly askew about them. They're not playing with a full deck, their cheese has slid off the cracker, so to speak. In many ways, you would never notice it. If you saw them at the supermarket or you were sitting around talking with them, you would never know.

The humor I use in this story helps heighten the horror. It gives you a window into the way the killers thought because they didn't see this as humorous at all, though it was humorous to the reader to see it from the outside. Because it's humorous, it's all the worse. You think, my God, I shouldn't be laughing at this; I shouldn't feel this kind of sensation.

We laugh at horrifying things to relieve tension. You go to a good horror movie, maybe one that's not even intentionally funny, and the horror gets so high that most people are kind of laughing. It's a way of inoculating yourself slowly against the inevitable. It's like when you tickle babies. There are these little places on the sides of babies, when you tickle them they giggle, but there are also little nerve centers there so the babies really don't know if it's friend or foe. They don't know what to do but giggle.

Early Influences

Where I grew up in east Texas, people used metaphors and similes a lot to express themselves. This is one you probably can't use in your book, but I'll give to you anyway: "I wouldn't take her to a dogfight if she were the defending champion." To me, that remark is humorous, but if you look behind it, think how mean and cruel that is. A lot of the humor was like that. It wasn't always meant to be cruel—don't misunderstand me—sometimes it was just meant to be a remark, but that kind of background and that kind of humor affected me.

My parents were older when I was born. My mother was forty, and she was a big fan of Will Rogers. She talked to me a lot about Will Rogers, and when I would see old things about him on TV I would pay attention to them. I loved his way of delivery. That kind of humor was always there for me. It was always a more earthy sort of humor. I was much more excited or interested in that than I was in, say, a Monty Python type of humor, which I also can appreciate; it's just a different way that didn't affect me as a writer.

It was particular things, like my father's storytelling and where I grew up, the way people expressed themselves, as well as the works of several writers. I grew up reading a lot of Mark Twain and Flannery O'Connor. Flannery O'Connor to me had the finest, driest sense of humor of any writer.

I think a lot of the hard-boiled writers that came out of the black-mass school of storytelling had that kind of dry, almost mean-spirited humor. I think that came out of the aftermath of World War II; these people came back from the war and they weren't laughing as hard, say, at some of the stuff they laughed at before, the real polite comedies. These guys had seen the most horrible things in the world, so the way their humor developed was different. That affected the way popular fiction and films were perceived, and therefore, the audience was influenced by that, too, in the same sense that the audience influences the material.

Dan Jenkins influenced me a little bit, especially his *Semi-Tough* and *Fairways and Greens*. Those books struck me as very funny because they struck me like people I knew. Therefore they had more impact on me. So did Raymond Chandler because he had a funny eye and the way he told things, primarily dialogue, was very humorous, as was the way he describes things; for example, "as inconspicuous as a tarantula on a slice of angel food cake." Neil Barrett is another example of a great writer of tremendous humor who writes crime novels and all sorts of things. People are not as aware of his works as they ought to be, but he's one of the funniest writers I've ever read.

When you're younger, I think you're drawn to a more mean-spirited sense of humor because you feel invincible, and you really don't feel like you're hurting anybody. I think as you get older, you begin to get a little more cautious about what you're going to say and how you're going to say it. That doesn't mean you should be reluctant to say what needs to be said, but you're no longer interested in just the humor itself. You want to say something funny because it has some impact and has some echo that makes the book seem stronger.

When people think of my work, they usually mention the fact that a lot of the stuff is funny or the dialogue is humorous, so there is no doubt that when people say they like my work because it's unique, if you press them on that, it's generally the humor they're talking about. I've always had pretty much the same kind of sense of humor. I think the difference is that I can better express it now through my writing than I could when I first started. It was always there, but I couldn't express it as well.

Sometimes people will say I talk about stuff nobody else talks about, but a lot of times I'm talking about stuff nobody else will talk about and it's funny when I do it. Sometimes if you talk about these things, it's just being rude. It's like saying I'm an honest person, to use that as a way of insulting somebody. You've got to do it in such a way that it develops logically out of the characters, out of the book.

All writers who are any good eventually cut themselves out of the pack by finding whatever it is that's their own particular personality or their own particular take on things. Of course, the problem is a lot of people cut themselves out of the pack and nobody's interested. You've got to hope that when you cut yourself out of the pack, that you're kind of a nice-looking wolf or that you're an interesting-looking dog, and don't cut yourself out of the pack because you're a runt.

Learning the Craft

I work in the mornings for three or four hours a day, depending on whatever story I'm writing. Humor is so much an integral part of who I am that I don't know that I stop and say, "Now I need to be humorous," or check to see if I have enough humor in the piece. I don't ever look at it like that. Humor really grows out of the characters and, of course, the characters must grow out of my own nature, my own attitudes, my own feelings about things. So I don't know that they are consciously ever set down to be humorous. It just comes out like that.

You can watch a TV sitcom as a series of one-liners and jokes that individually might be kind of humorous, but you can see the entire thing was written around the jokes. In other words, there's no core. But when you see something that's really good, for instance the old *Dick Van Dyke Show* or *Barney Miller* or *Taxi*, you actually saw something else going on there. There were interesting characters in these shows, and they had not necessarily an original story, but primarily interesting characters; the humor came out of them. Instead of just being a series of one-liners that anybody could have cracked wise about, what made it funny was who said it, because you knew who they were. That's why when books work and they are humorous, it's because you have conveyed to the reader who these people are, how they think, what their expectations are and how they can go wrong.

Charles Portis does this very well. If you read his *Norwood*, you have the example of the guy who never knows that any of what's going on is funny. It's hysterical. Those are usually the best books because the characters don't know it's funny.

Freezer Burn is a good example; I couldn't have written it straight. The fact is, people do rob firecracker stands, which is such a dumb crime. In other words, no matter how you tell that aspect of the story, it's humorous because it is such a stupid crime. It's hard not to look at the fact that some guy has his mother dead in the bedroom in plastic bags covered with Brut cologne as funny, but it's horrible. Horrible. You read something like that in the paper and you start chuckling a little bit, thinking God, how weird. You're not necessarily chuckling at the horrors of this poor person's life but the fact that anybody would go to this extreme. I don't think I could have told that story any other way.

I find that, if you can create the characters and the universe well enough, people understand it well enough that they will laugh. Now there are a lot of things that I really believe readers up North or wherever probably don't get. Sometimes I cut back on things I feel are perhaps too colloquial. Occasionally my editor will say that he didn't understand this, and if the editor doesn't understand it, then it probably ought to go because he's in another part of the country and doesn't get it.

Generally, I don't worry about that; I try to find a way of telling the story that pleases me and when I write, I try to write like everybody I know is dead. If I start trying to figure out what Old Joe Blow is going to think, or what the Yankees are going to think, or what the people out in California are going to think, or the good old boys in Texas are going to think, or what the people in Mexico are going to think or what my aunt's going to think, then I'm messed up because I'm trying to anticipate all of their different ways of thinking.

I have friends all over the country, but I don't consult them because I feel like if I do that, I'm no longer writing for me, I'm writing for them. If "them" was singular, that might be a worthwhile thing to do because I would love my books to sell out, but I'll always be me, no matter what I do. I think since it's impossible to choose what all these people want, you have no other alternative than to write for yourself.

I've never had anyone say to me, "That really wasn't very funny," but I have had people say to me, "That was offensive." That's another reason why you have to put all that on the back burner, and write it like everybody you know is dead. That's the only way you can do it.

I don't put any restraints on my humor if I feel it is something that will work within the context of what I'm trying to do. I don't necessarily say I have got to find a way to make this terrible scene humorous. It just sort of develops, but I never stop and think, I need to pull back here. I feel that at some point when you've done that, and you've done it to make a point, or you've done it to try and embrace the mysteries of life—why people like this exist or why they do those things—if you continue to embrace it, just to be humorous, just to be horrible, just to see who's the most disgusting, then it's sort of like a child's game. It's like going down there to hang out with the devil; you throw a steak on the grill, drink a Coke and talk about child molestation and all the horrible things in the world. It becomes too easy. It's like having a character that every time you don't know what to do with him, you have him take a puff of a cigarette or something. It becomes just a device, a mannerism, so you have to be very careful about that kind of thing.

I'm sure there are people out there who say humor can be taught. I guess you can learn it in the lowest common denominator sense. If a man goes to a Lions Club dinner and he's supposed to give a speech, and he gets four jokes that he heard and puts them in the speech, you could say OK, he's using humor. He's learned to use humor in his particular speech, but it doesn't mean he's funny. You could say he can memorize that kind of humor, but it's not the same thing as creating spontaneous humor that comes out of who you are.

If writers are observers of the human scene, then they know what's funny to them. That's the key. Instead of trying to figure out what's funny to others, know what's funny to yourself. If you know what's funny to you, then you can transfer that to others.

Whether you like it or not, or whether writers admit it or not, you're every character in the book. You're the bad guy, you're the female, you're the male, you're the dog that barks in the night because you created all of this. Even if you've seen it through, or were influenced by, some other character, it's still a character who comes through your viewpoint. Another person might know that same person you chose to base your character on and not see him that way at all. That's another way of knowing yourself, knowing what makes you laugh and finding a way to transfer it through your characters.

It almost sounds like one of those pop psychology "know thyself's," but that's exactly what writers are doing when they try to write. They're trying to know themselves. It's that ability, or the desire to try and find out at the core who you are, why you are like you are and why you relate to other people like you do. That's why you write. I don't care if you're writing a crime novel, a so-called serious novel or a western—when you're doing it well and when you're doing it with a heartfelt notion, that's what you're doing.

I don't think you can teach a person who doesn't have a sense of humor to have one. I don't think you can teach somebody particularly how to be humorous in the broader sense, but I think all writers can learn to use humor to at least some degree. That's not the same thing as being a humorist or being a basically humorous person. If you read my work, I think you feel there is a sense of humor at work there.

There are a lot of writers who aren't very funny but once in a while they at least make an attempt to be funny. If the readers are going along with them and they have all their ducks in a row, it's sort of like a well-balanced meal; you know, they need a little taters on the side there and so they put a little humor in. Everybody thinks they're funny, everybody thinks they know humor, but some people just aren't that damn funny. They can learn to interject, at least on some level, humor into the work to give the relief from tension and the other things we talked about, but I just don't think you can teach somebody to use humor in a masterful manner to really make an impact on the story.

Maybe you can't teach it, but maybe humor can be awakened. It may not be that you go to a class to learn it, but if you read enough or if it's a funny film or whatever, you may suddenly find that you have a greater reservoir for humor than you ever realized.

Joe R. Lansdale is the award-winning author of over a dozen novels, including *The Two Bear Mambo*, *Freezer Burn* and *Bad Chili*, as well as several short story collections. His latest novel, *The Bottoms*, won an Edgar for Best Novel.

CHAPTER 28

A Balancing Act in the Spotlight: Michael J. Rosen

My father has always been a repository of jokes. He remembers every joke. We would come to the table as kids, all excited to tell a new joke, and my father would know several variations on it. We almost never brought a new joke to him. A lot of his pleasure in joke telling participated in the tradition of Jewish humor. My father was great with accents, and this impressed us kids—it still does—when he managed to alternate, say, the voice of an elderly immigrant woman with the sound of a gentleman from India. His timing was perfect: never rushing, always allowing the right amount of buildup. There was such humor in his tone, too, and I think my ear must have been calibrated with that level of animation, that arena at the kitchen table where joke telling was an important thing to share.

I often think humor is one of the ways we have of recovering experience that evaded us somehow, or whose meaning eluded us. With humor's retelling or refiguring, we have a chance to go back to some episode or perception and see what it might have meant to us, cutting through the platitudes or apparent truths that the consensus of sentimentality typically inserts. Too much of what we do comes with facile, inherited, standardized responses. "This is what happened, so this is how you should feel." That's sentimentality: one emotion standing in place of a complex of emotions that more likely accompany the experience. And too often, we're more than content with the convenience that offers: It's "said and done," and on to the next item of business. But I think we're in dire need of further thought. Writing does that. Humor provides that chance to resist pat answers in favor of more genuine, personal responses. W.H. Auden used to define poetry as clear thinking about mixed feelings. I continue to feel that humor is allied with that same impulse.

What's key in all writing, and particularly humor, is that the writer wants to have the reader involved. Participation is necessary for empathy. And readers or viewers are more willing to laugh with the author than they are to weep with him—at least at first, which is why in movies where the screenwriter wants you to weep, the characters usually have a comedic side that's expressed earlier in the film. By laughing at a hero's escapades and personality, the audience has lowered its resistance and become susceptible to those overwhelming, universal topics that we're all familiar with: We're born, we die, we find love, we're frustrated, etc. In other words, we live one life, and we dream of another. Which can be unbearable or bearable. But humor is a salvation: It's one thing that makes up that difference.

There isn't one motive for humor, just as there isn't one motive for any action or desire. And we live in a culture that sentimentalizes everything, believing that if someone dies, you only feel one thing, and that's why you need this greeting card. Humor provides a way to let in another emotion, mitigating sentimentality. It really acknowledges the reader as an intelligent, empathic person by engaging his or her own understanding in the context of connections and inventions that the writer has brought to the page.

When I began to do my own writing, one great task was simply verbal fluency: acquisition of language, vocabulary, using words to reduce ideas into their components so that I could think about them clearly. I think a lot of people fail at writing humor because they're content to have a humorous idea and merely execute it in words. I feel that humor is more about the creation of an idea that is discovered through writing. Humor is "the mother and not the handmaid of your idea," to paraphrase Karl Kraus alluding to poetry. It isn't just, "Here's a funny concept, and now I will implement it," the way you might make ice cubes in a tray. It's more like making ice sculpture.

Humor as Sport, Act, Art

Of the many fundamental pitfalls in writing humor, two seem to be popular. One is just showing off with humor. A ranting pitch or a merciless parade of obscurity and verbal chicanery or choosing a subject that's so unfamiliar to the audience that the writer ends up spiking that ball of words onto your side, and that's that. The other players, the readers, aren't even able to return the ball (again, inviting the reader to participate, to bring his or her own experience to the table). It's peremptory, it's selfish, and all too often it's not nearly as smart as the writer imagines it to be.

The converse of this problem is performing humor with so little authority, confidence and freshness that the writing is like an interminable game, one where the reader knows exactly where the ball is going to land and, after a while, doesn't even bother trying hard to keep it in motion. The writer lulls the reader through the piece of humor as though it were kindergarten ("OK, everyone line up over here; everyone wash your hands . . ."). The majority of the pieces that I turn away for *Mirth of a Nation* are not poorly written or lacking humor in some way, but ultimately they're too predictable, and the author runs out of the inventiveness necessary to keep the game exciting, with the ball continually in play.

I often read submissions or whole books from fine writers whose primary resource for humor is one or another occurrence: "A funny thing happened to me, and let me tell you about it." Some of this can be funny, but so much anecdotal experience doesn't work on the page. A writer needs to recognize that the humor of an event is not the humor of the page without a whole other mastery of communication. "You had to be there," is true too often. Maybe there can be a written equivalent for the immediacy of being there, but there probably will need to be other elements involved because the verifiable fact that something really happened isn't sufficient to sustain a narrative. A writer has to be willing to stray from the strict truth in order to make the humor and the story work. The speaker's voice and tone and timing are lost. To recapture the humor on paper can require a cold and clear perspective that's painstaking and burdened—seemingly the antithesis of the joyful recounting of the story to a friend in person. The humor that we experience at parties or in conversations is spontaneous and contagious and volatile. But that rarely represents the method of composition a writer uses working at the sentences hour after discouraging hour, getting the humor down. As my colleague Henry Alford says, "It would all be so much easier if only the page would laugh."

Writing humor is a high-wire act. It's a bravura, the solo when the principal dancer comes center stage for the forty-five seconds of grand leaps and spins while the corps de ballet retreats to the wings. When you do humor, people are saying, "Oh, would you look at that! Wait, that wasn't as high as it should have been." Humorists must recognize that the audience is paying especial attention because the page has come forward and announced something funny is about to happen. So the stakes are higher. The vocabulary must be flawless. Any sloppiness will be immediately apparent. The writing must be finessed, and this requires practice that's as rigorous as that of principal dancers in the ballet. All right, not quite as rigorous, but still. For instance, humorists should read their work out loud. That offers a chance for the ear to be the audience. It can listen as though it were a different person. Is the pacing off, is the description too long, is something not working according to plan?

Humor on the Rebound

A few developments have really enabled humor to thrive in a way that it hasn't before. If you look at general magazines from thirty years ago, every one printed humor. That's hardly true now, but the Internet has begun to fill that gap. The Web has brought with it a new rush of humor, from online magazines, chat rooms, posted and circulated joke lists, and individuals who simply post their own columns. The fact that most material there arrives "self-published," without any editor to select it or revise it has given us a real jungle of new material, some of it thrillingly wild and some of it that ought to be tamed. But just as small presses in the sixties created a healthy culture for poetry and fiction, I think the Internet's publishing, since it can come without cost, warehouse demands or distribution problems, can be a great archive and showcase.

There has also been a lot more writing for television: for the late-night shows and talk shows, even for television cartoons for kids, that engage writers who otherwise wouldn't have found any livelihood in writing. Humor writing, other than stand-up, is not what you would call a profitable enterprise. There are very few best-selling books of humor. There are very few people who can write a 750-word or 2,000-word piece and make any kind of living by doing this once a month. And how many of these pieces could you possibly do each month and remain at the top of your form? That's partly why the field is filled primarily with well-educated white men. It's not a dabbler's field, exactly, but if a would-be writer feels any financial pressure to succeed, humor writing certainly won't seem like a realistic career choice.

There's a terrific vitality in contemporary humor right now that comes from having many sources and many voices. The sort of forms James Thurber and his *New Yorker* colleagues used are still popular. People such as Sandra Tsing Loh and David Sedaris are recounting their own family's foibles and fiascos with a tremendous selection of droll and dead-on details. There's real energy in adapting one form of discourse, say, nursery rhymes or the Zagat's rating system and then applying to some totally different subject, such as American presidents or stock analysis. I happen to love the sort of participatory journalism of Henry Alford, when, ill-prepared and intentionally unsuited, he tries out various occupations and experience just for a laugh. And there's no shortage of idioms and idiocies in our language and culture these days, which always can be a source of humor.

But political humor has become harder, so I hear from many colleagues. The political culture we're in just now is so overripe and ludicrous that invented humor can't keep up with it, can't take it to task with yet more humor. How can you top the facts of recent politics? How can you riff on something that the media have already mocked and mimicked into a numb state? So if a humorist had thought to push an idea into the realms of absurdity, in hopes of drawing out the humor, in hopes of awakening all of us to the apparent dangers, well, too late: The politicians have, as if on a soap opera, already taken things too far.

Michael J. Rosen is editor of the biennial *Mirth of a Nation: The Best Contemporary Humor* and a syndicated column of the same name that appears in many of the nation's alternative newspapers. He works as adviser to The Thurber House (www.thurberhouse.org), where he served for nearly twenty years as literary director. Rosen's own work includes three volumes of poetry, two dozen children's books and several compendiums of essays, stories, photographs and illustrations that benefit Share Our Strength's fight against hunger and The Company of Animals Fund's humane efforts.

CHAPTER 29

Talking Story With Lois-Ann Yamanaka

Where my humor comes from is kind of embedded in the dialect. It's embedded in the voice of the place, this Hawaiian-Creole-English dialect. I was watching this Latino comic on TV. He did a scene on the Martin Short show and he was coming at it like, how you know when you greet somebody; if you're white, it's like, "Hi, Bobby, how are you?" and you're kind of waving, right? The comic said in his family they all go, "Oh man, he coming over!" That's us too, you know, like we see somebody approaching a party; everybody that's sitting there is thinking about how we going to cut him down. It's not meant in any kind of malice, but it's kind of embedded in the culture, yeah?

There is a kind of way that we—I hate this term, you know, "people of color"—poke fun at ourselves and a way that we poke fun at mainstream culture. We all have other terms for somebody white. There is a whole kind of subculture. I don't know how it makes us different, but every place is unique. For us especially, because we come from a postcolonial kind of history, we have all these ethnic groups here that have been forced into this kind of cohabitation in a very small place as a way to get along. There are a lot of old stereotypes that now we can make fun of but are still real painful to certain groups.

A lot of our humor is ethnic humor, but people are getting very offended in this politically correct time, now that we're in the third or fourth generation past the plantation. My own humor is really like a dark kind of funny; it's very dark and it's not something that people will fall over on their sides laughing about because it's so embedded in the way that we address each other here, yeah? We are in a very small place with many different ethnic groups. Because we're into this native Hawaiian sovereignty movement here, they are very politically sensitive for anybody else that is not native to say things like "I'm Japanese-Hawaiian." I'm not Hawaiian by blood quantum. I'm a Japanese-American from Hawaii.

Because we come from such an oral kind of culture, there is a lot of what we call "talk story," and a lot of my stories are embedded in "talk story" where the old farts sit around outside. It's called *pau hana* time, you know, like at the end of the day, like Miller Time. The liquor comes out and the food and the old farts sitting around every day and you are privy to that; so many of the stories are there.

The story ideas come from everyday life. People are so funny. The events are unbelievable, you know, daily. I keep a real steady journal of the types of activities going on. Not the kind you sometimes see, especially with young writers who write things in their journal like, "I went to the grocery store and I bought Spam." That's not what I do. Something will catch me and then I will want to put it into a character's life. I know what books I'm writing, yeah? Many, many books at one time, so I know what characters I want to deal with. If I see something that will make me stop and focus on it for a while internally, in my internal life, I know it belongs somewhere in one of those lives. For example, I live in this real kind of ghetto place. I mean they don't come up here and clean the roadkill off the road, so there are all of these dead cats every morning. Somebody's cat is going to be roadkill. So I had to think now, why is this bugging me—something as small as roadkill? That kind of makes me branch outward to all the different kinds of roadkill that I've been fascinated by.

Some people have misunderstood my humor, but inevitably, you get that about all kinds of things, you know? From your narrative structure to some of the terms of dialect. All kinds of people won't get it, but a hell of a lot of people will get it. I think we assume, or I assume, that our readers are smart and I don't have to do that kind of direct definition of terms or like show you that "brown sticky substance"—you know what I mean. You don't need to do that because your readers are smart enough. They've read Zora Neale Hurston, they've read Alice Walker. They've read Toni Morrison and they've all done work in voice. They've read Mark Twain. At some point you have to assume that. You cannot be afraid of that.

Giving Voice to Your Characters

I think you must stick to the voice that's telling the story. Whatever that voice might say, whatever that character might say, is something you want to be true to. A lot of times, writers censor themselves in the writing process because a lot of things that people say, or characters say, are politically incorrect and very unpalatable. But if you stay true to the people, to the characters, they say some amazing things that are not politically correct but are extremely truthful and extremely funny in a dark way.

Especially old people. Old people characters say some very raunchy things. But if you start censoring yourself because you're sitting there at the computer thinking, oh, this critic is going to get me, or my friend at my writing group will be offended, you have defeated yourself.

I started writing when I was much older; I was twenty-seven years old. By that time I told myself three things: I was not going to censor myself anymore, I wasn't going to let others censor me, and that plays a real big part in how you're going to render something on paper, yeah? And the third thing is kind of funny, it has nothing to do with that. My third thing was giving back the gift that was so generously given to me; I do a lot of community things.

I think the more specific you are about your experience, the more it seems to resonate in other people as far away from your life experiences as you can imagine. This is something that young writers don't get. They think the more general you are, the more you will be able to reach other audiences. I don't mean more specific realistically, but more in terms of details. I read a lot of things by student writers, and they will say things that are very generic, like "I had a soda with a cigarette." I would say, "I was sitting outside the store smoking Benson & Hedges Ultra Lights, which are the most expensive kinds of cigarettes and I like to buy them in those two-pack kind of deals, drinking a Diet Pepsi and burping because . . . ," you know what I mean? The more specific you are, the more people understand what it is like to have to spend five bucks for a pack of cigarettes.

I think to write funny, it has to be accompanied by a hell of a lot of pain. Comedians and stand-up comics say that all the time, and the best of them are those that are riddled with neuroses, yeah? When you write, you finally take control of something that you may have not been able to control before, so you can make it worse, you can cry or you can make it entirely slapstick. You can turn it into something that makes you laugh when it didn't make you laugh then—my religious upbringing, for example. When you look at it differently, something that made you cry for weeks is something that can be rendered in a totally different way, and in that way you take control of something that hurt you.

The funniest people are those who are brutally honest with themselves and their experiences and are able to laugh about them. We are not laughing at them, we're laughing with them because their pain is universal, it's what we all experience, no matter where we experience it. It's that kind of brutality. You don't know whether to laugh or cry at the same time.

Learning to laugh at yourself is hard. Sometimes it's just too embarrassing or painful to admit that you did *that*. But that's also when you're ready to tell the story.

I taught at the college level, and what I found young people doing is, they tread around the story with different characters, different points of view, but it's the same story because they are so afraid of looking at it in the face. I told one student—because I finally got so fed up reading drafts of the same story—that there's a story that you were born to tell. Some of us are born to tell several stories, but this is the story that *you* were born to tell. It involved a lot of pain and honesty about it, you know what I mean? But she refused to get down into her *ki*. She just keeps it right at her throat so she can tell the story.

Some people never get ready, like that student who treads around the same subject. They might never be ready to tell their story.

Jumping Off the Cliff

A really important thing I never understood as a young writer was that, in order to write, you have to read randomly, but also read to inform the text that you are participating in. You read because somebody has to teach you about poetry, because somebody has to teach you about line and breadth, and because somebody has to teach you about creating nonfiction and fiction. Research is a part of writing and not just a small part. If I'm going to do stream of consciousness or a lot of interior dialogue, I want to read somebody who's done it well. That's where my mentor has been extraordinary, because I just tell her what I am trying to do now and she'll take me to the local bookstore, she'll pull books off the shelf and say, read this, read this, read this.

So, which writers influence me depends on what book I'm writing. For *Heads by Harry*, it was such a wide range of people—writers like Jerzy Kosinski, Jayne Anne Phillips, people who did work in voice, first-person voice. It's important to get their kind of sensibility into your body in order to produce your own work. Alice Walker, Sandra Cisneros, of course, Toni Morrison, Faulkner are others with that kind of voice.

There's a whole kind of information that comes from other writers. I read a lot of poets because poetry is like right there, yeah? It's kind of right in front of you, so you're either going to take it or put the book away.

I also like somebody who will crack me up. Fanny Flagg cracks me up, but I like to be a little more literary. I think with the other writers I mentioned, the humor is embedded in a lot of pain. It's nothing that is going to make you laugh out loud. It's something that makes you feel someplace deeper than that because it's a kind of dark humor, yeah?

Humor is something that comes with where you place the story, who you place in the story, what they do. In the case of *Heads by Harry*, the characters were outside the shop, there was that talk story, there was the brother who was just such a fantastic character for me, and his sister, who is also very flamboyant. They all held their own potential for humor as did the situation with the two brothers, and the white boy who she falls in love with, and all the kinds of comments she's going to receive for making that choice. I think it's just a matter of where you place the story and who's in the story. The humor just comes. You can try to write funny but it doesn't happen; it's immersed in the truth of that character.

A writer can lighten up his work by reading the whole manuscript and feeling the texture of the entire thing. There are points where the mood or the tone can be lifted, and it's in certain moments that are very tragic. It's looking at the whole and then deciding about the feel, the movement, of the text. But you cannot teach that to somebody, how to be intuitive about certain places where the whole will flow.

Finding a really good teacher helps, too. I was really blessed with them; I know they're not of this world, they're angels. After Seinfeld made that stupid episode about the girl who was always searching for a mentor, I'm ashamed to talk about that. One person I studied under was Molly Giles, and her humor is so sharp and wicked. She has several selections of short stories and she also worked with Amy Tan. She's very funny and not in a dry way, but sharp.

Maybe how humor can be taught—but you cannot even teach people to do this, because that's why everybody goes into therapy—is to access your pain and be able to stare it in the face. You have to go to a really dark place to find your pain. My friend calls it flirting with darkness, all the time, because it's like standing at the edge of a cliff. Having to go there and being able to stand there and then jump off the cliff is where you're going to find something. I don't want to say funny, because pain isn't funny, but at some point other people can relate to it. That's that jumping-off point. You just have to constantly do it.

Lois-Ann Yamanaka is the author of the award-winning poetry collection, *Saturday Night at the Pahala Theatre.* She has written a trilogy about coming-of-age in Hawaii, the final novel being *Heads by Harry.* A recipient of the Lannan Literary Award, she resides in Honolulu, Hawaii, where she also works with at-risk students and is a Distinguished Visiting Writer at the University of Hawaii.

CONCLUSION:
THE LAST LAUGH

The nice thing about being the editor of this book is that I get to speak first, to introduce the book to you, and to sum it up. But I don't think it's necessary for me to summarize the entire book for you. If you've read this far—avid reader that I know you are—you don't need that kind of gloss. Instead, I'd rather concentrate on the author interviews in the book and see if I can transform their words of wisdom into practical advice for you, maybe even give you some writing exercises to help you put their ideas into practice.

As I read over the interviews I conducted, I began to notice commonalities among them, not only in technique, but in what influences they thought helped shape their work, especially in regard to humor. As disparate as these writers were ethnically, chronologically and geographically, they were all united in their masterful use of humor in their writing. They proved that effective humor is ageless, color-blind and without boundaries.

Here are six items that our featured writers said contributed to their successful use of humor:

1. An imaginative and unconventional world vision.
2. Exaggerated or unlikely comparisons (metaphors and similes).
3. The notebook/journal habit.
4. Storytelling.
5. The influence of other writers.
6. The influence of movies and television.

Let's take a look at each one separately.

World Vision

As much as any visual artist, a writer sees the world differently from other people—and that has nothing to do with whether the writer wears glasses. A writer's world vision is internal. It is formed by what he knows of the world empirically, through his senses, and it is tempered by his own unique imagination. It is this imagination, the questioning of why things are the way they are and why they can't be something entirely different, that deepens the writer's vision of the world.

John Dufresne spoke of this world vision in his interview when he challenged us not to take a thing at face value but to always ask, "What else could it be?" This? Yes, but *that* also? Think of those mind-teaser puzzles we've all seen; is that a wine glass we see or two people about to kiss? Think of M.C. Escher's artwork for an actual representation of things changing before your eyes.

So, to develop an imaginative vision as a writer, mistrust what you experience as being *all* there is. Go deeper. What else is there? Peel that experience apart, one layer at a time, like an onion, and use Flannery O'Connor's anagogical vision to help you discover the multitude of meanings wrapped up in that one thing.

Then go have a drink, because this is hard work.

OK, here are some exercises you can try to help you develop a more imaginative vision:

1. Cut out interesting photos from a newspaper or magazine, but omit the captions (don't even read them if you can help it). Mix them up, then draw one out at random. Study the picture and write three entirely different scenarios that explain—no matter how ridiculously—what is going on in the photo. See beyond the image. Stretch your imagination. Note: This exercise can also be done using museum artwork as your writing prompts, although you probably won't be allowed to mix up the pictures.

2. Imagine that you are Superwriter and that your five senses are all developed to a superhuman degree. Write about what a typical day would be like for you with these supersensitive faculties. How would the world around you be different?

Unlikely Comparisons

Writing the perfect exaggerated or unlikely comparison is as easy as shaving a gorilla with a putty knife. It's like swimming in Jell-O. Yet, such comparisons are the building blocks of humor. Without them, your writing will be as funny as screen doors in a Russian nuclear submarine.

In their interviews, Lee K. Abbott, Roy Blount Jr., John Dufresne and Joe R. Lansdale all stressed the technique of adding humor to their writing by using unlikely or exaggerated metaphors and similes. These writers are masters of the English language and know exactly the right words to use in their metaphors and similes, to make them both funny and dead-on accurate. That is no easy feat. As Mark Twain said, "The difference between the right word and the almost right word is the difference between lightning and the lightning bug."

How do you write humorous comparisons? The first step, of course, is to employ the imagination, the world vision we noted earlier. What else could the situation or experience be? How can we think of it in an unusual, unorthodox way?

The second thing is to find exactly the right words that will bring your comparison to life, that will be highly visual, quirky, funny and accurate.

Let's examine the first simile—"as easy as shaving a gorilla with a putty knife"—to see why it works.

To demonstrate how difficult it was to write an unlikely comparison, I chose to increase the simile's being "unlikely" by contradicting my premise. I chose to show how difficult writing that simile would be by writing that it was *easy* but, after reading the complete simile, the reader understands the tongue-in-cheek contradiction.

The comparison works because it takes a familiar act, shaving, and sets it in a bizarre context. Who would shave a gorilla? Why? Further, by substituting a dull putty knife for a razor, the incongruity, the unlikelihood of the comparison is heightened.

Why did I decide to shave a gorilla over a rabbit, say, or a peach? How did I choose a putty knife over scissors, a machete? This is where word choice comes in. Once I imagined the situation I wanted to compare, I made word lists and mixed and matched until I found what I thought was the right combination. For example, a list of "things that can be shaved" could have included beards, heads, legs, apes, rabbits (and other furry/hairy critters), peaches, wood, points, etc. A similar list for "things that cut" would also have revealed several choices. How those images are mixed and matched is a personal judgment call. It is this mental "leap," as John Dufresne calls it—our own personal mixing and matching—that results in our coming up with funny comparisons.

When writing such comparisons, however, we need to be careful of

How to Write Funny

cliches. I used the screen door and submarine simile as an example of just such a cliche. I first heard the "screen door in a sub" simile when I was a kid—I'm sure you did, too—and it's still around, but now as a cliche. Even adding some new information—"Russian nuclear"—while making the simile more timely, does not rescue it, nor does it become less of a cliche. Strive for freshness, for originality, in your comparisons.

Unlikely comparisons can blossom into full-blown parodies with only a little tweaking. Tom Bodett suggested replacing a key noun in a newspaper headline with something ridiculous—"Truck Rollover on Interstate 5" becomes "Cow Rollover on Interstate 5"—and then proceeding to write the news story with the replacement noun. Parodies are an easy way to hone your humor-writing skills, since the basic structure (a newspaper article, a radio show, TV news) is already established. All you have to do is use your imagination to make it funny.

Try these exercises:

1. Describe yourself entirely in metaphor and simile. Remember Lee K. Abbott's "He looked like a toolbox," and try to think in such outlandish terms. Don't censor yourself. Nothing in this exercise should be considered ridiculous. Just go for it.

2. Read one of your favorite writers (they don't necessarily have to be funny), and pick out the metaphors and similes in his or her work. Ask yourself why they work. Then, revise each of them to make them unlikely and humorous. Use word lists, as previously, to help you.

Notebooks and Journals

It is not unusual for writers to keep notebooks or journals filled with their observations, musings and bits of information that appeal to their individual interests for whatever reasons. Andrei Codrescu referred to his notebook as the creative "mulch" that feeds some of his longer pieces; John Dufresne would never leave home without his notebook.

There are no rules when it comes to keeping journals or notebooks. Some writers admit to daily entries in their journals, while others find themselves jotting things down only when they are struck by something they find interesting. It could be a snippet of conversation overheard on a bus, a description of the Sonoran Desert while thumbing rides through

Arizona, a list of funny-sounding street names, a few remarks about a political column in the newspaper—anything is grist for the writer's mill. Sometimes, a writer will embellish her notebook with sketches, clipped newspaper articles, a purloined menu from a Chinese restaurant, any material that may help trip her memory at some future date.

Just like a pack rat, writers tend to stuff all these things into their notebooks, not quite sure how they will ever be used or when. Probably, most of this minutiae will never end up in any written piece but, every so often, writers find something beautiful and shiny among the rest, and it finds its way into their writing. Even the notes that may not be used can influence writers in subliminal levels. The very fact that they found the information interesting enough to be recorded in the first place means that their minds are thinking along those lines. The recording and reviewing of such notes is a continual mental prompt that gets those gray-matter neurons fired up. It may be that one specific notebook entry may never enter the writer's work, but how can we ever be sure that it didn't inspire some other line of thought that did eventually figure in the work? A writer's mind must always be open and receptive to any possibilities.

Akin to journal- and notebook-keeping, yet separate from it in some ways, is an idea file. The difference between the two is a matter of intention. Journals and notebooks are designed to capture the random musings of writers and the unexpected observations and experiences of their everyday lives. The idea file, on the other hand, is deliberately set up to gather information on a particular subject. For example, a travel writer may have an idea file—an actual manila file folder—labeled "Bali." Into that file the writer would put newspaper and magazine articles about Bali, travel brochures, Internet postings, postcards and photos, book reviews and book titles about Bali, etc. This is a deliberate intent by the writer to accumulate raw information about a particular subject that he can then sift through for specific writing ideas.

No one system is better than the other, nor does the usage of one preclude using the other. Further, there is nothing wrong with jotting down an idea on a cocktail napkin or the back of an envelope. Whatever works for you is the best system.

If you are not currently keeping a journal or idea file, now would be a good time to give them a try. Try this:

1. For the next three weeks, try keeping a journal and entering something into it every day. Don't be intimidated by the blank page. One way to get started is by doing what is called a "free write." For five minutes write down whatever comes into your mind. Keep your hand always moving. Do not stop. Don't worry if you are not writing complete sentences or if your writing does not make sense. The important thing here is to try and develop the habit of journal-keeping. With practice, your jottings will become more coherent.

2. Start an idea file. May I suggest "political humor" as your subject? Enter anything you read or hear that tickles your funny bone. After three weeks of collecting material, review the file and see if you can write a humorous political piece.

Storytelling

What is a writer if not a storyteller? Several of the interviewed writers had fond recollections of listening to family and friends relate stories and remembered how their own writing was influenced by those stories. Andrei Codrescu, John Dufresne and Lois-Ann Yamanaka all recalled listening to extended families and friends swapping stories when they gathered together. The stories of his Native American family and friends on the reservation influenced Sherman Alexie's work, and both Joe R. Lansdale and Bill Bryson considered their parents to be great storytellers and jokers.

Simply by carefully listening to such familial stories, the writers learned much about jokes, comic timing, word choice, dialect, innuendo, puns, suspense and comic relief. Without even being aware of it, they developed an "ear" for language and story, a skill as important to a writer as his powers of observation.

Lois-Ann Yamanaka said that everyone is born with a story to tell. Before writers can tell their stories, however, they must first develop an ear for language and the structure of story, just as Yamanaka did in her Hawaiian neighborhood by listening to the "old futs talk story."

I remember family gatherings of my mother's Italian-American relatives and can recall that volume seemed to play an important part in their conversations and storytelling as did theatrical hand gestures and even making faces. Although none of these aunts and uncles were fluent in the language of their immigrant parents, their language was studded with choice Italian words—not the pure Italian of Dante but a Sicilian-American dialect— many of which, as a youth, I knew I had no business repeating.

As well, I remember my father's equally large Ukrainian family coming together and being as vocal, aided by beer, which illustrated one of the primal laws of physics—volume is directly proportional to the amount of beer consumed. Similar to my mother's family, my father's family had only a rudimentary knowledge of Ukrainian, and again, their conversation was sprinkled with interesting, sometimes inappropriate, words. But there was also a tonal quality in their speech, even in English, that mimicked how I thought most Eastern European languages sounded, sort of a sibilant "shushing" sound. I wondered if that came from their parents and grand-parents or from their predominantly Eastern European neighbors in the small Pennsylvania coal-mining town in which they all were raised.

It has taken some time for these family influences in language and story-telling to emerge in my own writing, but they had always been there, ever since I was a child, dormant and ready to awaken at just the right time.

It doesn't have to be family that helps you develop your writer's ear, of course. You may learn the art by listening to your friends and neighbors, local TV and radio stations, strangers in a restaurant or at a ball game (writers are permitted to eavesdrop). The point is to pay attention, to listen, to hear not just the words, but the emotion behind them, the nuances, and to understand the complex psychology of the speakers themselves. That's what it means to develop a writer's ear.

These may help you develop an ear toward better storytelling:

1. Ask a relative to tell you a funny story from his or her past: first job, marriage, first child, military service, etc. Tape record the story. Before playing the tape back, write your relative's story as you heard it. Now play the tape. How does the oral version differ from your written version of the story? Are there elements from the oral version that you could have included in your written version that would have made the story funnier? More authentic?

2. Create a fictional persona for yourself: Texas cowboy, Russian balle-

rina, Midwest corn farmer, Marie Antoinette, Spanish conquistador, New York City cop, etc. Keeping in mind your persona's ethnic, historic and cultural influences, write a story in your persona's voice. After, have a friend read it aloud to you. How does it sound? Is it authentic? Have you captured your persona's unique personality?

Other Writers

Not all readers are writers, but certainly, all writers are readers. Long before their writing skills were ever developed, the interviewed writers—as indeed, probably all writers—were voracious readers. They were not circumscribed in their reading, but read anything they could get their hands on, some of them, like Andrei Codrescu, experiencing the joy of reading officially banned works.

Writers are curious by nature. The best of them read widely. In addition to reading books directly related to the subject matter of their own writing, they also read out of their specific genres and fields of interest, expanding their knowledge, their experiences.

Developing writers are influenced by the writers they read and often find themselves imitating favorite writers in their own work, both consciously and unconsciously. Roy Blount Jr. admitted to sounding a lot like Robert Benchley in his early days, before his own voice matured and kicked into his writing. Many of the other writers in this book could point to similar early doppelgangers.

In terms of humor, specifically, there were several writers whose works were cited by the writers in this book as having exerted some influence on their own sense of humor and writing style. Here is a list of some of these writers and their works that you may find helpful in developing your sense of humor:

> Aristophanes—*The Birds, The Frogs*
> Robert Benchley—*Benchley Beside Himself*
> Miguel Cervantes—*Don Quixote*
> Nora Ephron—*Heartburn, When Harry Met Sally*
> Veronica Geng—*Love Trouble Is My Business, Partners*
> Molly Giles—*Rough Translations*
> Jaroslav Hasek—*The Good Soldier Svejk*

Joseph Heller—*Catch-22*

Carl Hiaasen—*Strip Tease*

Dan Jenkins—*Semi-Tough, Fairways and Greens*

Garrison Keillor—*Lake Wobegon Days*

Fran Lebowitz—*Metropolitan Life, Social Studies*

Flannery O'Connor—*A Good Man Is Hard to Find*

S.J. Perelman—*Most of the Most of S.J. Perelman*

Charles Portis—*Norwood*

Francois Rabelais—*Gargantua and Pantagruel*

James Thurber—*The Thurber Carnival*

Calvin Trillin—*Family Man*

Mark Twain—*Life on the Mississippi* and everything else he wrote

Kurt Vonnegut—*Breakfast of Champions, Slaughterhouse-Five*

Eudora Welty—*The Ponder Heart,* "Why I Live at the P.O."

P.G. Wodehouse—*Carry On Jeeves* and other Jeeves books

Movies and Television

Since writers are influenced in great part by what they see and hear, it would make sense that movies and television can affect their writing, especially in regard to humor.

The comedies of the Marx Brothers, *Duck Soup* in particular, were mentioned by some of the writers in this book as having had an influence upon their sense of humor. So, too, were some of the "classic" comedies such as *Mr. Deeds Goes to Town, The Apartment* and *Some Like It Hot.*

Some of the younger writers found their sense of humor affected by television more so than movies; in a previous interview I had with him for a magazine, Sherman Alexie called himself the "first graduate of the Brady Bunch School of Writing." In addition to Alexie's seventies sitcom favorite, other TV shows that provided some inspiration for the writers in this book included *The Dick Van Dyke Show, Barney Miller, Taxi* and *Seinfeld.*

There is a huge difference between making something funny on the screen and making it funny in print. A comedian who relies on expression, gesticulation and a supporting cast in order to be funny may fail dismally to be funny on the printed page; the bookstores are full of such examples.

There are rare exceptions—Woody Allen and Steve Martin are two—who have the ability to be funny in both formats.

The writers in this book recognized that fact; they did not simply try to re-create movies and television programs on paper. They said they were not necessarily influenced by movies or TV shows in their entirety, but rather by specific elements in them. Joe R. Lansdale, who says the humor in his books comes naturally from his characters, cited *Barney Miller* and *Taxi* as TV shows that had some influence upon his sense of humor since both shows emphasized character development over zany plots.

With the possible exception of Sherman Alexie, who is now producing movies and doing stand-up comedy in addition to writing, our featured writers did not study TV and movies to learn how to be funny. For most of them, movies and television worked on their writing sensibilities in a subliminal way. Language, plot, character development and comic timing were just some of the lessons they learned from movies and TV, probably without knowing they were learning anything at all. Like all good writers, funny or serious, they learned to open their minds to the influence and stimulation of whatever the world had to offer. They learned to apply their imaginations to the material gathered in their spongelike minds. The results have benefited us all.

INDEX

How to Write Funny

How to Write Funny